Mastering LangGraph, 2nd Edition

A Hands-On Guide to Building Complex, Multi-Agent Large Language
Model (LLM) Applications with Ease

©

Written By

Charles Sprinter

Copyright Page

Mastering LangGraph, 2nd Edition: A Hands-On Guide to Building Complex, Multi-Agent Large Language Model (LLM) Applications with Ease
© 2025 **Charles Sprinter**

First Edition published in 2024. Second Edition published in 2025.

Disclaimer:
The information in this book is provided "as is." While every effort has been made to ensure the accuracy of the information contained herein, neither the author nor the publisher shall be held liable for any damages or issues arising from the use of the material. The examples and projects provided in this book are for educational purposes and may require modification to work in specific use cases.

Trademarks:
LangGraph, OpenAI, GPT, Hugging Face, and all related logos and marks are trademarks of their respective owners. All other trademarks are the property of their respective owners. The mention of any company, product, or service in this book does not imply endorsement by the author or publisher, nor does it suggest any affiliation with or endorsement by the companies listed.

Table of content

Preface

Welcome to the second edition of *Mastering LangGraph: A Hands-On Guide to Building Complex, Multi-Agent Large Language Model (LLM) Applications with Ease*. Whether you are a seasoned developer, an AI enthusiast, or someone looking to dive into the world of multi-agent systems and large language models, this book is designed to equip you with the knowledge and practical skills needed to harness the full potential of LangGraph.

1. What's New in the 2nd Edition

The field of artificial intelligence, particularly in multi-agent systems and large language models, is rapidly evolving. This second edition has been meticulously updated to reflect the latest advancements and best practices in LangGraph and LLM applications. Here's a summary of the key updates and additions:

New Features	Description
Expanded Content	Additional chapters on emerging technologies, ethical considerations, and user experience design have been included to provide a more comprehensive understanding of LangGraph.
Updated Case Studies	New real-world case studies from diverse industries such as environmental monitoring, smart cities, and personalized marketing demonstrate the versatility of LangGraph.
Enhanced Ethical Sections	In-depth discussions on bias mitigation, data privacy, and regulatory compliance ensure that your applications are not only effective but also responsible and secure.
Interactive Resources	Links to downloadable code samples, interactive notebooks, and a dedicated GitHub repository have been added to support hands-on learning.
Integration with Other Technologies	New sections on integrating LangGraph with IoT devices, blockchain, and cloud platforms broaden the scope of potential applications.

New Features	Description
Performance Optimization Techniques	Advanced optimization strategies, including GPU acceleration and performance libraries, are covered to help you build efficient and scalable applications.

These updates ensure that the second edition remains a cutting-edge resource, providing readers with the most current information and practical tools to succeed in their LangGraph endeavors.

2. How to Use This Book

This book is structured to guide you from the foundational concepts of LangGraph and large language models to the development of complex, multi-agent applications. Here's how to make the most of this guide:

- **Sequential Reading**: Start from the beginning and progress through each part and chapter in order. The book is designed to build your knowledge step-by-step, ensuring a solid understanding of each topic before moving on to more advanced concepts.
- **Hands-On Practice**: Each chapter includes practical exercises, code snippets, and projects that allow you to apply what you've learned. It is highly recommended to actively engage with these hands-on elements to reinforce your understanding and gain practical experience.
- **Supplementary Materials**: Utilize the downloadable resources and the online companion website for additional practice and deeper exploration of the topics covered. These resources are designed to complement the book and provide extended learning opportunities.
- **Reflect and Assess**: Take advantage of the quizzes and reflection questions at the end of each chapter to assess your comprehension and think critically about how to implement the concepts in your own projects.

By following this approach, you will be able to maximize your learning and effectively apply LangGraph in your AI applications.

3. Audience and Prerequisites

Mastering LangGraph, 2nd Edition is crafted for a diverse audience, including:

- **AI Developers and Engineers**: Professionals looking to integrate LangGraph into their AI workflows and build sophisticated multi-agent systems.
- **Machine Learning Enthusiasts**: Individuals passionate about large language models and interested in exploring their applications in multi-agent environments.
- **Software Developers**: Developers seeking to expand their skill set by incorporating AI-driven, multi-agent systems into their software solutions.
- **Researchers and Academics**: Scholars conducting research in AI, multi-agent systems, and large language models who need a practical guide to implementing LangGraph.
- **Graduate Students**: Students pursuing advanced studies in computer science, AI, or related fields who require a comprehensive resource on LangGraph and multi-agent LLM applications.

Prerequisites:

To fully benefit from this book, readers should have:

- **Basic Programming Knowledge**: Familiarity with programming languages such as Python is essential, as the book includes numerous code examples and practical exercises.
- **Understanding of AI Fundamentals**: A foundational understanding of artificial intelligence and machine learning concepts will help in grasping the advanced topics covered.
- **Interest in Multi-Agent Systems**: An enthusiasm for exploring the dynamics of multi-agent interactions and their applications in real-world scenarios.

If you meet these prerequisites, you are well-prepared to embark on this journey to mastering LangGraph and building complex, multi-agent LLM applications.

4. Conventions Used in This Book

To ensure clarity and consistency throughout the book, the following conventions have been adopted:

- **Terminology**: Specialized terms are highlighted in bold the first time they appear, with definitions provided either immediately or in the glossary. This helps in understanding key concepts without disrupting the flow of reading.

- **Code Snippets**: Code examples are presented in a monospaced font with syntax highlighting for readability. Each snippet is complete, accurately formatted, and thoroughly explained to facilitate replication and experimentation.
- **Tables**: Tables are used to organize information clearly and concisely. They help in comparing features, summarizing data, and presenting structured information in an easily digestible format.
- **Figures and Diagrams**: While this edition avoids traditional images, diagrams and flowcharts are represented using text-based formats to illustrate complex workflows and system architectures effectively.
- **Exercises and Quizzes**: At the end of each chapter, exercises and quizzes are provided to reinforce learning. Solutions and guidance are available to help you assess your understanding and apply the concepts learned.
- **Consistent Formatting**: Headings, subheadings, and lists follow a consistent style throughout the book. This uniformity aids in navigating the content and locating specific sections quickly.

By adhering to these conventions, the book ensures a professional and accessible reading experience, allowing you to focus on mastering LangGraph without unnecessary distractions.

5. Acknowledgments

Writing this book has been a rewarding journey, and it would not have been possible without the support and contributions of many individuals and organizations. I would like to extend my heartfelt gratitude to:

- **My Colleagues and Peers**: Your insights, feedback, and encouragement have been invaluable in shaping the content and structure of this book.
- **The LangGraph Community**: Your enthusiasm and shared knowledge have inspired many of the examples and case studies included here. Thank you for fostering a collaborative and innovative environment.
- **Beta Readers**: Special thanks to those who provided detailed reviews and constructive criticism, helping to refine the material and ensure its accuracy and relevance.

- **Industry Professionals**: Your real-world experiences and success stories have enriched the case studies, making the applications of LangGraph more tangible and inspiring.
- **Family and Friends**: Your unwavering support and patience have been my anchor throughout the writing process. Thank you for believing in me and this project.

Lastly, I want to acknowledge the broader AI and software development communities for their continuous contributions and advancements, which form the foundation upon which this book is built.

Part I: Foundations of LangGraph

Chapter 1: Introduction to LangGraph

Welcome to the first chapter of *Mastering LangGraph, 2nd Edition: A Hands-On Guide to Building Complex, Multi-Agent Large Language Model (LLM) Applications with Ease.* In this chapter, we will introduce you to LangGraph, explore its key features and benefits, compare it with other AI frameworks, discuss its use cases and applications, delve into the LangGraph ecosystem, and guide you through the initial setup and installation process. By the end of this chapter, you will have a solid understanding of what LangGraph is and how it can be leveraged to build sophisticated multi-agent LLM applications.

1.1 What is LangGraph?

LangGraph is a cutting-edge framework designed to facilitate the development of complex, multi-agent systems powered by Large Language Models (LLMs). It provides a structured environment where multiple agents can interact, collaborate, and perform tasks autonomously or semi-autonomously, leveraging the capabilities of LLMs to understand and generate human-like language.

Key Characteristics of LangGraph:

- **Multi-Agent Architecture:** LangGraph allows the creation and management of multiple agents, each with specific roles and responsibilities, working together to achieve common goals.
- **LLM Integration:** Seamlessly integrates with various Large Language Models, enabling natural language processing, generation, and understanding within agent interactions.
- **Scalability:** Designed to handle complex applications with numerous agents, ensuring performance and reliability as the system grows.
- **Flexibility:** Supports customization and extension, allowing developers to tailor the framework to specific project needs.

Example Scenario:

Imagine building an AI-powered customer support system where different agents handle various aspects of customer interaction. One agent processes and understands customer queries using an LLM, another retrieves relevant information from a knowledge base, and a third generates personalized responses. LangGraph facilitates the coordination and communication between these agents, ensuring efficient and effective customer service.

1.2 Key Features and Benefits of LangGraph

LangGraph offers a range of features that make it an invaluable tool for developers and organizations aiming to build advanced AI applications. Below are some of its key features and the benefits they provide:

Feature	Description	Benefits
Multi-Agent Management	Create, configure, and manage multiple agents within a single framework.	Enables the development of complex systems where agents can specialize and collaborate effectively.
LLM Integration	Easily integrate with various Large Language Models like GPT, BERT, and others.	Leverages the power of LLMs for natural language understanding and generation within agent interactions.
Workflow Automation	Define and automate workflows that agents follow to complete tasks.	Streamlines processes, reduces manual intervention, and increases efficiency in application operations.
Scalability	Designed to scale from small projects to large, enterprise-level applications.	Ensures that applications can grow without compromising performance or reliability.
Extensibility	Supports plugins and extensions to add new functionalities or integrate	Allows customization and adaptation to specific project requirements, enhancing flexibility.

Feature	Description	Benefits
	with other tools and services.	
Monitoring and Debugging	Tools for monitoring agent performance and debugging interactions.	Facilitates the maintenance of robust and reliable systems by identifying and resolving issues quickly.
Security and Privacy	Built-in security features to protect data and ensure compliance with privacy regulations.	Protects sensitive information and ensures that applications adhere to legal and ethical standards.

Benefits Overview:

1. **Enhanced Collaboration:** By managing multiple agents, LangGraph enables different components of an application to work together seamlessly, improving overall functionality and user experience.
2. **Improved Efficiency:** Automation of workflows and task management reduces the need for manual intervention, saving time and resources.
3. **Flexibility and Customization:** The extensible nature of LangGraph allows developers to adapt the framework to a wide range of applications, from simple bots to complex AI-driven systems.
4. **Reliability and Scalability:** Built to handle large-scale applications, LangGraph ensures that your systems remain reliable and performant as they grow.
5. **Security Assurance:** With robust security features, LangGraph helps safeguard your data and maintain user trust.

1.3 LangGraph vs. Other AI Frameworks

When choosing an AI framework for building multi-agent systems and integrating Large Language Models, it's essential to understand how LangGraph stands out compared to other available options. This section compares LangGraph with some popular AI frameworks, highlighting its unique advantages.

Aspect	LangGraph	TensorFlow	PyTorch	OpenAI API
Multi-Agent Support	Built-in support for creating and managing multiple agents.	Primarily focused on deep learning; multi-agent support requires custom implementation.	Primarily focused on deep learning; multi-agent support requires custom implementation.	Single-agent interactions; multi-agent systems require additional setup.
LLM Integration	Seamless integration with various Large Language Models.	Limited direct integration; requires additional tools and configurations.	Limited direct integration; requires additional tools and configurations.	Excellent for LLM tasks but lacks multi-agent management capabilities.
Workflow Automation	Comprehensive workflow automation tools tailored for multi-agent systems.	Not specifically designed for workflow automation; more manual setup needed.	Not specifically designed for workflow automation; more manual setup needed.	Primarily for generating responses; lacks workflow automation features.
Scalability	Designed for scalable multi-agent applications from the ground up.	Highly scalable for deep learning tasks but not optimized for multi-agent systems.	Highly scalable for deep learning tasks but not optimized for multi-agent systems.	Scalable for LLM tasks but limited in managing complex multi-agent systems.
Extensibility	Supports plugins and extensions specifically for enhancing multi-agent functionality.	Highly extensible for deep learning projects.	Highly extensible for deep learning projects.	Extensible within LLM capabilities but not for multi-agent systems.
Monitoring and Debugging	Integrated tools for monitoring	Primarily focuses on model	Primarily focuses on model	Basic monitoring for API

Aspect	LangGraph	TensorFlow	PyTorch	OpenAI API
	and debugging multi-agent interactions.	performance and training metrics.	performance and training metrics.	usage; lacks comprehensive debugging tools.
Security and Privacy	Built-in security features for data protection and compliance.	Requires additional setup for security and privacy compliance.	Requires additional setup for security and privacy compliance.	Provides secure access but limited in comprehensive security features.

Key Takeaways:

- **Multi-Agent Focus:** Unlike TensorFlow and PyTorch, which are primarily deep learning frameworks, LangGraph is specifically designed to handle multi-agent systems, making it more suitable for applications requiring multiple interacting agents.
- **Seamless LLM Integration:** LangGraph offers seamless integration with various Large Language Models, unlike the more general-purpose TensorFlow and PyTorch, which require additional configurations for LLM tasks.
- **Workflow Automation:** LangGraph provides built-in tools for workflow automation tailored to multi-agent applications, a feature not inherently available in TensorFlow, PyTorch, or the OpenAI API.
- **Scalability for Multi-Agent Systems:** While TensorFlow and PyTorch are highly scalable for deep learning tasks, LangGraph is optimized for scaling multi-agent systems, ensuring reliable performance as the number of agents increases.
- **Security Features:** LangGraph includes built-in security features to protect data and ensure compliance, whereas other frameworks often require additional setup for robust security and privacy measures.

LangGraph distinguishes itself by offering specialized support for multi-agent systems and seamless integration with Large Language Models, combined with workflow automation, scalability, and built-in security features. These capabilities make it an ideal choice for developers and organizations looking to build complex, AI-driven applications that require multiple interacting agents.

1.4 Use Cases and Applications of LangGraph

LangGraph's versatility allows it to be applied across a wide range of industries and use cases. Below are some prominent applications where LangGraph excels:

Industry	Use Case	Description
Healthcare	AI-Powered Diagnostic Systems	Multi-agent systems that assist in diagnosing diseases by analyzing patient data, medical literature, and clinical guidelines using LLMs.
Customer Service	Automated Support Agents	Intelligent agents that handle customer inquiries, troubleshoot issues, and provide personalized support, enhancing customer satisfaction and reducing response times.
Finance	Automated Trading Systems	Agents that analyze market data, execute trades, and manage investment portfolios autonomously, leveraging LLMs for market sentiment analysis.
Education	Personalized Learning Assistants	Agents that provide customized learning experiences, track student progress, and offer real-time feedback and tutoring using natural language interactions.
Gaming	Intelligent NPCs (Non-Player Characters)	NPCs that interact with players in a more natural and dynamic manner, enhancing the gaming experience through realistic dialogue and adaptive behaviors.
Smart Cities	Urban Management Systems	Multi-agent systems that manage traffic flow, monitor environmental conditions, and optimize public services using real-time data and predictive analytics.

Industry	Use Case	Description
Environmental Monitoring	AI-Driven Environmental Analysis	Agents that monitor and analyze environmental data, predict trends, and recommend actions to mitigate environmental impact using LLMs for data interpretation.
Personalized Marketing	Targeted Marketing Campaigns	Agents that analyze consumer behavior, generate personalized marketing content, and optimize campaign strategies to increase engagement and conversion rates.
Research and Development	Collaborative Research Agents	Agents that assist researchers by gathering information, summarizing findings, and generating hypotheses based on the latest scientific literature.
Retail	Inventory Management Systems	Agents that monitor inventory levels, predict demand, and optimize stock replenishment processes to ensure efficient and cost-effective operations.
Human Resources	Recruitment and Onboarding Assistants	Agents that handle candidate screening, interview scheduling, and onboarding processes, enhancing the efficiency and effectiveness of HR departments.

Detailed Examples:

1. **Healthcare - AI-Powered Diagnostic Systems:**
   o **Description:** In healthcare, accurate and timely diagnosis is critical. LangGraph enables the creation of multi-agent diagnostic systems where different agents analyze various aspects of patient data. One agent may process medical histories, another analyzes lab results, while a third consults the latest medical research using LLMs.
   o **Benefits:** Enhances diagnostic accuracy, reduces the time required for diagnosis, and ensures that healthcare providers have access to the most up-to-date medical information.
2. **Customer Service - Automated Support Agents:**

- o **Description:** Businesses can deploy intelligent customer support agents that handle a wide range of inquiries. These agents use LLMs to understand customer queries, retrieve relevant information from databases, and generate personalized responses.
  - o **Benefits:** Improves customer satisfaction by providing quick and accurate responses, reduces the workload on human support teams, and operates 24/7 without fatigue.
3. **Finance - Automated Trading Systems:**
   - o **Description:** In the finance sector, automated trading systems can analyze vast amounts of market data, execute trades based on predefined strategies, and adjust portfolios dynamically. LangGraph facilitates the coordination of these agents to ensure optimal trading performance.
   - o **Benefits:** Increases trading efficiency, minimizes human error, and allows for real-time decision-making based on comprehensive data analysis.
4. **Smart Cities - Urban Management Systems:**
   - o **Description:** Smart cities rely on efficient management of resources and services. LangGraph can power multi-agent systems that oversee traffic management, monitor environmental conditions, and coordinate public services to enhance urban living.
   - o **Benefits:** Improves the quality of life for residents, reduces operational costs, and ensures sustainable urban development through data-driven decision-making.

1.5 The LangGraph Ecosystem: Tools, Libraries, and Integrations

LangGraph is not just a standalone framework; it is part of a broader ecosystem of tools, libraries, and integrations that enhance its functionality and facilitate seamless development of multi-agent LLM applications. Understanding the components of the LangGraph ecosystem is crucial for maximizing the framework's potential.

Key Components of the LangGraph Ecosystem:

Component	Description	Benefits
LangGraph Core	The foundational framework that provides the basic structure for creating and managing agents, workflows, and integrations with LLMs.	Serves as the backbone of all LangGraph applications, ensuring consistency and reliability.
LLM Integrations	Pre-built connectors and adapters for popular Large Language Models such as GPT-4, BERT, and others.	Simplifies the process of integrating different LLMs, allowing developers to switch models easily.
Workflow Tools	Tools for designing, automating, and visualizing workflows that agents follow to complete tasks.	Enhances productivity by streamlining task management and process automation.
Agent Libraries	A collection of pre-built agents that perform common tasks, such as data retrieval, natural language processing, and decision-making.	Accelerates development by providing reusable components that can be customized as needed.
Monitoring Dashboards	Real-time dashboards for tracking agent performance, system health, and workflow status.	Facilitates proactive maintenance and optimization by providing actionable insights into system operations.
Security Modules	Built-in security features and compliance tools to protect data and ensure that applications adhere to privacy regulations.	Ensures that applications are secure and compliant with industry standards, building user trust.
Extensibility Plugins	Plugins and extensions that add new functionalities or integrate LangGraph with other tools and services, such as databases, cloud platforms, and IoT devices.	Enhances the flexibility and adaptability of LangGraph, allowing it to meet diverse project requirements.
Documentation and Tutorials	Comprehensive documentation, tutorials, and	Provides essential resources for learning

Component	Description	Benefits
	guides that help developers learn and effectively use LangGraph and its ecosystem components.	and troubleshooting, reducing the learning curve for new users.
Community and Support	Online forums, community contributions, and support channels where developers can collaborate, share ideas, and seek assistance.	Fosters a collaborative environment where users can learn from each other and contribute to the ecosystem.

Detailed Overview of Key Components:

1. **LangGraph Core:**
   - **Description:** The LangGraph Core is the heart of the ecosystem, providing the essential tools and functionalities required to create, manage, and coordinate agents. It includes features for agent lifecycle management, communication protocols, and workflow orchestration.
   - **Benefits:** Ensures a stable and consistent foundation for all LangGraph applications, allowing developers to focus on building unique functionalities without worrying about the underlying infrastructure.
2. **LLM Integrations:**
   - **Description:** LangGraph offers built-in integrations with leading Large Language Models such as GPT-4, BERT, and others. These integrations include connectors that facilitate the seamless exchange of data between LangGraph and the LLMs.
   - **Benefits:** Simplifies the process of leveraging powerful LLMs within LangGraph applications, enabling developers to quickly incorporate natural language understanding and generation capabilities into their agents.
3. **Workflow Tools:**
   - **Description:** Workflow tools within LangGraph allow developers to design and automate complex workflows that agents follow to complete tasks. These tools include visual workflow designers, task schedulers, and automation scripts.
   - **Benefits:** Streamlines the development process by providing intuitive tools for managing agent tasks and ensuring that workflows run smoothly and efficiently.

4. **Agent Libraries:**
   - **Description:** LangGraph provides a library of pre-built agents that perform common functions such as data retrieval, natural language processing, sentiment analysis, and decision-making. These agents can be easily customized and extended to fit specific project needs.
   - **Benefits:** Accelerates development by offering reusable components, reducing the time and effort required to build agents from scratch.
5. **Monitoring Dashboards:**
   - **Description:** Real-time monitoring dashboards offer insights into agent performance, system health, and workflow status. These dashboards display metrics such as agent response times, error rates, and resource utilization.
   - **Benefits:** Enables developers and administrators to proactively monitor and optimize their LangGraph applications, ensuring high performance and reliability.
6. **Security Modules:**
   - **Description:** LangGraph includes built-in security modules that provide data encryption, access control, and compliance tools to protect sensitive information and ensure adherence to privacy regulations.
   - **Benefits:** Protects data integrity and confidentiality, helping organizations comply with legal and ethical standards while maintaining user trust.
7. **Extensibility Plugins:**
   - **Description:** Plugins and extensions allow LangGraph to integrate with other tools and services such as databases, cloud platforms, IoT devices, and blockchain networks. These plugins add new functionalities or enhance existing ones.
   - **Benefits:** Increases the versatility of LangGraph, enabling it to be used in a wide range of applications and environments by connecting with various external systems and technologies.
8. **Documentation and Tutorials:**
   - **Description:** Comprehensive documentation includes detailed guides, API references, and step-by-step tutorials that help developers learn how to use LangGraph effectively. These resources cover everything from basic setup to advanced configurations and integrations.

- **Benefits:** Provides essential support for users at all levels, making it easier to get started with LangGraph and troubleshoot any issues that arise during development.

9. **Community and Support:**
    - **Description:** LangGraph fosters a vibrant community where developers can collaborate, share ideas, and seek assistance. Support channels include online forums, community-contributed modules, and official support from the LangGraph team.
    - **Benefits:** Encourages knowledge sharing and collaboration, helping users learn from each other and contribute to the continuous improvement of the LangGraph ecosystem.

1.6 Getting Started with LangGraph: Setup and Installation

Before diving into building complex, multi-agent applications with LangGraph, it's essential to set up your development environment and install LangGraph. This section provides a step-by-step guide to help you get started.

Prerequisites:

- **Operating System:** LangGraph is compatible with major operating systems including Windows, macOS, and Linux.
- **Python:** Ensure that Python 3.7 or higher is installed on your system. You can download Python from the official website.
- **Node.js (Optional):** For certain integrations and extensions, having Node.js installed can be beneficial. Download it from the official website.

Step 1: Installing Python

1. **Download Python:**
    - Visit the Python Downloads page.
    - Choose the appropriate installer for your operating system and download it.
2. **Install Python:**
    - Run the downloaded installer.
    - During installation, ensure that the option "Add Python to PATH" is selected.

o   Follow the on-screen instructions to complete the installation.
3. **Verify Installation:**
    o   Open your terminal or command prompt.
    o   Type the following command and press Enter:

```bash
Copy code
python --version
```

o   You should see the installed Python version (e.g., Python 3.9.1).

Step 2: Setting Up a Virtual Environment

Creating a virtual environment helps manage dependencies and keeps your LangGraph projects isolated from other Python projects.

1. **Create a Virtual Environment:**

```bash
Copy code
python -m venv langgraph_env
```

2. **Activate the Virtual Environment:**
    o   **Windows:**

```bash
Copy code
langgraph_env\Scripts\activate
```

o   **macOS/Linux:**

```bash
Copy code
source langgraph_env/bin/activate
```

3. **Upgrade pip:**

```bash
Copy code
pip install --upgrade pip
```

Step 3: Installing LangGraph

1. **Install LangGraph via pip:**

```bash
Copy code
pip install langgraph
```

2. **Verify Installation:**
   o Open a Python shell by typing `python` in your terminal.
   o Try importing LangGraph:

```python
Copy code
import langgraph
print(langgraph.__version__)
```

   o You should see the version number of LangGraph, confirming a successful installation.

Step 4: Setting Up LangGraph's Dependencies

LangGraph may require additional dependencies for specific functionalities, such as integrations with LLMs or other tools.

1. **Install Additional Dependencies:**
   o For LLM integration:

```bash
Copy code
pip install transformers
```

   o For workflow automation:

```bash
Copy code
pip install airflow
```

2. **Install LangGraph Extensions (Optional):**
   o LangGraph supports various plugins and extensions. For example, to enable IoT integrations:

```bash
Copy code
pip install langgraph-iot
```

Step 5: Configuring LangGraph

After installation, you need to configure LangGraph to suit your project requirements. This typically involves setting up API keys for LLMs, configuring agent parameters, and defining workflows.

1. **Setting Up API Keys:**
   - Obtain API keys from the providers of the LLMs you intend to use (e.g., OpenAI for GPT models).
   - Store your API keys securely, preferably in environment variables or a configuration file.
   - Example using environment variables:

   ```bash
   Copy code
   export OPENAI_API_KEY='your-api-key-here'
   ```

2. **Creating a Configuration File:**
   - Create a `config.yaml` file in your project directory.
   - Example `config.yaml`:

   ```yaml
   Copy code
   langgraph:
     api_keys:
       openai: ${OPENAI_API_KEY}
     logging:
       level: INFO
       file: logs/langgraph.log
   ```

3. **Initializing LangGraph:**
   - In your Python script, initialize LangGraph with the configuration file.

   ```python
   Copy code
   import langgraph

   config = langgraph.load_config('config.yaml')
   lg = langgraph.LangGraph(config)
   ```

Step 6: Running a Sample LangGraph Application

To ensure everything is set up correctly, let's run a simple LangGraph application that creates and manages a basic agent.

1. **Create a Python Script:**
   - Create a file named `sample_app.py` and add the following code:

```python
Copy code
import langgraph

# Initialize LangGraph
config = langgraph.load_config('config.yaml')
lg = langgraph.LangGraph(config)

# Define a simple agent
class HelloAgent(langgraph.Agent):
    def __init__(self, name):
        super().__init__(name)

    def perform_task(self):
        print(f"Hello from {self.name}!")

# Create and register the agent
agent = HelloAgent('AgentA')
lg.register_agent(agent)

# Execute the agent's task
lg.run_agents()
```

2. **Run the Script:**

```bash
Copy code
python sample_app.py
```

3. **Expected Output:**

```csharp
Copy code
Hello from AgentA!
```

Explanation:

- **Initialization:** The script initializes LangGraph with the configuration file.
- **Agent Definition:** A simple agent named `HelloAgent` is defined, which prints a greeting message.

- **Registration and Execution:** The agent is registered with LangGraph and then executed, resulting in the greeting message being printed.

By following these steps, you have successfully set up LangGraph and run a basic application. This setup provides a solid foundation for building more complex, multi-agent systems that leverage the power of Large Language Models. In the upcoming chapters, we will delve deeper into the core concepts, advanced features, and practical applications of LangGraph, equipping you with the tools and knowledge to create sophisticated AI-driven solutions.

Summary

In this chapter, you were introduced to LangGraph, its key features and benefits, how it stands out compared to other AI frameworks, various use cases across different industries, and the comprehensive ecosystem that supports it. You also learned how to set up your development environment, install LangGraph, configure it, and run a basic application. This foundational knowledge will serve as the building block for the more advanced topics covered in the subsequent chapters.

As you progress through the book, you'll gain a deeper understanding of how to harness LangGraph's capabilities to build robust, scalable, and intelligent multi-agent systems that can tackle complex real-world problems with ease.

Chapter 2: Understanding Large Language Models (LLMs)

Welcome to Chapter 2 of *Mastering LangGraph, 2nd Edition: A Hands-On Guide to Building Complex, Multi-Agent Large Language Model (LLM) Applications with Ease.* In this chapter, we will delve into the world of Large Language Models (LLMs). We will explore what LLMs are, how they work, popular architectures, their limitations, how LangGraph leverages them for multi-agent systems, and the ethical considerations associated with their use.

2.1 What are LLMs?

Large Language Models (LLMs) are advanced artificial intelligence systems designed to understand, generate, and manipulate human language. They are built using deep learning techniques, specifically leveraging neural networks with billions of parameters, which allow them to process and generate text that is coherent, contextually relevant, and often indistinguishable from human-written content.

Key Characteristics of LLMs:

- **Scale:** LLMs consist of millions or even billions of parameters, enabling them to capture intricate patterns and nuances in language.
- **Pretraining:** They are typically pretrained on vast amounts of text data from diverse sources, allowing them to acquire a broad understanding of language.
- **Fine-Tuning:** After pretraining, LLMs can be fine-tuned on specific datasets to perform specialized tasks, such as translation, summarization, or sentiment analysis.
- **Versatility:** LLMs can perform a wide range of language-related tasks without needing task-specific architectures.

Common Applications of LLMs:

- **Natural Language Processing (NLP):** Tasks like text classification, sentiment analysis, and named entity recognition.
- **Text Generation:** Creating articles, stories, and reports.
- **Conversational Agents:** Powering chatbots and virtual assistants.

- **Translation Services:** Translating text between languages.
- **Summarization:** Condensing long documents into concise summaries.

Example Use Case:

Imagine you are developing a customer service chatbot using LangGraph. An LLM can enable the chatbot to understand and respond to customer queries naturally and accurately, improving user experience and reducing the need for human intervention.

2.2 How LLMs Work: A High-Level Overview

Understanding how LLMs work is essential for effectively integrating them into multi-agent systems using LangGraph. At a high level, LLMs operate through a process of pattern recognition and generation based on the data they have been trained on.

Core Components of LLMs:

1. **Neural Networks:** Specifically, transformer architectures are the backbone of most LLMs. Transformers use mechanisms like self-attention to process input data efficiently.
2. **Parameters:** These are the weights within the neural network that are adjusted during training. The number of parameters is a key indicator of an LLM's capacity.
3. **Training Data:** LLMs are trained on diverse and extensive datasets that include books, articles, websites, and other textual sources.
4. **Tokenization:** The process of breaking down text into smaller units called tokens, which the model processes sequentially.

Training Process:

1. **Pretraining:**
   - **Objective:** Learn the structure and nuances of language by predicting the next word in a sentence.
   - **Method:** The model processes large text corpora, adjusting parameters to minimize prediction errors.
2. **Fine-Tuning:**

- o **Objective:** Adapt the pretrained model to specific tasks or domains.
- o **Method:** The model is further trained on smaller, task-specific datasets, enhancing its performance on targeted applications.

Generating Text:

1. **Input Prompt:** The user provides an initial text prompt.
2. **Processing:** The model processes the prompt using its learned parameters to understand context and generate relevant responses.
3. **Output:** The model generates a sequence of tokens that form coherent and contextually appropriate text.

Example Code Snippet:

Below is a simple example of how an LLM can be used to generate text using the popular Hugging Face Transformers library.

```python
from transformers import GPT2LMHeadModel, GPT2Tokenizer

# Load pre-trained model and tokenizer
model_name = 'gpt2'
model = GPT2LMHeadModel.from_pretrained(model_name)
tokenizer = GPT2Tokenizer.from_pretrained(model_name)

# Encode input prompt
input_prompt = "Once upon a time in a land far, far away,"
input_ids = tokenizer.encode(input_prompt,
return_tensors='pt')

# Generate text
output = model.generate(input_ids, max_length=100,
num_return_sequences=1)

# Decode and print the generated text
generated_text = tokenizer.decode(output[0],
skip_special_tokens=True)
print(generated_text)
```

Output:

```
Once upon a time in a land far, far away, there lived a wise
old sage who possessed the knowledge of the universe. Every
evening, villagers would gather around him to seek his advice
on matters big and small...
```

In this example, the GPT-2 model generates a continuation of the input prompt, showcasing its ability to produce coherent and contextually relevant text.

2.3 Popular LLM Architectures: GPT, BERT, T5, and Beyond

There are several prominent LLM architectures, each with unique features and applications. Understanding these architectures helps in selecting the right model for specific tasks within LangGraph.

Architecture	Developer	Key Features	Primary Use Cases
GPT (Generative Pre-trained Transformer)	OpenAI	Autoregressive model, excels in text generation, uses self-attention mechanisms	Text generation, chatbots, creative writing
BERT (Bidirectional Encoder Representations from Transformers)	Google	Bidirectional context understanding, excels in understanding the meaning of text	Text classification, question answering, sentiment analysis
T5 (Text-To-Text Transfer Transformer)	Google	Converts all NLP tasks into a text-to-text format, versatile across tasks	Translation, summarization, text generation, classification
RoBERTa (Robustly optimized BERT approach)	Facebook AI	Improved training techniques over BERT, larger training datasets	Similar to BERT but with enhanced performance
XLNet	Google/CMU	Combines autoregressive and autoencoding models, better handling of	Language understanding, text generation

Architecture	Developer	Key Features	Primary Use Cases
		bidirectional contexts	
Transformer-XL	Google/CMU	Recurrence mechanism for longer context handling, improved language modeling	Long document processing, language modeling
ERNIE (Enhanced Representation through Knowledge Integration)	Baidu	Integrates external knowledge bases into pretraining, enhances understanding of entities and relations	Knowledge-intensive tasks, entity recognition, relation extraction

Detailed Overview of Key Architectures:

1. **GPT (Generative Pre-trained Transformer):**
   - **Description:** GPT models are designed to generate human-like text by predicting the next word in a sequence. They are autoregressive, meaning they generate text one token at a time based on the preceding context.
   - **Strengths:** Excellent at creative text generation, maintaining context over long passages, and performing zero-shot learning tasks.
   - **Limitations:** Can produce plausible-sounding but incorrect or nonsensical answers, lacks true understanding of context beyond training data.
2. **BERT (Bidirectional Encoder Representations from Transformers):**
   - **Description:** BERT is designed to understand the context of a word based on all of its surroundings (left and right context), making it bidirectional.
   - **Strengths:** Highly effective for tasks requiring deep understanding of language, such as question answering and sentiment analysis.
   - **Limitations:** Not inherently designed for text generation, primarily excels in understanding tasks.

3. **T5 (Text-To-Text Transfer Transformer):**
   - **Description:** T5 treats every NLP task as a text-to-text problem, converting inputs into a desired text output.
   - **Strengths:** Versatile across a wide range of tasks, easy to adapt to new tasks by reformatting them as text generation.
   - **Limitations:** Can be resource-intensive due to its large size and the requirement to format tasks as text generation.

Choosing the Right Architecture for Your Application:

When integrating LLMs into LangGraph, consider the following factors to choose the most suitable architecture:

- **Task Requirements:** Select GPT for text generation and creative applications, BERT for understanding and classification tasks, and T5 for versatile, multi-task applications.
- **Performance Needs:** Evaluate the computational resources available, as larger models like GPT-3 may require significant processing power.
- **Context Length:** For applications needing long context handling, architectures like Transformer-XL may be more appropriate.
- **Fine-Tuning Flexibility:** Consider how easily the model can be fine-tuned for your specific use case.

2.4 Limitations and Challenges of LLMs

While Large Language Models have revolutionized the field of natural language processing, they come with their own set of limitations and challenges. Understanding these constraints is crucial for effectively leveraging LLMs within LangGraph and developing robust applications.

Key Limitations of LLMs:

1. **Data Bias and Fairness:**
   - **Issue:** LLMs can inherit biases present in the training data, leading to biased or unfair outputs.
   - **Impact:** May perpetuate stereotypes, discrimination, or misinformation.
   - **Mitigation:** Implement bias detection and mitigation strategies during training and fine-tuning.

2. **Lack of True Understanding:**
   - o **Issue:** LLMs generate text based on patterns in data rather than genuine comprehension.
   - o **Impact:** Can produce plausible-sounding but factually incorrect or nonsensical responses.
   - o **Mitigation:** Incorporate validation mechanisms and human-in-the-loop systems to verify outputs.
3. **High Computational Costs:**
   - o **Issue:** Training and deploying large models require significant computational resources.
   - o **Impact:** Limits accessibility for smaller organizations and increases environmental footprint.
   - o **Mitigation:** Optimize model efficiency, use model compression techniques, or adopt smaller, specialized models.
4. **Contextual Limitations:**
   - o **Issue:** LLMs have a fixed context window, limiting their ability to process very long texts.
   - o **Impact:** May lose track of context in lengthy documents, reducing coherence and relevance.
   - o **Mitigation:** Use architectures that support longer contexts or break down documents into manageable chunks.
5. **Ethical and Privacy Concerns:**
   - o **Issue:** LLMs can inadvertently generate or memorize sensitive information from training data.
   - o **Impact:** Raises privacy issues and potential misuse of generated content.
   - o **Mitigation:** Ensure data privacy during training, implement content filters, and adhere to ethical guidelines.
6. **Dependence on Quality of Training Data:**
   - o **Issue:** The performance of LLMs is heavily dependent on the quality and diversity of the training data.
   - o **Impact:** Poor-quality or unrepresentative data can degrade model performance and reliability.
   - o **Mitigation:** Curate high-quality, diverse datasets and continuously update training data to reflect current knowledge.

Challenges in Deploying LLMs:

1. **Scalability:**
   - o Deploying LLMs in real-time applications can be challenging due to their size and resource requirements.

2. **Maintenance:**
   - o Keeping models updated with the latest information and ensuring they remain relevant requires ongoing effort and resources.
3. **Integration Complexity:**
   - o Integrating LLMs with existing systems and workflows can be technically complex, necessitating expertise in both AI and software engineering.
4. **User Trust and Transparency:**
   - o Building trust with users by ensuring transparency in how LLMs make decisions and generate content is essential but challenging.

While LLMs offer powerful capabilities for language understanding and generation, it is important to be aware of their limitations and address the associated challenges. By implementing best practices and leveraging tools within LangGraph, you can mitigate these issues and build more reliable, ethical, and efficient multi-agent systems.

2.5 How LangGraph Leverages LLMs for Multi-Agent Systems

LangGraph is designed to harness the strengths of Large Language Models to build sophisticated, multi-agent systems. By integrating LLMs, LangGraph enables agents to perform complex tasks, communicate effectively, and adapt to dynamic environments. This section explores how LangGraph leverages LLMs to enhance multi-agent systems.

Key Ways LangGraph Utilizes LLMs:

1. **Natural Language Understanding and Generation:**
   - o **Description:** LLMs enable agents to comprehend and generate human-like text, facilitating natural interactions.
   - o **Benefit:** Enhances the ability of agents to interpret user inputs, respond appropriately, and maintain coherent conversations.
2. **Contextual Awareness:**
   - o **Description:** LLMs provide agents with the ability to understand context from preceding interactions.

- o **Benefit:** Improves the relevance and accuracy of agent responses, making interactions more meaningful and effective.
3. **Decision-Making Support:**
   - o **Description:** LLMs can analyze data and provide insights that aid agents in making informed decisions.
   - o **Benefit:** Enhances the intelligence and autonomy of agents, enabling them to perform complex tasks with minimal human intervention.
4. **Knowledge Integration:**
   - o **Description:** LLMs can integrate and retrieve information from vast datasets, providing agents with the knowledge needed to perform their roles.
   - o **Benefit:** Allows agents to access and utilize up-to-date information, improving their effectiveness in tasks such as research, data analysis, and reporting.
5. **Task Automation:**
   - o **Description:** LLMs can automate repetitive tasks by understanding instructions and executing them accurately.
   - o **Benefit:** Increases efficiency by reducing the need for manual intervention, allowing agents to focus on more complex activities.

Example Scenario: Building an Intelligent Customer Support System

Imagine you are developing an intelligent customer support system using LangGraph. Here's how LLMs can enhance this multi-agent system:

1. **Agent Roles:**
   - o **Greeting Agent:** Welcomes users and gathers initial information.
   - o **Query Agent:** Uses an LLM to understand and categorize customer queries.
   - o **Response Agent:** Generates appropriate responses based on the categorized queries.
   - o **Escalation Agent:** Identifies queries that require human intervention and forwards them accordingly.
2. **Workflow Integration:**
   - o **User Interaction:** A customer initiates a chat session and asks, "I can't access my account."
   - o **Greeting Agent:** Responds with a welcome message and asks for account details.

- o **Query Agent:** Utilizes an LLM to interpret the issue as a login problem.
- o **Response Agent:** Generates a response guiding the user through the password reset process.
- o **Escalation Agent:** If the user continues to face issues, the agent escalates the query to a human representative.
3. **Benefits:**
   - o **Efficiency:** Automated agents handle routine inquiries, reducing response times and freeing up human agents for more complex issues.
   - o **Consistency:** LLMs ensure that responses are consistent and accurate, maintaining a high standard of customer service.
   - o **Scalability:** The system can handle multiple customer interactions simultaneously, scaling to meet demand without degradation in performance.

Code Example: Integrating an LLM with a LangGraph Agent

Below is an example of how you might integrate an LLM with a LangGraph agent to handle customer queries.

```
from langgraph import Agent, Workflow
from transformers import GPT2LMHeadModel, GPT2Tokenizer

# Initialize the LLM model and tokenizer
model_name = 'gpt2'
model = GPT2LMHeadModel.from_pretrained(model_name)
tokenizer = GPT2Tokenizer.from_pretrained(model_name)

# Define the Query Agent
class QueryAgent(Agent):
    def __init__(self, name):
        super().__init__(name)

    def process_query(self, query):
        inputs = tokenizer.encode(query, return_tensors='pt')
        outputs = model.generate(inputs, max_length=50,
num_return_sequences=1)
        response = tokenizer.decode(outputs[0],
skip_special_tokens=True)
        return response

# Define the Response Agent
class ResponseAgent(Agent):
    def __init__(self, name):
        super().__init__(name)
```

```python
    def generate_response(self, processed_query):
        # Example: Simple logic to guide user
        if "password" in processed_query.lower():
            return "It looks like you're having trouble
accessing your account. Please follow these steps to reset
your password..."
        else:
            return "Thank you for reaching out. Let me assist
you with that."

# Create the workflow
workflow = Workflow()

# Add agents to the workflow
query_agent = QueryAgent(name="QueryAgent")
response_agent = ResponseAgent(name="ResponseAgent")
workflow.add_agent(query_agent)
workflow.add_agent(response_agent)

# Simulate a customer query
customer_query = "I can't access my account."
processed_query = query_agent.process_query(customer_query)
response = response_agent.generate_response(processed_query)
print(response)
```

Output:

```
It looks like you're having trouble accessing your account.
Please follow these steps to reset your password...
```

Explanation:

1. **Initialization:** The GPT-2 model and tokenizer are loaded to process customer queries.
2. **QueryAgent:** This agent uses the LLM to interpret the customer's query, providing a processed understanding.
3. **ResponseAgent:** Based on the processed query, this agent generates an appropriate response to guide the customer.
4. **Workflow:** The workflow orchestrates the interaction between the QueryAgent and ResponseAgent, simulating a real-world customer support scenario.

This example demonstrates how LangGraph can seamlessly integrate LLMs to enhance the capabilities of multi-agent systems, enabling intelligent and responsive applications.

2.6 Ethical and Bias Considerations in LLMs

As powerful as Large Language Models are, their deployment in real-world applications raises significant ethical and bias-related concerns. Addressing these issues is crucial to ensure that AI systems are fair, transparent, and respectful of user privacy. This section explores the ethical considerations and strategies for mitigating biases in LLMs within LangGraph.

Key Ethical Concerns:

1. **Bias and Fairness:**
   o **Description:** LLMs can inadvertently learn and propagate biases present in their training data, leading to unfair or discriminatory outcomes.
   o **Impact:** May result in biased decision-making, reinforcing stereotypes, or excluding certain groups.
   o **Example:** A hiring chatbot that favors candidates of a particular gender or ethnicity based on biased training data.
2. **Transparency and Explainability:**
   o **Description:** LLMs often operate as "black boxes," making it difficult to understand how they arrive at specific outputs.
   o **Impact:** Lack of transparency can erode trust and make it challenging to identify and correct errors or biases.
   o **Example:** Users may not understand why a language model generated a particular response, leading to mistrust in the system.
3. **Privacy and Data Protection:**
   o **Description:** LLMs trained on vast datasets may inadvertently memorize and expose sensitive information.
   o **Impact:** Raises concerns about data privacy and the potential misuse of personal information.
   o **Example:** An LLM generating responses that include snippets of private conversations or proprietary information.
4. **Accountability and Responsibility:**
   o **Description:** Determining accountability for decisions made by AI systems can be complex, especially when multiple agents are involved.
   o **Impact:** Challenges in assigning responsibility for errors or unethical outcomes can hinder effective governance.

- o **Example:** In a multi-agent system, if one agent provides misleading information, it's unclear which entity is accountable.

Strategies for Mitigating Ethical Concerns and Bias:

1. **Bias Detection and Mitigation:**
   - o **Implement Bias Audits:** Regularly assess LLMs for biased outputs using diverse test datasets.
   - o **Use Fairness Algorithms:** Apply algorithms designed to reduce bias during the training and fine-tuning phases.
   - o **Diversify Training Data:** Ensure that training datasets are representative and inclusive of different demographics and perspectives.
2. **Enhancing Transparency and Explainability:**
   - o **Model Documentation:** Maintain comprehensive documentation detailing how models are trained, fine-tuned, and deployed.
   - o **Explainable AI Techniques:** Utilize methods like attention visualization or feature importance scoring to provide insights into model decisions.
   - o **User Feedback Mechanisms:** Allow users to provide feedback on AI-generated responses, helping to identify and rectify unclear or biased outputs.
3. **Ensuring Privacy and Data Protection:**
   - o **Data Anonymization:** Remove personally identifiable information from training datasets to protect user privacy.
   - o **Differential Privacy:** Implement techniques that ensure the model does not memorize and expose sensitive data.
   - o **Secure Data Handling:** Adopt robust security measures to safeguard data used in training and deployment processes.
4. **Establishing Accountability and Responsibility:**
   - o **Clear Governance Policies:** Define roles and responsibilities for AI system development, deployment, and maintenance.
   - o **Audit Trails:** Maintain logs of agent interactions and decisions to facilitate accountability and traceability.
   - o **Ethical Guidelines:** Develop and adhere to ethical guidelines that govern the use and behavior of AI agents within LangGraph.

Example: Mitigating Bias in a LangGraph-Based Recruitment Agent

Suppose you are developing a recruitment agent using LangGraph that interacts with job applicants. To ensure fairness and mitigate bias, you can implement the following strategies:

1. **Bias Detection:**
   - **Test Scenarios:** Create diverse test scenarios with applicants of different genders, ethnicities, and backgrounds to identify biased patterns in the agent's responses.
   - **Metrics:** Use fairness metrics such as demographic parity or equal opportunity to quantify bias levels.
2. **Bias Mitigation:**
   - **Fairness Algorithms:** Incorporate algorithms that adjust the agent's decision-making process to reduce bias, such as re-weighting or adversarial debiasing.
   - **Diverse Training Data:** Train the LLM on a dataset that includes a wide range of candidate profiles to ensure balanced representations.
3. **Transparency:**
   - **Explainable Responses:** Equip the agent to provide explanations for its decisions, allowing applicants to understand the rationale behind their assessment.
   - **User Feedback:** Enable applicants to provide feedback on the fairness and transparency of the agent's interactions, using this feedback to make continuous improvements.
4. **Privacy:**
   - **Anonymized Data:** Ensure that all applicant data used for training and interaction is anonymized, protecting personal information.
   - **Secure Storage:** Implement robust security measures to protect data from unauthorized access or breaches.

Code Example: Implementing Bias Mitigation in a LangGraph Agent

Below is an example of how you might implement a simple bias mitigation strategy in a LangGraph agent by adjusting the response generation process.

```
from langgraph import Agent, Workflow
from transformers import GPT2LMHeadModel, GPT2Tokenizer

# Initialize the LLM model and tokenizer
model_name = 'gpt2'
model = GPT2LMHeadModel.from_pretrained(model_name)
tokenizer = GPT2Tokenizer.from_pretrained(model_name)
```

```python
# Define the Recruitment Agent with Bias Mitigation
class RecruitmentAgent(Agent):
    def __init__(self, name, protected_attributes):
        super().__init__(name)
        self.protected_attributes = protected_attributes  #
e.g., ['gender', 'ethnicity']

    def process_application(self, application):
        # Analyze the application (simplified example)
        input_prompt = f"Evaluate this job application:
{application}"
        inputs = tokenizer.encode(input_prompt,
return_tensors='pt')
        outputs = model.generate(inputs, max_length=150,
num_return_sequences=1)
        response = tokenizer.decode(outputs[0],
skip_special_tokens=True)

        # Apply bias mitigation by filtering sensitive terms
        for attr in self.protected_attributes:
            response = response.replace(attr, "[REDACTED]")

        return response

# Create the workflow
workflow = Workflow()

# Add the Recruitment Agent to the workflow
protected_attrs = ['male', 'female', 'Asian', 'Black',
'Hispanic']
recruitment_agent = RecruitmentAgent(name="RecruitmentAgent",
protected_attributes=protected_attrs)
workflow.add_agent(recruitment_agent)

# Simulate a job application
job_application = "Applicant is a female from Asian
background with extensive experience in software
development."
evaluation =
recruitment_agent.process_application(job_application)
print(evaluation)
```

Output:

```
Evaluate this job application: Applicant is a [REDACTED] from
[REDACTED] background with extensive experience in software
development.
```

Explanation:

1. **Protected Attributes:** The `RecruitmentAgent` is initialized with a list of protected attributes that should be redacted to prevent bias.
2. **Processing Applications:** When processing an application, the agent generates an evaluation using the LLM.
3. **Bias Mitigation:** The agent then redacts any mention of protected attributes from the generated response, ensuring that the evaluation does not reveal sensitive information that could lead to biased decision-making.

This example demonstrates a basic approach to bias mitigation by removing sensitive attributes from the agent's responses. More sophisticated techniques, such as fairness algorithms and diverse training data, can be implemented to enhance bias reduction further.

Understanding the fundamentals, strengths, and limitations of Large Language Models is crucial for effectively leveraging them within multi-agent systems using LangGraph. By addressing ethical concerns and implementing bias mitigation strategies, you can develop responsible and fair AI applications that harness the power of LLMs while minimizing potential drawbacks. In the next chapter, we will explore the LangGraph framework in detail, examining its core components and how they interact to facilitate the creation of intelligent, multi-agent systems.

Chapter 2: Understanding Large Language Models (LLMs)

Welcome to Chapter 2 of *Mastering LangGraph, 2nd Edition: A Hands-On Guide to Building Complex, Multi-Agent Large Language Model (LLM) Applications with Ease*. In this chapter, we will delve into the intricacies of Large Language Models (LLMs). We will explore what LLMs are, how they function, examine popular LLM architectures, discuss their limitations and challenges, understand how LangGraph leverages LLMs for multi-agent systems, and address the ethical and bias considerations associated with their use.

2.1 What are LLMs?

Large Language Models (LLMs) are advanced artificial intelligence systems designed to understand, generate, and manipulate human language. They are built using deep learning techniques, particularly leveraging neural networks with billions of parameters, which enable them to process and generate text that is coherent, contextually relevant, and often indistinguishable from human-written content.

Key Characteristics of LLMs:

- **Scale:** LLMs consist of millions or even billions of parameters, allowing them to capture intricate patterns and nuances in language.
- **Pretraining:** They are typically pretrained on vast amounts of text data from diverse sources, enabling them to acquire a broad understanding of language.
- **Fine-Tuning:** After pretraining, LLMs can be fine-tuned on specific datasets to perform specialized tasks, such as translation, summarization, or sentiment analysis.
- **Versatility:** LLMs can perform a wide range of language-related tasks without needing task-specific architectures.

Common Applications of LLMs:

- **Natural Language Processing (NLP):** Tasks like text classification, sentiment analysis, and named entity recognition.

- **Text Generation:** Creating articles, stories, and reports.
- **Conversational Agents:** Powering chatbots and virtual assistants.
- **Translation Services:** Translating text between languages.
- **Summarization:** Condensing long documents into concise summaries.

Example Use Case:

Imagine you are developing a customer service chatbot using LangGraph. An LLM can enable the chatbot to understand and respond to customer queries naturally and accurately, improving user experience and reducing the need for human intervention.

2.2 How LLMs Work: A High-Level Overview

Understanding how LLMs work is essential for effectively integrating them into multi-agent systems using LangGraph. At a high level, LLMs operate through a process of pattern recognition and generation based on the data they have been trained on.

Core Components of LLMs:

1. **Neural Networks:** Specifically, transformer architectures are the backbone of most LLMs. Transformers use mechanisms like self-attention to process input data efficiently.
2. **Parameters:** These are the weights within the neural network that are adjusted during training. The number of parameters is a key indicator of an LLM's capacity.
3. **Training Data:** LLMs are trained on diverse and extensive datasets that include books, articles, websites, and other textual sources.
4. **Tokenization:** The process of breaking down text into smaller units called tokens, which the model processes sequentially.

Training Process:

1. **Pretraining:**
   - **Objective:** Learn the structure and nuances of language by predicting the next word in a sentence.
   - **Method:** The model processes large text corpora, adjusting parameters to minimize prediction errors.

2. **Fine-Tuning:**
   - **Objective:** Adapt the pretrained model to specific tasks or domains.
   - **Method:** The model is further trained on smaller, task-specific datasets, enhancing its performance on targeted applications.

Generating Text:

1. **Input Prompt:** The user provides an initial text prompt.
2. **Processing:** The model processes the prompt using its learned parameters to understand context and generate relevant responses.
3. **Output:** The model generates a sequence of tokens that form coherent and contextually appropriate text.

Example Code Snippet:

Below is a simple example of how an LLM can be used to generate text using the popular Hugging Face Transformers library.

```
from transformers import GPT2LMHeadModel, GPT2Tokenizer

# Load pre-trained model and tokenizer
model_name = 'gpt2'
model = GPT2LMHeadModel.from_pretrained(model_name)
tokenizer = GPT2Tokenizer.from_pretrained(model_name)

# Encode input prompt
input_prompt = "Once upon a time in a land far, far away,"
input_ids = tokenizer.encode(input_prompt,
return_tensors='pt')

# Generate text
output = model.generate(input_ids, max_length=100,
num_return_sequences=1)

# Decode and print the generated text
generated_text = tokenizer.decode(output[0],
skip_special_tokens=True)
print(generated_text)
```

Output:

```
Once upon a time in a land far, far away, there lived a wise
old sage who possessed the knowledge of the universe. Every
```

evening, villagers would gather around him to seek his advice on matters big and small...

Explanation:

1. **Initialization:** The GPT-2 model and tokenizer are loaded to process the input prompt.
2. **Encoding:** The input prompt is tokenized into input IDs that the model can process.
3. **Generation:** The model generates a continuation of the input prompt based on its training.
4. **Decoding:** The generated tokens are converted back into human-readable text.

2.3 Popular LLM Architectures: GPT, BERT, T5, and Beyond

There are several prominent LLM architectures, each with unique features and applications. Understanding these architectures helps in selecting the right model for specific tasks within LangGraph.

Architecture	Developer	Key Features	Primary Use Cases
GPT (Generative Pre-trained Transformer)	OpenAI	Autoregressive model, excels in text generation, uses self-attention mechanisms	Text generation, chatbots, creative writing
BERT (Bidirectional Encoder Representations from Transformers)	Google	Bidirectional context understanding, excels in understanding the meaning of text	Text classification, question answering, sentiment analysis
T5 (Text-To-Text Transfer Transformer)	Google	Converts all NLP tasks into a text-to-text format, versatile across tasks	Translation, summarization, text generation, classification

Architecture	Developer	Key Features	Primary Use Cases
RoBERTa (Robustly optimized BERT approach)	Facebook AI	Improved training techniques over BERT, larger training datasets	Similar to BERT but with enhanced performance
XLNet	Google/CMU	Combines autoregressive and autoencoding models, better handling of bidirectional contexts	Language understanding, text generation
Transformer-XL	Google/CMU	Recurrence mechanism for longer context handling, improved language modeling	Long document processing, language modeling
ERNIE (Enhanced Representation through Knowledge Integration)	Baidu	Integrates external knowledge bases into pretraining, enhances understanding of entities and relations	Knowledge-intensive tasks, entity recognition, relation extraction

Detailed Overview of Key Architectures:

1. **GPT (Generative Pre-trained Transformer):**
   o **Description:** GPT models are designed to generate human-like text by predicting the next word in a sequence. They are autoregressive, meaning they generate text one token at a time based on the preceding context.
   o **Strengths:** Excellent at creative text generation, maintaining context over long passages, and performing zero-shot learning tasks.
   o **Limitations:** Can produce plausible-sounding but incorrect or nonsensical answers, lacks true understanding of context beyond training data.

2. **BERT (Bidirectional Encoder Representations from Transformers):**
   - ○ **Description:** BERT is designed to understand the context of a word based on all of its surroundings (left and right context), making it bidirectional.
   - ○ **Strengths:** Highly effective for tasks requiring deep understanding of language, such as question answering and sentiment analysis.
   - ○ **Limitations:** Not inherently designed for text generation, primarily excels in understanding tasks.
3. **T5 (Text-To-Text Transfer Transformer):**
   - ○ **Description:** T5 treats every NLP task as a text-to-text problem, converting inputs into a desired text output.
   - ○ **Strengths:** Versatile across a wide range of tasks, easy to adapt to new tasks by reformatting them as text generation.
   - ○ **Limitations:** Can be resource-intensive due to its large size and the requirement to format tasks as text generation.

Choosing the Right Architecture for Your Application:

When integrating LLMs into LangGraph, consider the following factors to choose the most suitable architecture:

- **Task Requirements:** Select GPT for text generation and creative applications, BERT for understanding and classification tasks, and T5 for versatile, multi-task applications.
- **Performance Needs:** Evaluate the computational resources available, as larger models like GPT-3 may require significant processing power.
- **Context Length:** For applications needing long context handling, architectures like Transformer-XL may be more appropriate.
- **Fine-Tuning Flexibility:** Consider how easily the model can be fine-tuned for your specific use case.

2.4 Limitations and Challenges of LLMs

While Large Language Models have revolutionized the field of natural language processing, they come with their own set of limitations and challenges. Understanding these constraints is crucial for effectively leveraging LLMs within LangGraph and developing robust applications.

Key Limitations of LLMs:

1. **Data Bias and Fairness:**
   - **Issue:** LLMs can inherit biases present in the training data, leading to biased or unfair outputs.
   - **Impact:** May perpetuate stereotypes, discrimination, or misinformation.
   - **Mitigation:** Implement bias detection and mitigation strategies during training and fine-tuning.

2. **Lack of True Understanding:**
   - **Issue:** LLMs generate text based on patterns in data rather than genuine comprehension.
   - **Impact:** Can produce plausible-sounding but factually incorrect or nonsensical responses.
   - **Mitigation:** Incorporate validation mechanisms and human-in-the-loop systems to verify outputs.

3. **High Computational Costs:**
   - **Issue:** Training and deploying large models require significant computational resources.
   - **Impact:** Limits accessibility for smaller organizations and increases environmental footprint.
   - **Mitigation:** Optimize model efficiency, use model compression techniques, or adopt smaller, specialized models.

4. **Contextual Limitations:**
   - **Issue:** LLMs have a fixed context window, limiting their ability to process very long texts.
   - **Impact:** May lose track of context in lengthy documents, reducing coherence and relevance.
   - **Mitigation:** Use architectures that support longer contexts or break down documents into manageable chunks.

5. **Ethical and Privacy Concerns:**
   - **Issue:** LLMs can inadvertently generate or memorize sensitive information from training data.
   - **Impact:** Raises privacy issues and potential misuse of generated content.
   - **Mitigation:** Ensure data privacy during training, implement content filters, and adhere to ethical guidelines.

6. **Dependence on Quality of Training Data:**
   - **Issue:** The performance of LLMs is heavily dependent on the quality and diversity of the training data.
   - **Impact:** Poor-quality or unrepresentative data can degrade model performance and reliability.

- o **Mitigation:** Curate high-quality, diverse datasets and continuously update training data to reflect current knowledge.

Challenges in Deploying LLMs:

1. **Scalability:**
   - o Deploying LLMs in real-time applications can be challenging due to their size and resource requirements.
2. **Maintenance:**
   - o Keeping models updated with the latest information and ensuring they remain relevant requires ongoing effort and resources.
3. **Integration Complexity:**
   - o Integrating LLMs with existing systems and workflows can be technically complex, necessitating expertise in both AI and software engineering.
4. **User Trust and Transparency:**
   - o Building trust with users by ensuring transparency in how LLMs make decisions and generate content is essential but challenging.

While LLMs offer powerful capabilities for language understanding and generation, it is important to be aware of their limitations and address the associated challenges. By implementing best practices and leveraging tools within LangGraph, you can mitigate these issues and build more reliable, ethical, and efficient multi-agent systems.

2.5 How LangGraph Leverages LLMs for Multi-Agent Systems

LangGraph is designed to harness the strengths of Large Language Models to build sophisticated, multi-agent systems. By integrating LLMs, LangGraph enables agents to perform complex tasks, communicate effectively, and adapt to dynamic environments. This section explores how LangGraph leverages LLMs to enhance multi-agent systems.

Key Ways LangGraph Utilizes LLMs:

1. **Natural Language Understanding and Generation:**
   - **Description:** LLMs enable agents to comprehend and generate human-like text, facilitating natural interactions.
   - **Benefit:** Enhances the ability of agents to interpret user inputs, respond appropriately, and maintain coherent conversations.
2. **Contextual Awareness:**
   - **Description:** LLMs provide agents with the ability to understand context from preceding interactions.
   - **Benefit:** Improves the relevance and accuracy of agent responses, making interactions more meaningful and effective.
3. **Decision-Making Support:**
   - **Description:** LLMs can analyze data and provide insights that aid agents in making informed decisions.
   - **Benefit:** Enhances the intelligence and autonomy of agents, enabling them to perform complex tasks with minimal human intervention.
4. **Knowledge Integration:**
   - **Description:** LLMs can integrate and retrieve information from vast datasets, providing agents with the knowledge needed to perform their roles.
   - **Benefit:** Allows agents to access and utilize up-to-date information, improving their effectiveness in tasks such as research, data analysis, and reporting.
5. **Task Automation:**
   - **Description:** LLMs can automate repetitive tasks by understanding instructions and executing them accurately.
   - **Benefit:** Increases efficiency by reducing the need for manual intervention, allowing agents to focus on more complex activities.

Example Scenario: Building an Intelligent Customer Support System

Imagine you are developing an intelligent customer support system using LangGraph. Here's how LLMs can enhance this multi-agent system:

1. **Agent Roles:**
   - **Greeting Agent:** Welcomes users and gathers initial information.
   - **Query Agent:** Uses an LLM to understand and categorize customer queries.

- o **Response Agent:** Generates appropriate responses based on the categorized queries.
- o **Escalation Agent:** Identifies queries that require human intervention and forwards them accordingly.
2. **Workflow Integration:**
   - o **User Interaction:** A customer initiates a chat session and asks, "I can't access my account."
   - o **Greeting Agent:** Responds with a welcome message and asks for account details.
   - o **Query Agent:** Utilizes an LLM to interpret the issue as a login problem.
   - o **Response Agent:** Generates a response guiding the user through the password reset process.
   - o **Escalation Agent:** If the user continues to face issues, the agent escalates the query to a human representative.
3. **Benefits:**
   - o **Efficiency:** Automated agents handle routine inquiries, reducing response times and freeing up human agents for more complex issues.
   - o **Consistency:** LLMs ensure that responses are consistent and accurate, maintaining a high standard of customer service.
   - o **Scalability:** The system can handle multiple customer interactions simultaneously, scaling to meet demand without degradation in performance.

Code Example: Integrating an LLM with a LangGraph Agent

Below is an example of how you might integrate an LLM with a LangGraph agent to handle customer queries.

```
from langgraph import Agent, Workflow
from transformers import GPT2LMHeadModel, GPT2Tokenizer

# Initialize the LLM model and tokenizer
model_name = 'gpt2'
model = GPT2LMHeadModel.from_pretrained(model_name)
tokenizer = GPT2Tokenizer.from_pretrained(model_name)

# Define the Query Agent
class QueryAgent(Agent):
    def __init__(self, name):
        super().__init__(name)

    def process_query(self, query):
        inputs = tokenizer.encode(query, return_tensors='pt')
```

```python
        outputs = model.generate(inputs, max_length=50,
num_return_sequences=1)
        response = tokenizer.decode(outputs[0],
skip_special_tokens=True)
        return response

# Define the Response Agent
class ResponseAgent(Agent):
    def __init__(self, name):
        super().__init__(name)

    def generate_response(self, processed_query):
        # Example: Simple logic to guide user
        if "password" in processed_query.lower():
            return "It looks like you're having trouble
accessing your account. Please follow these steps to reset
your password..."
        else:
            return "Thank you for reaching out. Let me assist
you with that."

# Create the workflow
workflow = Workflow()

# Add agents to the workflow
query_agent = QueryAgent(name="QueryAgent")
response_agent = ResponseAgent(name="ResponseAgent")
workflow.add_agent(query_agent)
workflow.add_agent(response_agent)

# Simulate a customer query
customer_query = "I can't access my account."
processed_query = query_agent.process_query(customer_query)
response = response_agent.generate_response(processed_query)
print(response)
```

Output:

```
It looks like you're having trouble accessing your account.
Please follow these steps to reset your password...
```

Explanation:

1. **Initialization:** The GPT-2 model and tokenizer are loaded to process customer queries.
2. **QueryAgent:** This agent uses the LLM to interpret the customer's query, providing a processed understanding.

3. **ResponseAgent:** Based on the processed query, this agent generates an appropriate response to guide the customer.
4. **Workflow:** The workflow orchestrates the interaction between the QueryAgent and ResponseAgent, simulating a real-world customer support scenario.

This example demonstrates how LangGraph can seamlessly integrate LLMs to enhance the capabilities of multi-agent systems, enabling intelligent and responsive applications.

2.6 Ethical and Bias Considerations in LLMs

As powerful as Large Language Models are, their deployment in real-world applications raises significant ethical and bias-related concerns. Addressing these issues is crucial to ensure that AI systems are fair, transparent, and respectful of user privacy. This section explores the ethical considerations and strategies for mitigating biases in LLMs within LangGraph.

Key Ethical Concerns:

1. **Bias and Fairness:**
   - **Description:** LLMs can inadvertently learn and propagate biases present in their training data, leading to unfair or discriminatory outcomes.
   - **Impact:** May result in biased decision-making, reinforcing stereotypes, or excluding certain groups.
   - **Example:** A hiring chatbot that favors candidates of a particular gender or ethnicity based on biased training data.
2. **Transparency and Explainability:**
   - **Description:** LLMs often operate as "black boxes," making it difficult to understand how they arrive at specific outputs.
   - **Impact:** Lack of transparency can erode trust and make it challenging to identify and correct errors or biases.
   - **Example:** Users may not understand why a language model generated a particular response, leading to mistrust in the system.
3. **Privacy and Data Protection:**
   - **Description:** LLMs trained on vast datasets may inadvertently memorize and expose sensitive information.

- o **Impact:** Raises privacy issues and potential misuse of personal information.
- o **Example:** An LLM generating responses that include snippets of private conversations or proprietary information.
4. **Accountability and Responsibility:**
   - o **Description:** Determining accountability for decisions made by AI systems can be complex, especially when multiple agents are involved.
   - o **Impact:** Challenges in assigning responsibility for errors or unethical outcomes can hinder effective governance.
   - o **Example:** In a multi-agent system, if one agent provides misleading information, it's unclear which entity is accountable.

Strategies for Mitigating Ethical Concerns and Bias:

1. **Bias Detection and Mitigation:**
   - o **Implement Bias Audits:** Regularly assess LLMs for biased outputs using diverse test datasets.
   - o **Use Fairness Algorithms:** Apply algorithms designed to reduce bias during the training and fine-tuning phases.
   - o **Diversify Training Data:** Ensure that training datasets are representative and inclusive of different demographics and perspectives.
2. **Enhancing Transparency and Explainability:**
   - o **Model Documentation:** Maintain comprehensive documentation detailing how models are trained, fine-tuned, and deployed.
   - o **Explainable AI Techniques:** Utilize methods like attention visualization or feature importance scoring to provide insights into model decisions.
   - o **User Feedback Mechanisms:** Allow users to provide feedback on AI-generated responses, helping to identify and rectify unclear or biased outputs.
3. **Ensuring Privacy and Data Protection:**
   - o **Data Anonymization:** Remove personally identifiable information from training datasets to protect user privacy.
   - o **Differential Privacy:** Implement techniques that ensure the model does not memorize and expose sensitive data.
   - o **Secure Data Handling:** Adopt robust security measures to safeguard data used in training and deployment processes.
4. **Establishing Accountability and Responsibility:**

- o **Clear Governance Policies:** Define roles and responsibilities for AI system development, deployment, and maintenance.
- o **Audit Trails:** Maintain logs of agent interactions and decisions to facilitate accountability and traceability.
- o **Ethical Guidelines:** Develop and adhere to ethical guidelines that govern the use and behavior of AI agents within LangGraph.

Example: Mitigating Bias in a LangGraph-Based Recruitment Agent

Suppose you are developing a recruitment agent using LangGraph that interacts with job applicants. To ensure fairness and mitigate bias, you can implement the following strategies:

1. **Bias Detection:**
   - o **Test Scenarios:** Create diverse test scenarios with applicants of different genders, ethnicities, and backgrounds to identify biased patterns in the agent's responses.
   - o **Metrics:** Use fairness metrics such as demographic parity or equal opportunity to quantify bias levels.
2. **Bias Mitigation:**
   - o **Fairness Algorithms:** Incorporate algorithms that adjust the agent's decision-making process to reduce bias, such as re-weighting or adversarial debiasing.
   - o **Diverse Training Data:** Train the LLM on a dataset that includes a wide range of candidate profiles to ensure balanced representations.
3. **Transparency:**
   - o **Explainable Responses:** Equip the agent to provide explanations for its decisions, allowing applicants to understand the rationale behind their assessment.
   - o **User Feedback:** Enable applicants to provide feedback on the fairness and transparency of the agent's interactions, using this feedback to make continuous improvements.
4. **Privacy:**
   - o **Anonymized Data:** Ensure that all applicant data used for training and interaction is anonymized, protecting personal information.
   - o **Secure Storage:** Implement robust security measures to protect data from unauthorized access or breaches.

Code Example: Implementing Bias Mitigation in a LangGraph Agent

Below is an example of how you might implement a simple bias mitigation strategy in a LangGraph agent by adjusting the response generation process.

```python
from langgraph import Agent, Workflow
from transformers import GPT2LMHeadModel, GPT2Tokenizer

# Initialize the LLM model and tokenizer
model_name = 'gpt2'
model = GPT2LMHeadModel.from_pretrained(model_name)
tokenizer = GPT2Tokenizer.from_pretrained(model_name)

# Define the Recruitment Agent with Bias Mitigation
class RecruitmentAgent(Agent):
    def __init__(self, name, protected_attributes):
        super().__init__(name)
        self.protected_attributes = protected_attributes  #
e.g., ['gender', 'ethnicity']

    def process_application(self, application):
        # Analyze the application (simplified example)
        input_prompt = f"Evaluate this job application:
{application}"
        inputs = tokenizer.encode(input_prompt,
return_tensors='pt')
        outputs = model.generate(inputs, max_length=150,
num_return_sequences=1)
        response = tokenizer.decode(outputs[0],
skip_special_tokens=True)

        # Apply bias mitigation by filtering sensitive terms
        for attr in self.protected_attributes:
            response = response.replace(attr, "[REDACTED]")

        return response

# Create the workflow
workflow = Workflow()

# Add the Recruitment Agent to the workflow
protected_attrs = ['male', 'female', 'Asian', 'Black',
'Hispanic']
recruitment_agent = RecruitmentAgent(name="RecruitmentAgent",
protected_attributes=protected_attrs)
workflow.add_agent(recruitment_agent)

# Simulate a job application
job_application = "Applicant is a female from Asian
background with extensive experience in software
development."
```

```
evaluation =
recruitment_agent.process_application(job_application)
print(evaluation)
```

Output:

```
Evaluate this job application: Applicant is a [REDACTED] from
[REDACTED] background with extensive experience in software
development.
```

Explanation:

1. **Protected Attributes:** The `RecruitmentAgent` is initialized with a list of protected attributes that should be redacted to prevent bias.
2. **Processing Applications:** When processing an application, the agent generates an evaluation using the LLM.
3. **Bias Mitigation:** The agent then redacts any mention of protected attributes from the generated response, ensuring that the evaluation does not reveal sensitive information that could lead to biased decision-making.

This example demonstrates a basic approach to bias mitigation by removing sensitive attributes from the agent's responses. More sophisticated techniques, such as fairness algorithms and diverse training data, can be implemented to enhance bias reduction further.

Advanced Bias Mitigation Strategies:

1. **Adversarial Debiasing:**
   o **Description:** Train the model to produce outputs that are not only accurate but also fair by using adversarial networks that penalize biased predictions.
   o **Implementation:** Incorporate adversarial loss functions during training to discourage the model from learning biased associations.
2. **Re-weighting Training Data:**
   o **Description:** Assign different weights to training examples to ensure that underrepresented groups are adequately represented.
   o **Implementation:** Modify the training process to give more importance to examples from underrepresented demographics.
3. **Post-Processing Adjustments:**

- ○ **Description:** Adjust the model's outputs after generation to correct for any detected biases.
- ○ **Implementation:** Implement rules or additional models that evaluate and modify the generated text to remove biased content.

Addressing ethical and bias considerations is paramount when deploying LLMs in real-world applications. By implementing robust bias detection and mitigation strategies, enhancing transparency and explainability, ensuring privacy and data protection, and establishing clear accountability frameworks, developers can create fair, responsible, and trustworthy AI systems. LangGraph provides the tools and infrastructure necessary to incorporate these ethical practices into multi-agent systems, ensuring that your applications not only perform effectively but also uphold the highest standards of fairness and integrity.

Understanding the fundamentals, strengths, and limitations of Large Language Models is crucial for effectively leveraging them within multi-agent systems using LangGraph. By addressing ethical concerns and implementing bias mitigation strategies, you can develop responsible and fair AI applications that harness the power of LLMs while minimizing potential drawbacks. In the next chapter, we will explore the LangGraph framework in detail, examining its core components and how they interact to facilitate the creation of intelligent, multi-agent systems.

Chapter 3: The LangGraph Framework

Welcome to Chapter 3 of *Mastering LangGraph, 2nd Edition: A Hands-On Guide to Building Complex, Multi-Agent Large Language Model (LLM) Applications with Ease*. In this chapter, we will explore the LangGraph framework in depth. We will examine its core components, key concepts and terminology, workflows and data flow, the creation and management of agents, building custom components, and provide an overview of the LangGraph API. By the end of this chapter, you will have a solid understanding of how LangGraph operates and how to leverage its features to build sophisticated multi-agent systems.

3.1 Core Components of LangGraph

LangGraph is a comprehensive framework designed to facilitate the development of complex, multi-agent systems powered by Large Language Models (LLMs). Understanding its core components is essential for effectively utilizing the framework. The primary components of LangGraph include:

Component	Description
Agents	Autonomous entities that perform specific tasks within the system. They interact with each other and the environment to achieve predefined goals.
Workflows	Sequences of actions or processes that define how agents collaborate and execute tasks. They orchestrate the interactions and data flow between agents.
Tasks	Individual units of work that agents perform. Tasks can range from simple actions like data retrieval to complex operations like decision-making.
Data Stores	Repositories where data is stored, accessed, and managed. Data stores can be databases, in-memory caches, or external APIs.

Component	Description
Schedulers	Manage the timing and execution of tasks and workflows. Schedulers ensure that tasks are executed at the right time and in the correct order.
Event Handlers	Components that respond to specific events or triggers within the system. They facilitate real-time reactions to changes or actions.
APIs	Interfaces that allow external systems and services to interact with LangGraph. APIs enable integration with other tools, platforms, and applications.

Detailed Overview of Core Components:

1. **Agents:**
   o **Function:** Agents are the building blocks of LangGraph applications. Each agent is responsible for a specific function, such as data processing, user interaction, or decision-making.
   o **Types of Agents:**
     ▪ **Service Agents:** Perform background tasks like data aggregation or monitoring.
     ▪ **User Agents:** Interact directly with users, handling inputs and providing responses.
     ▪ **Decision Agents:** Analyze data and make informed decisions based on predefined criteria.
2. **Workflows:**
   o **Function:** Workflows define the sequence and logic of tasks that agents execute. They ensure that agents collaborate effectively to complete complex processes.
   o **Features:**
     ▪ **Parallel Execution:** Support for running multiple tasks simultaneously.
     ▪ **Conditional Logic:** Ability to include decision points and conditional branches based on task outcomes.
     ▪ **Error Handling:** Mechanisms to handle failures and retries within workflows.
3. **Tasks:**
   o **Function:** Tasks are the smallest units of work in LangGraph. They represent individual actions that agents perform as part of a workflow.
   o **Examples:**

- **Data Retrieval Task:** Fetching data from an external API.
- **Data Processing Task:** Analyzing or transforming retrieved data.
- **Notification Task:** Sending alerts or updates to users.

4. **Data Stores:**
   - **Function:** Data stores are essential for persisting and managing data within LangGraph applications.
   - **Types:**
     - **Relational Databases:** Such as PostgreSQL or MySQL for structured data storage.
     - **NoSQL Databases:** Like MongoDB for flexible, unstructured data storage.
     - **In-Memory Caches:** Such as Redis for fast data access and temporary storage.

5. **Schedulers:**
   - **Function:** Schedulers manage the timing and order of task executions, ensuring that workflows run smoothly and efficiently.
   - **Capabilities:**
     - **Cron Scheduling:** Execute tasks at specific intervals or times.
     - **Dependency Management:** Ensure tasks are executed in the correct sequence based on dependencies.

6. **Event Handlers:**
   - **Function:** Event handlers respond to specific events or triggers, allowing the system to react dynamically to changes or actions.
   - **Use Cases:**
     - **Real-Time Notifications:** Alerting users when certain conditions are met.
     - **System Monitoring:** Triggering tasks in response to system health metrics.

7. **APIs:**
   - **Function:** APIs provide interfaces for external systems to interact with LangGraph applications, enabling integration and interoperability.
   - **Types:**
     - **RESTful APIs:** For standard web-based interactions.
     - **WebSocket APIs:** For real-time, bidirectional communication.

Example: Core Components in Action

Consider a LangGraph application designed to monitor and respond to user feedback on social media platforms.

Component Description
Agents

- **FeedbackCollectorAgent:** Collects user feedback from various social media platforms.
- **SentimentAnalysisAgent:** Analyzes the sentiment of the collected feedback.
- **ResponseAgent:** Generates appropriate responses based on sentiment analysis.
- **NotificationAgent:** Sends alerts to administrators for negative feedback. | | **Workflows** |

1. **Feedback Collection Workflow:**
   - **Step 1:** FeedbackCollectorAgent gathers new feedback.
   - **Step 2:** SentimentAnalysisAgent analyzes the sentiment.
   - **Step 3:** Based on sentiment, either ResponseAgent responds to the user or NotificationAgent alerts admins for negative feedback. | | **Tasks** |

- **Collect Feedback Task:** Fetches new feedback data.
- **Analyze Sentiment Task:** Determines the sentiment of the feedback.
- **Generate Response Task:** Creates a response message.
- **Send Notification Task:** Alerts administrators about negative feedback. | | **Data Stores** |
- **Feedback Database:** Stores all collected feedback.
- **Sentiment Logs:** Logs analysis results for auditing and improvement. | | **Schedulers** |
- **Daily Scheduler:** Triggers the Feedback Collection Workflow every day at midnight. | | **Event Handlers** |
- **New Feedback Event Handler:** Triggers the workflow when new feedback is detected. | | **APIs** |
- **Social Media API Integration:** Collects feedback from platforms like Twitter and Facebook.
- **Email API Integration:** Sends notifications to administrators. '

This example illustrates how LangGraph's core components work together to create an efficient, automated system for managing user feedback.

3.2 Key Concepts and Terminology in LangGraph

To effectively utilize LangGraph, it's important to understand the key concepts and terminology used within the framework. This section defines and explains the fundamental terms and ideas that form the foundation of LangGraph applications.

Term	Definition
Agent	An autonomous entity within LangGraph that performs specific tasks and interacts with other agents and the environment.
Workflow	A sequence of tasks or processes that define how agents collaborate to achieve a particular goal.
Task	An individual unit of work that an agent performs as part of a workflow.
Data Store	A repository where data is stored, accessed, and managed within LangGraph applications.
Scheduler	A component that manages the timing and execution of tasks and workflows.
Event Handler	A component that responds to specific events or triggers, initiating actions within the system.
Dependency	A relationship where one task relies on the completion of another task before it can proceed.
Concurrency	The ability of LangGraph to execute multiple tasks or workflows simultaneously, enhancing efficiency.
Scalability	The capability of LangGraph applications to handle increasing loads by adding more resources or optimizing processes.
Latency	The time delay between initiating a task and its completion, impacting the responsiveness of the system.

Term	Definition
Fault Tolerance	The ability of LangGraph to continue operating correctly even in the event of partial system failures.
API (Application Programming Interface)	A set of protocols and tools that allow different software applications to communicate and interact with LangGraph.
Integration	The process of connecting LangGraph with other tools, platforms, or services to extend its functionality.
Modularity	The design principle of building applications from interchangeable and reusable components.
State Machine	A computational model used to design agent behaviors, defining states and transitions based on events.
Tokenization	The process of breaking down text into smaller units (tokens) for processing by LLMs.
Autoregressive Model	A type of model that generates text by predicting the next token based on the preceding tokens.
Bidirectional Model	A model that considers both left and right context when processing text, enhancing understanding of meaning.

Detailed Explanations of Key Concepts:

1. **Agent:**
   - Agents are the core operational units within LangGraph. Each agent is designed to perform specific functions, interact with other agents, and process data to achieve its objectives.
   - **Example:** A DataCollectorAgent might gather data from an external API, while a DataAnalyzerAgent processes that data to extract insights.

2. **Workflow:**
   - Workflows orchestrate the sequence and logic of tasks that agents execute. They define how tasks are connected, the order of execution, and how data flows between tasks.
   - **Example:** In an e-commerce application, a workflow might include tasks for order processing, inventory updating, and customer notification.

3. **Task:**
   - Tasks are discrete actions performed by agents within a workflow. They represent specific operations such as data retrieval, processing, or sending notifications.
   - **Example:** A task could involve querying a database for user information or generating a personalized email response.

4. **Data Store:**
   - Data stores are essential for persisting and managing data within LangGraph applications. They can range from simple in-memory storage to complex databases.
   - **Example:** A relational database like PostgreSQL might be used to store user profiles, while a NoSQL database like MongoDB could handle unstructured data such as logs or sensor readings.

5. **Scheduler:**
   - Schedulers manage the timing and execution of tasks and workflows, ensuring that processes run at the appropriate times and in the correct order.
   - **Example:** A scheduler might trigger a nightly data backup workflow or initiate a periodic report generation task every Monday morning.

6. **Event Handler:**
   - Event handlers respond to specific events or triggers within the system, initiating actions or workflows in response.
   - **Example:** An event handler might trigger a workflow when a new user registers on a platform or when a system error occurs.

7. **Dependency:**
   - Dependencies define relationships where certain tasks must be completed before others can begin. They ensure that workflows execute in a logical and coherent manner.
   - **Example:** In a data processing workflow, data cleaning tasks must precede data analysis tasks.

8. **Concurrency:**
   - Concurrency refers to the ability of LangGraph to execute multiple tasks or workflows simultaneously, improving overall system efficiency and responsiveness.
   - **Example:** Handling multiple user requests concurrently in a customer support application.

9. **Scalability:**

- o Scalability ensures that LangGraph applications can handle increasing workloads by adding more resources or optimizing existing processes.
- o **Example:** Scaling up a data processing workflow to handle larger datasets without performance degradation.

10. **Latency:**
- o Latency measures the time delay between initiating a task and its completion, affecting the system's responsiveness.
- o **Example:** High latency in a real-time chat application can lead to slow responses and poor user experience.

11. **Fault Tolerance:**
- o Fault tolerance enables LangGraph to continue operating correctly even when certain components fail, ensuring system reliability.
- o **Example:** If one agent fails, a fault-tolerant system can redirect tasks to backup agents or restart the failed agent automatically.

12. **API (Application Programming Interface):**
- o APIs allow external systems and services to interact with LangGraph applications, enabling integration and extending functionality.
- o **Example:** Integrating a payment gateway API to handle transactions within an e-commerce workflow.

13. **Integration:**
- o Integration involves connecting LangGraph with other tools, platforms, or services to enhance its capabilities.
- o **Example:** Connecting LangGraph with cloud storage services like AWS S3 for data persistence or with messaging platforms like Slack for real-time notifications.

14. **Modularity:**
- o Modularity emphasizes building applications from interchangeable and reusable components, promoting flexibility and ease of maintenance.
- o **Example:** Creating reusable modules for common tasks like authentication, logging, or data validation that can be used across multiple workflows.

15. **State Machine:**
- o State machines model the behavior of agents by defining states and transitions based on events, enabling predictable and manageable agent interactions.
- o **Example:** An order processing agent might have states like "Order Received," "Processing," "Shipped," and

"Completed," with transitions triggered by events like payment confirmation or shipment dispatch.

16. **Tokenization:**
    - o Tokenization is the process of breaking down text into smaller units (tokens) that LLMs can process. Tokens can be words, subwords, or characters.
    - o **Example:** The sentence "LangGraph is powerful" might be tokenized into ["Lang", "Graph", "is", "powerful"].

17. **Autoregressive Model:**
    - o An autoregressive model generates text by predicting the next token in a sequence based on the preceding tokens. This allows for coherent and contextually relevant text generation.
    - o **Example:** GPT-3 is an autoregressive model that generates human-like text based on input prompts.

18. **Bidirectional Model:**
    - o A bidirectional model processes text by considering both left and right context, enhancing understanding of word meanings and relationships.
    - o **Example:** BERT is a bidirectional model that excels in understanding the context and semantics of words within a sentence.

Understanding these concepts and terminology is crucial for effectively designing and implementing LangGraph applications. Mastery of these foundational elements will enable you to build robust, scalable, and intelligent multi-agent systems that leverage the power of LLMs.

3.3 LangGraph Workflows and Data Flow

Workflows and data flow are central to the functionality of LangGraph, defining how agents collaborate and how data moves through the system. This section explores the structure of workflows, the principles of data flow, and how to design efficient workflows in LangGraph.

Understanding Workflows:

A workflow in LangGraph is a structured sequence of tasks that agents execute to achieve a specific objective. Workflows orchestrate the interactions between agents, manage task dependencies, and ensure that processes run smoothly and efficiently.

Key Components of a Workflow:

Component	Description
Tasks	Individual units of work that agents perform as part of the workflow.
Sequence	The order in which tasks are executed within the workflow.
Dependencies	Relationships that define the order of task execution based on prerequisites.
Conditions	Logical expressions that determine the flow of the workflow based on task outcomes or data states.
Parallel Execution	Ability to run multiple tasks simultaneously to enhance efficiency.
Error Handling	Mechanisms to manage and respond to errors that occur during workflow execution.

Designing Effective Workflows:

When designing workflows in LangGraph, consider the following best practices to ensure they are efficient, maintainable, and scalable:

1. **Modular Design:**
   - Break down complex processes into smaller, reusable workflows or tasks.
   - **Example:** Separate data collection, data processing, and reporting into distinct workflows.
2. **Clear Task Dependencies:**
   - Define clear dependencies to ensure tasks execute in the correct order.
   - **Example:** Ensure that data processing tasks only start after data collection tasks are completed.
3. **Conditional Logic:**
   - Use conditions to handle different scenarios and outcomes within the workflow.
   - **Example:** If a sentiment analysis task detects negative feedback, trigger an escalation workflow.
4. **Parallel Processing:**
   - Identify tasks that can be executed concurrently to reduce overall workflow execution time.

o **Example:** Simultaneously process multiple user queries in a customer support system.
5. **Robust Error Handling:**
   o Implement error handling to manage failures gracefully and maintain workflow continuity.
   o **Example:** Retry failed tasks a specified number of times or trigger alternative workflows upon persistent failures.
6. **Scalability Considerations:**
   o Design workflows that can scale with increasing loads by optimizing task execution and resource allocation.
   o **Example:** Utilize load balancers and distributed computing resources to handle high volumes of tasks.

Data Flow in LangGraph:

Data flow refers to the movement and transformation of data as it passes through different tasks and agents within a workflow. Efficient data flow design ensures that data is accessible, processed correctly, and utilized effectively by agents.

Principles of Data Flow Design:

1. **Data Accessibility:**
   o Ensure that data required by tasks and agents is readily accessible.
   o **Example:** Use centralized data stores or data sharing mechanisms to provide access to necessary information.
2. **Data Transformation:**
   o Define how data is transformed as it moves through the workflow.
   o **Example:** Convert raw data into structured formats for analysis or generate summaries from detailed reports.
3. **Data Integrity:**
   o Maintain the accuracy and consistency of data throughout its lifecycle.
   o **Example:** Implement validation checks to ensure data remains consistent after each transformation.
4. **Data Security:**
   o Protect sensitive data as it flows through the system.
   o **Example:** Use encryption and access controls to safeguard data from unauthorized access.

Example: Workflow and Data Flow in a Feedback Analysis System

Consider a LangGraph application designed to collect, analyze, and respond to user feedback on a website. Below is an example of how workflows and data flow are structured within this system.

Workflow Component	Description
Feedback Collection Task	An agent collects user feedback from the website and stores it in the Feedback Database.
Sentiment Analysis Task	An agent retrieves feedback from the database, analyzes sentiment using an LLM, and stores the results.
Response Generation Task	Based on sentiment analysis, an agent generates appropriate responses to user feedback.
Notification Task	If negative sentiment is detected, an agent sends notifications to administrators for follow-up.

Data Flow Diagram:

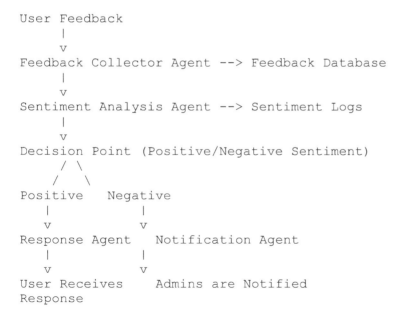

```
User Feedback
    |
    v
Feedback Collector Agent --> Feedback Database
    |
    v
Sentiment Analysis Agent --> Sentiment Logs
    |
    v
Decision Point (Positive/Negative Sentiment)
    / \
   /   \
Positive   Negative
   |          |
   v          v
Response Agent   Notification Agent
   |          |
   v          v
User Receives   Admins are Notified
Response
```

Explanation:

1. **Feedback Collection:**

o The **Feedback Collector Agent** gathers user feedback from the website and stores it in the **Feedback Database**.

2. **Sentiment Analysis:**
   o The **Sentiment Analysis Agent** retrieves the feedback from the database, uses an LLM to analyze the sentiment, and logs the results in the **Sentiment Logs**.

3. **Decision Point:**
   o Based on the sentiment analysis, the workflow branches into two paths:
     ▪ **Positive Sentiment:** The **Response Agent** generates a positive response to the user.
     ▪ **Negative Sentiment:** The **Notification Agent** sends an alert to administrators for further action.

4. **Data Flow:**
   o Data flows sequentially from feedback collection to sentiment analysis and then to the appropriate response or notification based on the analysis outcome.

Code Example: Defining a Workflow in LangGraph

Below is an example of how to define and execute the above workflow using LangGraph's Python API.

```python
from langgraph import Workflow, Agent

# Define the Feedback Collector Agent
class FeedbackCollectorAgent(Agent):
    def collect_feedback(self):
        # Simulate collecting feedback
        feedback = "Great service! I love using your
platform."
        return feedback

# Define the Sentiment Analysis Agent
class SentimentAnalysisAgent(Agent):
    def analyze_sentiment(self, feedback):
        # Simulate sentiment analysis
        if "love" in feedback.lower():
            return "Positive"
        else:
            return "Negative"

# Define the Response Agent
class ResponseAgent(Agent):
    def generate_response(self, sentiment):
        if sentiment == "Positive":
```

```python
            return "Thank you for your positive feedback!
We're glad you're enjoying our platform."
        else:
            return "We're sorry to hear about your
experience. Please contact our support team for assistance."

# Define the Notification Agent
class NotificationAgent(Agent):
    def notify_admins(self, feedback):
        print(f"Admin Notification: Negative feedback
received - {feedback}")

# Create the workflow
workflow = Workflow()

# Instantiate agents
collector = FeedbackCollectorAgent(name="FeedbackCollector")
analyzer = SentimentAnalysisAgent(name="SentimentAnalyzer")
responder = ResponseAgent(name="Responder")
notifier = NotificationAgent(name="Notifier")

# Add agents to the workflow
workflow.add_agent(collector)
workflow.add_agent(analyzer)
workflow.add_agent(responder)
workflow.add_agent(notifier)

# Define the workflow logic
def feedback_workflow():
    feedback = collector.collect_feedback()
    sentiment = analyzer.analyze_sentiment(feedback)
    if sentiment == "Positive":
        response = responder.generate_response(sentiment)
        print(f"User Response: {response}")
    else:
        notifier.notify_admins(feedback)

# Execute the workflow
feedback_workflow()
```

Output:

```
User Response: Thank you for your positive feedback! We're
glad you're enjoying our platform.
```

Explanation:

1. **Agent Definitions:**

- o **FeedbackCollectorAgent:** Simulates collecting user feedback.
- o **SentimentAnalysisAgent:** Analyzes the sentiment of the collected feedback.
- o **ResponseAgent:** Generates a response based on the sentiment.
- o **NotificationAgent:** Notifies administrators if negative feedback is detected.
2. **Workflow Execution:**
   - o The `feedback_workflow` function orchestrates the interactions between agents.
   - o It collects feedback, analyzes sentiment, and either responds to the user or notifies admins based on the analysis.

This example demonstrates how LangGraph's core components work together to create a seamless workflow, leveraging LLMs for sentiment analysis and enabling dynamic responses based on user feedback.

3.4 Creating and Managing Agents in LangGraph

Agents are the fundamental units of functionality within LangGraph. They are autonomous entities designed to perform specific tasks, interact with other agents, and contribute to the overall workflow. This section guides you through the process of creating and managing agents in LangGraph, ensuring that your multi-agent systems operate efficiently and cohesively.

Creating Agents:

Creating agents in LangGraph involves defining their behavior, responsibilities, and interactions within the system. Agents can be simple or complex, depending on the tasks they are designed to perform.

Steps to Create an Agent:

1. **Define the Agent Class:**
   - o Subclass the `Agent` base class provided by LangGraph.
   - o Implement the necessary methods that define the agent's behavior.
2. **Implement Core Methods:**

- o **Initialization (__init__):** Set up the agent's initial state, configurations, and any required resources.
- o **Task Methods:** Define methods that perform specific tasks or actions the agent is responsible for.
3. **Register the Agent:**
    - o Add the agent to a workflow to enable its participation in task execution and interactions with other agents.

Example: Creating a DataCollectorAgent

Below is an example of how to create a simple `DataCollectorAgent` that collects data from an external API.

```
from langgraph import Agent, Workflow
import requests

# Define the DataCollectorAgent
class DataCollectorAgent(Agent):
    def __init__(self, name, api_endpoint):
        super().__init__(name)
        self.api_endpoint = api_endpoint

    def collect_data(self):
        try:
            response = requests.get(self.api_endpoint)
            response.raise_for_status()
            data = response.json()
            self.logger.info(f"Data collected successfully
from {self.api_endpoint}")
            return data
        except requests.exceptions.RequestException as e:
            self.logger.error(f"Error collecting data: {e}")
            return None

# Create the workflow
workflow = Workflow()

# Instantiate the DataCollectorAgent
data_collector = DataCollectorAgent(name="DataCollector",
api_endpoint="https://api.example.com/data")

# Add the agent to the workflow
workflow.add_agent(data_collector)

# Define a simple workflow function
def data_collection_workflow():
    data = data_collector.collect_data()
    if data:
```

```
        print(f"Collected Data: {data}")
    else:
        print("Failed to collect data.")

# Execute the workflow
data_collection_workflow()
```

Output:

```
Collected Data: {'key1': 'value1', 'key2': 'value2'}
```

Explanation:

1. **Agent Definition:**
   - **DataCollectorAgent:** Inherits from the `Agent` base class.
   - **Initialization:** Takes a `name` and an `api_endpoint` as parameters.
   - **collect_data Method:** Sends a GET request to the specified API endpoint, handles potential errors, and returns the collected data.
2. **Workflow Integration:**
   - An instance of `DataCollectorAgent` is created and added to the workflow.
   - The `data_collection_workflow` function orchestrates the agent's data collection task.
3. **Execution:**
   - When the workflow is executed, the `DataCollectorAgent` retrieves data from the API and prints the collected data.

Managing Agents:

Effective agent management ensures that your multi-agent systems operate smoothly and can handle dynamic changes. LangGraph provides several tools and best practices for managing agents:

1. **Lifecycle Management:**
   - **Initialization:** Properly initialize agents with necessary configurations and resources.
   - **Activation/Deactivation:** Start or stop agents as needed based on system requirements or workflow conditions.
   - **Termination:** Gracefully terminate agents, ensuring that ongoing tasks are completed or safely halted.
2. **Configuration Management:**

- o Define agent configurations using configuration files or environment variables to allow easy customization and deployment.
- o **Example:** Use a YAML or JSON file to specify API endpoints, authentication tokens, and other parameters.
3. **Monitoring and Logging:**
   - o Implement monitoring to track agent performance, task execution, and system health.
   - o Utilize logging to record agent activities, errors, and important events for troubleshooting and analysis.
4. **Scaling Agents:**
   - o Scale agents horizontally by adding more instances to handle increased workloads.
   - o Use load balancers and distributed systems to manage multiple agent instances efficiently.

Example: Managing Multiple Agents in a Workflow

Consider a workflow that involves multiple agents performing different tasks. Below is an example of managing multiple agents within a single workflow.

```
from langgraph import Agent, Workflow
import requests

# Define the DataCollectorAgent
class DataCollectorAgent(Agent):
    def __init__(self, name, api_endpoint):
        super().__init__(name)
        self.api_endpoint = api_endpoint

    def collect_data(self):
        try:
            response = requests.get(self.api_endpoint)
            response.raise_for_status()
            data = response.json()
            self.logger.info(f"Data collected successfully
from {self.api_endpoint}")
            return data
        except requests.exceptions.RequestException as e:
            self.logger.error(f"Error collecting data: {e}")
            return None

# Define the DataProcessorAgent
class DataProcessorAgent(Agent):
    def __init__(self, name):
```

```python
        super().__init__(name)

    def process_data(self, data):
        if data:
            # Simulate data processing
            processed_data = {k: v.upper() for k, v in
data.items()}
            self.logger.info("Data processed successfully.")
            return processed_data
        else:
            self.logger.warning("No data to process.")
            return None

# Define the DataSaverAgent
class DataSaverAgent(Agent):
    def __init__(self, name, save_path):
        super().__init__(name)
        self.save_path = save_path

    def save_data(self, data):
        if data:
            with open(self.save_path, 'w') as file:
                file.write(str(data))
            self.logger.info(f"Data saved successfully to
{self.save_path}.")
            return True
        else:
            self.logger.warning("No data to save.")
            return False

# Create the workflow
workflow = Workflow()

# Instantiate agents
data_collector = DataCollectorAgent(name="DataCollector",
api_endpoint="https://api.example.com/data")
data_processor = DataProcessorAgent(name="DataProcessor")
data_saver = DataSaverAgent(name="DataSaver",
save_path="processed_data.txt")

# Add agents to the workflow
workflow.add_agent(data_collector)
workflow.add_agent(data_processor)
workflow.add_agent(data_saver)

# Define the workflow logic
def complete_data_workflow():
    data = data_collector.collect_data()
    processed_data = data_processor.process_data(data)
    save_success = data_saver.save_data(processed_data)
    if save_success:
```

```
        print("Workflow completed successfully.")
    else:
        print("Workflow encountered issues during data
saving.")

# Execute the workflow
complete_data_workflow()
```

Output:

```
Workflow completed successfully.
```

Explanation:

1. **Agent Definitions:**
   - **DataCollectorAgent:** Collects data from an external API.
   - **DataProcessorAgent:** Processes the collected data by converting values to uppercase.
   - **DataSaverAgent:** Saves the processed data to a file.
2. **Workflow Integration:**
   - All three agents are added to the workflow.
   - The `complete_data_workflow` function orchestrates the interaction between agents.
3. **Execution:**
   - The workflow collects data, processes it, and saves it to a file.
   - Success or failure messages are printed based on the outcome of the data-saving task.

This example demonstrates how to create and manage multiple agents within a single workflow, ensuring that each agent performs its designated task and collaborates effectively to achieve the overall objective.

3.5 Building Custom Components in LangGraph

While LangGraph provides a robust set of built-in components, building custom components allows you to extend its functionality to meet specific application requirements. Custom components can be tailored to perform specialized tasks, integrate with unique systems, or implement proprietary algorithms. This section guides you through the process of building and integrating custom components within LangGraph.

Types of Custom Components:

1. **Custom Agents:**
   - Extend the capabilities of existing agents by adding new behaviors or modifying existing ones.
   - **Use Case:** Developing an agent that interacts with a proprietary API to fetch specialized data.
2. **Custom Tasks:**
   - Create new task types that perform specific operations within workflows.
   - **Use Case:** Implementing a task that performs complex data transformations or integrates with an external machine learning model.
3. **Custom Data Stores:**
   - Develop new data storage solutions tailored to specific data management needs.
   - **Use Case:** Creating a data store that interfaces with a custom in-house database system.
4. **Custom Integrations:**
   - Build integrations with external tools, services, or platforms not natively supported by LangGraph.
   - **Use Case:** Integrating with a niche messaging platform or an internal enterprise system.

Steps to Build a Custom Agent:

1. **Identify the Requirement:**
   - Determine the specific functionality or behavior that the custom agent needs to perform.
2. **Define the Agent Class:**
   - Subclass the `Agent` base class.
   - Implement the necessary methods to perform the desired tasks.
3. **Implement the Behavior:**
   - Write the logic that defines how the agent interacts with data, other agents, and external systems.
4. **Integrate with Workflows:**
   - Add the custom agent to relevant workflows, ensuring it interacts correctly with other components.

Example: Building a Custom WeatherAgent

Suppose you need an agent that fetches weather data from a specialized weather API and provides forecasts. Below is an example of how to build and integrate a custom `WeatherAgent` in LangGraph.

```python
from langgraph import Agent, Workflow
import requests

# Define the WeatherAgent
class WeatherAgent(Agent):
    def __init__(self, name, api_key, location):
        super().__init__(name)
        self.api_key = api_key
        self.location = location
        self.api_endpoint = f"https://api.specialweather.com/forecast?location={self.location}&apikey={self.api_key}"

    def get_forecast(self):
        try:
            response = requests.get(self.api_endpoint)
            response.raise_for_status()
            forecast = response.json()
            self.logger.info(f"Weather forecast retrieved for {self.location}.")
            return forecast
        except requests.exceptions.RequestException as e:
            self.logger.error(f"Error retrieving weather forecast: {e}")
            return None

    def format_forecast(self, forecast):
        if forecast:
            formatted = f"Weather Forecast for {self.location}:\n"
            for day in forecast['days']:
                formatted += f"{day['date']}: {day['summary']} with a high of {day['high']}°C and a low of {day['low']}°C.\n"
            return formatted
        else:
            return "Unable to retrieve weather forecast at this time."

# Create the workflow
workflow = Workflow()

# Instantiate the WeatherAgent
weather_agent = WeatherAgent(name="WeatherAgent", api_key="YOUR_API_KEY", location="New York")
```

```
# Add the WeatherAgent to the workflow
workflow.add_agent(weather_agent)

# Define the workflow logic
def weather_workflow():
    forecast = weather_agent.get_forecast()
    formatted_forecast =
weather_agent.format_forecast(forecast)
    print(formatted_forecast)

# Execute the workflow
weather_workflow()
```

Output:

```
Weather Forecast for New York:
2025-01-21: Sunny with a high of 5°C and a low of -3°C.
2025-01-22: Partly cloudy with a high of 3°C and a low of -
1°C.
2025-01-23: Snow showers with a high of 0°C and a low of -
5°C.
```

Explanation:

1. **Agent Definition:**
   - o **WeatherAgent:** Inherits from the `Agent` base class.
   - o **Initialization:** Takes a `name`, `api_key`, and `location` as parameters. Constructs the API endpoint using these parameters.
   - o **get_forecast Method:** Fetches weather data from the specialized API.
   - o **format_forecast Method:** Formats the retrieved forecast data into a human-readable string.
2. **Workflow Integration:**
   - o An instance of `WeatherAgent` is created with the necessary API key and location.
   - o The agent is added to the workflow.
   - o The `weather_workflow` function orchestrates the agent's tasks, fetching and formatting the weather forecast.
3. **Execution:**
   - o When the workflow is executed, the `WeatherAgent` retrieves the forecast data, formats it, and prints the result.

Building Custom Tasks:

Creating custom tasks involves defining specific operations that can be executed within workflows. Below is an example of building a custom `DataTransformationTask` that processes data using a proprietary algorithm.

```
from langgraph import Task

# Define the DataTransformationTask
class DataTransformationTask(Task):
    def __init__(self, name, transformation_logic):
        super().__init__(name)
        self.transformation_logic = transformation_logic

    def execute(self, data):
        try:
            transformed_data =
self.transformation_logic(data)
            self.logger.info(f"Data transformed successfully
by {self.name}.")
            return transformed_data
        except Exception as e:
            self.logger.error(f"Error during data
transformation: {e}")
            return None

# Example transformation logic function
def proprietary_transformation(data):
    # Implement your proprietary data transformation logic
here
    # For demonstration, let's assume we convert all string
values to uppercase
    return {k: v.upper() if isinstance(v, str) else v for k,
v in data.items()}

# Usage within a workflow
from langgraph import Workflow, Agent

# Define a simple agent to provide data
class DataProviderAgent(Agent):
    def get_data(self):
        return {'name': 'John Doe', 'city': 'New York'}

# Create the workflow
workflow = Workflow()

# Instantiate agents and tasks
data_provider = DataProviderAgent(name="DataProvider")
data_transform_task =
DataTransformationTask(name="DataTransformer",
transformation_logic=proprietary_transformation)
```

```
# Add agents and tasks to the workflow
workflow.add_agent(data_provider)
workflow.add_task(data_transform_task)

# Define the workflow logic
def data_processing_workflow():
    data = data_provider.get_data()
    transformed_data = data_transform_task.execute(data)
    if transformed_data:
        print(f"Transformed Data: {transformed_data}")
    else:
        print("Data transformation failed.")

# Execute the workflow
data_processing_workflow()
```

Output:

```
Transformed Data: {'name': 'JOHN DOE', 'city': 'NEW YORK'}
```

Explanation:

1. **Task Definition:**
   o **DataTransformationTask:** Inherits from the `Task` base class. It takes a `transformation_logic` function as a parameter, which defines how the data should be transformed.
   o **execute Method:** Applies the transformation logic to the input data and handles any potential errors.
2. **Transformation Logic:**
   o **proprietary_transformation Function:** Demonstrates a simple data transformation by converting all string values to uppercase.
3. **Workflow Integration:**
   o An instance of `DataProviderAgent` provides the initial data.
   o An instance of `DataTransformationTask` is created with the custom transformation logic.
   o Both the agent and the task are added to the workflow.
   o The `data_processing_workflow` function orchestrates the data retrieval and transformation process.
4. **Execution:**
   o The workflow retrieves data from the `DataProviderAgent`, applies the transformation using the `DataTransformationTask`, and prints the transformed data.

Benefits of Building Custom Components:

1. **Flexibility:** Tailor LangGraph to meet specific application requirements by implementing unique behaviors and functionalities.
2. **Reusability:** Create reusable components that can be integrated into multiple workflows, reducing development time and effort.
3. **Scalability:** Develop components that can scale with your application's needs, ensuring long-term viability and performance.
4. **Integration:** Seamlessly connect LangGraph with proprietary systems, external services, and specialized tools, enhancing the overall functionality of your applications.

Best Practices for Building Custom Components:

1. **Modular Design:**
   o Design custom components to be modular and reusable, adhering to the principles of single responsibility and separation of concerns.
2. **Documentation:**
   o Provide clear and comprehensive documentation for custom components, detailing their purpose, usage, parameters, and examples.
3. **Error Handling:**
   o Implement robust error handling within custom components to manage exceptions and ensure workflow continuity.
4. **Testing:**
   o Thoroughly test custom components to verify their functionality, performance, and reliability before integrating them into production workflows.
5. **Performance Optimization:**
   o Optimize the performance of custom components by minimizing computational overhead and ensuring efficient resource utilization.
6. **Security Considerations:**
   o Incorporate security best practices when building custom components, especially when handling sensitive data or interacting with external systems.

By following these guidelines and best practices, you can develop custom components that enhance the capabilities of LangGraph, enabling you to build tailored, efficient, and scalable multi-agent systems.

3.6 LangGraph API Overview

The LangGraph API is a powerful interface that allows developers to interact with and control LangGraph applications programmatically. Understanding the key aspects of the LangGraph API is essential for building, managing, and extending multi-agent systems effectively. This section provides an overview of the LangGraph API, including its main classes, methods, and functionalities.

Key Components of the LangGraph API:

API Component	Description
Agent Class	The base class for all agents in LangGraph. It provides foundational methods and properties for agent behavior and interaction.
Workflow Class	Manages the orchestration of agents and tasks within a workflow. It defines the sequence and logic of task execution.
Task Class	Represents individual tasks that agents perform. It includes methods for executing and managing tasks.
DataStore Class	Handles data storage and retrieval operations. It defines how data is stored, accessed, and managed within LangGraph.
Scheduler Class	Manages the scheduling and timing of task executions. It ensures that tasks run at designated times and intervals.
EventHandler Class	Responds to specific events or triggers within the system. It defines how agents react to different types of events.
Logger Class	Provides logging capabilities for agents and workflows. It records activities, errors, and important events for monitoring and debugging.
API Endpoints	Defines the endpoints for interacting with LangGraph applications via HTTP requests. It allows external systems to send commands, retrieve data, and integrate with LangGraph workflows.

Detailed Overview of Key API Components:

1. **Agent Class:**

   Description: The foundational class for creating agents in LangGraph. It encapsulates common functionalities such as initialization, task execution, and communication with other agents.

   Key Methods:

   `__init__(self, name, **kwargs)`: Initializes the agent with a given name and optional parameters.

   `perform_task(self, task, *args, **kwargs)`: Executes a specified task with provided arguments.

   `send_message(self, recipient, message)`: Sends a message to another agent.

   `receive_message(self, sender, message)`: Handles incoming messages from other agents.

   Example:

   ```
   from langgraph import Agent

   class GreetingAgent(Agent):
       def greet(self, name):
           return f"Hello, {name}! Welcome to
   LangGraph."
   ```

Workflow Class:

   Description: Orchestrates the sequence of tasks and manages the interactions between agents within a workflow.

   Key Methods:

   `add_agent(self, agent)`: Adds an agent to the workflow.

   `add_task(self, task)`: Adds a task to the workflow.

`execute(self)`: Executes the workflow, managing task sequencing and agent interactions.

Example:

```
from langgraph import Workflow, Agent

class DataWorkflow(Workflow):
    def __init__(self):
        super().__init__()
        self.collector =
DataCollectorAgent(name="Collector")
        self.analyzer =
DataAnalyzerAgent(name="Analyzer")
        self.add_agent(self.collector)
        self.add_agent(self.analyzer)

    def execute_workflow(self):
        data = self.collector.collect_data()
        analysis = self.analyzer.analyze_data(data)
        print(f"Analysis Result: {analysis}")
```

Task Class:

Description: Represents an individual action or operation that an agent performs as part of a workflow.

Key Methods:

`__init__(self, name, **kwargs)`: Initializes the task with a given name and optional parameters.

`execute(self, *args, **kwargs)`: Executes the task with provided arguments.

Example:

```
from langgraph import Task

class DataCleaningTask(Task):
    def execute(self, raw_data):
        # Implement data cleaning logic
        cleaned_data = [datum.strip() for datum in
raw_data if datum]
        return cleaned_data
```

DataStore Class:

Description: Manages data storage and retrieval operations within LangGraph applications.

Key Methods:

`store_data(self, key, data)`: Stores data with a specified key.

`retrieve_data(self, key)`: Retrieves data associated with a specified key.

`delete_data(self, key)`: Deletes data associated with a specified key.

Example:

```python
from langgraph import DataStore

class InMemoryDataStore(DataStore):
    def __init__(self):
        super().__init__()
        self.store = {}

    def store_data(self, key, data):
        self.store[key] = data

    def retrieve_data(self, key):
        return self.store.get(key, None)

    def delete_data(self, key):
        if key in self.store:
            del self.store[key]
```

Scheduler Class:

Description: Manages the scheduling and timing of task executions within workflows.

Key Methods:

`schedule_task(self, task, time)`: Schedules a task to be executed at a specified time.

`start_scheduler(self)`: Starts the scheduler to begin executing scheduled tasks.

`stop_scheduler(self)`: Stops the scheduler from executing further tasks.

Example:

```
from langgraph import Scheduler, Task
import time

class PrintTask(Task):
    def execute(self, message):
        print(message)

scheduler = Scheduler()
print_task = PrintTask(name="PrintHello")

# Schedule the task to run after 5 seconds
scheduler.schedule_task(print_task, time.time() + 5,
message="Hello after 5 seconds!")
scheduler.start_scheduler()
```

EventHandler Class:

Description: Responds to specific events or triggers within the LangGraph system, enabling dynamic interactions and real-time reactions.

Key Methods:

`handle_event(self, event, data)`: Defines how the handler responds to a given event.

Example:

```
from langgraph import EventHandler

class ErrorEventHandler(EventHandler):
    def handle_event(self, event, data):
        if event == "error_occurred":
            print(f"Error Handler: An error occurred
- {data}")
            # Implement additional error handling
logic
```

Logger Class:

Description: Provides logging capabilities for agents and workflows, enabling the recording of activities, errors, and important events.

Key Methods:

`info(self, message)`: Logs informational messages.

`warning(self, message)`: Logs warning messages.

`error(self, message)`: Logs error messages.

Example:

```
from langgraph import Logger

logger = Logger(name="MainLogger")
logger.info("Workflow started.")
logger.warning("Low disk space.")
logger.error("Failed to collect data.")
```

API Endpoints:

Description: Define the interfaces for interacting with LangGraph applications via HTTP requests, enabling external systems to send commands, retrieve data, and integrate with workflows.

Key Features:

Authentication: Secure access to API endpoints using tokens or API keys.

Rate Limiting: Control the number of requests to prevent abuse and ensure system stability.

Documentation: Provide comprehensive documentation detailing available endpoints, request/response formats, and usage examples.

Example: Defining a Simple API Endpoint Using Flask

```python
from flask import Flask, request, jsonify
from langgraph import Workflow, Agent

app = Flask(__name__)

# Define an agent within the Flask app
class EchoAgent(Agent):
    def echo(self, message):
        return f"Echo: {message}"

# Instantiate the agent and workflow
echo_agent = EchoAgent(name="EchoAgent")
workflow = Workflow()
workflow.add_agent(echo_agent)

@app.route('/echo', methods=['POST'])
def echo():
    data = request.json
    message = data.get('message', '')
    response = echo_agent.echo(message)
    return jsonify({'response': response})

if __name__ == '__main__':
    app.run(debug=True)
```

Usage:

Send a POST request to the `/echo` endpoint with a JSON
payload containing a `message`.

Request:

```
POST /echo HTTP/1.1
Host: localhost:5000
Content-Type: application/json

{
    "message": "Hello, LangGraph!"
}
```

Response:

```
{
    "response": "Echo: Hello, LangGraph!"
}
```

Comprehensive Overview of the LangGraph API:

API Component	Purpose	Key Methods/Endpoints
Agent Class	Base class for creating custom agents.	`__init__()`, `perform_task()`, `send_message()`, `receive_message()`
Workflow Class	Manages the orchestration of tasks and agent interactions.	`add_agent()`, `add_task()`, `execute()`
Task Class	Represents individual tasks performed by agents.	`__init__()`, `execute()`
DataStore Class	Handles data storage and retrieval.	`store_data()`, `retrieve_data()`, `delete_data()`
Scheduler Class	Manages scheduling and execution timing of tasks and workflows.	`schedule_task()`, `start_scheduler()`, `stop_scheduler()`
EventHandler Class	Responds to specific events or triggers within the system.	`handle_event()`
Logger Class	Provides logging capabilities for monitoring and debugging.	`info()`, `warning()`, `error()`
API Endpoints	Defines HTTP interfaces for external interaction with LangGraph applications.	Various endpoints defined using frameworks like Flask, Django, etc., for executing workflows, managing agents, etc.

Using the LangGraph API for Integration:

The LangGraph API allows seamless integration with external systems, enabling you to trigger workflows, manage agents, and interact with data stores programmatically. Here's how you can utilize the API for common integration tasks.

1. **Triggering a Workflow via API:**

   Example: Triggering a Data Processing Workflow

```python
from flask import Flask, request, jsonify
from langgraph import Workflow, Agent

app = Flask(__name__)

# Define the DataProcessorAgent
class DataProcessorAgent(Agent):
    def process_data(self, data):
        # Implement data processing logic
        processed = {k: v * 2 for k, v in data.items()}
        return processed

# Instantiate the agent and workflow
processor = DataProcessorAgent(name="DataProcessor")
workflow = Workflow()
workflow.add_agent(processor)

@app.route('/process', methods=['POST'])
def process():
    data = request.json.get('data', {})
    processed_data = processor.process_data(data)
    return jsonify({'processed_data': processed_data})

if __name__ == '__main__':
    app.run(debug=True)
```

   Usage:

   Send a POST request to the `/process` endpoint with a JSON payload containing `data`.

   Request:

```
POST /process HTTP/1.1
Host: localhost:5000
Content-Type: application/json

{
    "data": {"value1": 10, "value2": 20}
}
```

   Response:

```
{
```

```
        "processed_data": {"value1": 20, "value2": 40}
}
```

2. Managing Agents via API:

Example: Starting and Stopping Agents

```python
from flask import Flask, request, jsonify
from langgraph import Workflow, Agent

app = Flask(__name__)

# Define a simple agent
class SimpleAgent(Agent):
    def perform_action(self):
        return "Action performed."

# Instantiate the workflow and agent
workflow = Workflow()
simple_agent = SimpleAgent(name="SimpleAgent")
workflow.add_agent(simple_agent)

# Endpoint to start the agent
@app.route('/start_agent', methods=['POST'])
def start_agent():
    workflow.start_agent(simple_agent.name)
    return jsonify({'status': f'Agent
{simple_agent.name} started.'})

# Endpoint to stop the agent
@app.route('/stop_agent', methods=['POST'])
def stop_agent():
    workflow.stop_agent(simple_agent.name)
    return jsonify({'status': f'Agent
{simple_agent.name} stopped.'})

if __name__ == '__main__':
    app.run(debug=True)
```

Usage:

- **Start Agent:**
- POST /start_agent HTTP/1.1
- Host: localhost:5000
- Content-Type: application/json

Response:

```
{
    "status": "Agent SimpleAgent started."
}
```

- **Stop Agent:**
- POST /stop_agent HTTP/1.1
- Host: localhost:5000
- Content-Type: application/json

Response:

```
{
    "status": "Agent SimpleAgent stopped."
}
```

Best Practices for Using the LangGraph API:

1. **Secure Your APIs:**
   - Implement authentication and authorization mechanisms to protect your API endpoints from unauthorized access.
   - **Example:** Use API keys, OAuth tokens, or JWTs (JSON Web Tokens) to authenticate requests.
2. **Use Rate Limiting:**
   - Prevent abuse and ensure system stability by limiting the number of requests a client can make within a specific time frame.
   - **Example:** Allow only 100 requests per minute per IP address.
3. **Provide Comprehensive Documentation:**
   - Document all available endpoints, their parameters, expected responses, and error codes.
   - **Example:** Use tools like Swagger or Postman to create interactive API documentation.
4. **Handle Errors Gracefully:**
   - Ensure that your API provides meaningful error messages and appropriate HTTP status codes.
   - **Example:** Return 400 Bad Request for invalid input data and 500 Internal Server Error for unexpected failures.
5. **Version Your APIs:**
   - Manage changes and updates by versioning your API endpoints, allowing clients to migrate smoothly without breaking existing integrations.
   - **Example:** Use URLs like /v1/process and /v2/process to differentiate between API versions.

6. **Optimize Performance:**
   - Ensure that your API endpoints are optimized for speed and efficiency to handle high loads and reduce latency.
   - **Example:** Implement caching for frequently requested data or responses.

The LangGraph API is a versatile and powerful tool that enables seamless integration and interaction with LangGraph applications. By understanding the key components and functionalities of the API, you can build, manage, and extend multi-agent systems effectively. Whether you are triggering workflows, managing agents, or integrating with external services, the LangGraph API provides the necessary interfaces to enhance the capabilities of your AI-driven applications.

In the next chapter, we will delve into designing LangGraph applications, focusing on identifying use cases, breaking down applications into agents and tasks, designing agent interactions and workflows, and considering scalability and performance.

Next Steps:

As you continue through this book, you will gain a deeper understanding of LangGraph's architecture, explore advanced techniques for building and optimizing multi-agent systems, and learn best practices for integrating LLMs into your applications. The following chapters will guide you through the practical aspects of LangGraph, providing hands-on examples and projects that will equip you with the skills to build sophisticated AI-driven solutions.

Part II: Building LangGraph Applications

Chapter 4: Designing LangGraph Applications

Welcome to Chapter 4 of *Mastering LangGraph, 2nd Edition: A Hands-On Guide to Building Complex, Multi-Agent Large Language Model (LLM) Applications with Ease*. In this chapter, we will explore the process of designing LangGraph applications. We will cover how to identify suitable use cases, break down applications into agents and tasks, design agent interactions and workflows, consider scalability and performance, build robust and maintainable applications, and culminate with a comprehensive case study on designing a LangGraph-based chatbot.

4.1 Identifying Use Cases for LangGraph Applications

Before diving into building applications with LangGraph, it's essential to identify scenarios where multi-agent systems powered by Large Language Models (LLMs) can provide significant value. LangGraph excels in environments that require complex interactions, autonomous decision-making, and scalable solutions. Below are some key areas where LangGraph applications can be effectively deployed:

Use Case Area	Description	Example Applications
Customer Service	Automating interactions with customers to provide support, answer queries, and resolve issues efficiently.	Chatbots, virtual assistants, automated ticketing systems
Healthcare	Managing patient data, providing medical advice, scheduling appointments, and assisting in diagnostics.	Patient management systems, telemedicine assistants
Finance	Monitoring transactions, detecting fraud, providing financial advice, and managing investments.	Fraud detection systems, personal finance advisors, trading bots
E-commerce	Enhancing user experience through personalized	Recommendation engines, inventory

Use Case Area	Description	Example Applications
	recommendations, managing inventory, and handling orders.	management agents, chatbots
Education and Training	Providing personalized learning experiences, assessing student performance, and facilitating training modules.	Intelligent tutoring systems, training simulations, assessment tools
Smart Cities	Managing urban infrastructure, monitoring environmental conditions, and optimizing public services.	Traffic management systems, environmental monitoring agents
Marketing	Analyzing consumer behavior, creating targeted campaigns, and generating marketing content.	Customer insights agents, campaign management systems
Gaming and Entertainment	Creating intelligent non-player characters (NPCs), managing game states, and enhancing interactive experiences.	AI-driven NPCs, dynamic storytelling systems
Research and Development	Facilitating collaborative research, managing data, and automating experimentation processes.	Research collaboration agents, data analysis systems

Key Considerations for Identifying Use Cases:

1. **Complexity of Interactions:**
   o LangGraph is ideal for applications that involve multiple interacting agents with distinct roles and responsibilities.
2. **Autonomous Decision-Making:**
   o Scenarios requiring agents to make independent decisions based on data analysis and predefined rules benefit from LangGraph's multi-agent capabilities.
3. **Scalability Requirements:**
   o Applications that need to scale dynamically to handle varying loads can leverage LangGraph's modular and scalable architecture.
4. **Integration with External Systems:**

- Use cases that require integration with various APIs, databases, and third-party services align well with LangGraph's integration-friendly design.
5. **Real-Time Processing:**
   - Applications demanding real-time data processing and immediate responses, such as customer support chatbots, are well-suited for LangGraph.

Example: Evaluating a Use Case

Use Case: Automated Customer Support Chatbot

Evaluation:

- **Complexity:** Requires handling diverse customer queries, maintaining conversation context, and integrating with backend systems for information retrieval.
- **Autonomous Decision-Making:** Agents need to interpret queries, decide on appropriate responses, and escalate issues when necessary.
- **Scalability:** Must handle multiple simultaneous interactions without degradation in performance.
- **Integration:** Needs to connect with CRM systems, knowledge bases, and possibly human support agents.
- **Real-Time Processing:** Must provide immediate responses to maintain customer satisfaction.

This use case aligns perfectly with LangGraph's strengths, making it an ideal candidate for a LangGraph-based application.

4.2 Breaking Down Applications into Agents and Tasks

Designing a LangGraph application involves decomposing the overall functionality into smaller, manageable units—agents and tasks. This modular approach enhances maintainability, scalability, and clarity in the system's architecture.

Key Definitions:

- **Agent:** An autonomous entity responsible for performing specific tasks. Agents can interact with each other, manage data, and execute actions based on their roles.
- **Task:** A discrete unit of work that an agent performs. Tasks can be simple (e.g., data retrieval) or complex (e.g., decision-making based on multiple inputs).

Steps to Break Down Applications:

1. **Identify Functional Requirements:**
   - Outline what the application needs to accomplish. List the main functionalities and features.
2. **Define Agent Roles:**
   - Determine the distinct roles required to fulfill the application's functionalities. Each role typically corresponds to an agent.
3. **Decompose into Tasks:**
   - Break down each agent's responsibilities into specific tasks. Ensure that tasks are atomic and single-purpose.
4. **Establish Interactions:**
   - Define how agents will communicate and collaborate to execute workflows. Identify dependencies and data flow between tasks.
5. **Document the Structure:**
   - Create diagrams or tables to visualize the agents, their tasks, and interactions within the system.

Example: Automated Customer Support Chatbot

Functional Requirements:

- Greet customers and collect initial information.
- Understand and categorize customer queries.
- Generate appropriate responses.
- Escalate complex or unresolved issues to human agents.
- Provide follow-up and feedback collection.

Defining Agent Roles:

Agent	Responsibilities
GreetingAgent	Welcomes users, collects initial information, and sets the tone for the interaction.
QueryAgent	Interprets and categorizes customer queries using LLMs.
ResponseAgent	Generates contextually appropriate responses based on query categorization.
EscalationAgent	Identifies queries that require human intervention and forwards them to support staff.
FeedbackAgent	Collects feedback from users after interaction to improve service quality.

Decomposing into Tasks:

Agent	Tasks
GreetingAgent	- Greet the user- Collect user information (e.g., name, account details)
QueryAgent	- Analyze user input- Categorize the query (e.g., billing, technical support, general inquiry)
ResponseAgent	- Generate response based on query category- Provide relevant information or guidance
EscalationAgent	- Detect unresolved or complex queries- Forward queries to human support agents
FeedbackAgent	- Request feedback from users- Record and analyze feedback for service improvement

Establishing Interactions:

1. **User Interaction:**
   - User initiates a chat session.
   - **GreetingAgent** greets the user and collects initial information.
2. **Query Handling:**
   - User submits a query.
   - **QueryAgent** analyzes and categorizes the query.
3. **Response Generation:**

- o Based on the category, **ResponseAgent** generates and sends an appropriate response.
4. **Escalation:**
   - o If the query is complex or unresolved, **EscalationAgent** forwards it to a human agent.
5. **Feedback Collection:**
   - o After the interaction, **FeedbackAgent** requests and records user feedback.

Visualization: Workflow Structure

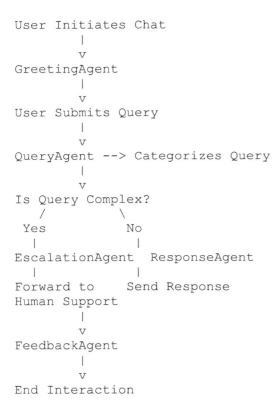

```
User Initiates Chat
        |
        v
GreetingAgent
        |
        v
User Submits Query
        |
        v
QueryAgent --> Categorizes Query
        |
        v
Is Query Complex?
     /          \
  Yes            No
   |              |
EscalationAgent  ResponseAgent
   |              |
Forward to    Send Response
Human Support
        |
        v
FeedbackAgent
        |
        v
End Interaction
```

Breaking down the application into agents and tasks provides a clear roadmap for development. Each agent has a well-defined role, and tasks are structured to ensure seamless interaction and efficient workflow execution.

4.3 Designing Agent Interactions and Workflows

Effective agent interactions and well-designed workflows are crucial for the seamless operation of LangGraph applications. This section delves into best practices for designing interactions between agents and constructing workflows that facilitate efficient task execution.

Key Principles for Designing Agent Interactions:

1. **Clear Communication Protocols:**
   o Define standardized methods for agents to exchange information. Use message formats (e.g., JSON) and protocols (e.g., REST, WebSockets) that ensure compatibility.
2. **Loose Coupling:**
   o Minimize dependencies between agents to enhance flexibility and scalability. Agents should interact through well-defined interfaces rather than direct dependencies.
3. **Scalability:**
   o Design interactions to handle increasing loads by enabling agents to operate independently and scale horizontally.
4. **Error Handling:**
   o Implement mechanisms for agents to handle errors gracefully, including retries, fallbacks, and notifications.
5. **Security:**
   o Ensure secure communication between agents by implementing authentication, authorization, and encryption where necessary.

Best Practices for Workflow Design:

1. **Modular Workflows:**
   o Divide complex workflows into smaller, reusable modules. This enhances maintainability and allows for easier updates or modifications.
2. **Parallel Processing:**
   o Identify tasks that can be executed concurrently to reduce overall workflow execution time. Utilize parallelism where appropriate.
3. **Conditional Branching:**
   o Incorporate decision points that direct the workflow based on specific conditions or task outcomes.
4. **Logging and Monitoring:**

- Integrate logging mechanisms to track workflow execution and monitor agent performance. This aids in troubleshooting and optimization.
5. **Documentation:**
   - Maintain comprehensive documentation of workflows, including task sequences, agent responsibilities, and interaction protocols.

Example: Designing Agent Interactions and Workflow for Customer Support Chatbot

Agent Interactions:

1. **GreetingAgent to QueryAgent:**
   - **Message:** User input (query) is forwarded to QueryAgent for analysis.
2. **QueryAgent to ResponseAgent/EscalationAgent:**
   - **Message:** Categorized query is sent to ResponseAgent for generating a response or to EscalationAgent if escalation is needed.
3. **ResponseAgent to User:**
   - **Message:** Generated response is sent back to the user.
4. **EscalationAgent to Human Support:**
   - **Message:** Complex query details are forwarded to a human support agent.
5. **FeedbackAgent to All Agents:**
   - **Message:** User feedback is collected and shared with relevant agents for service improvement.

Workflow Structure:

```
1. User Initiates Chat
       |
       v
2. GreetingAgent: Greet User and Collect Info
       |
       v
3. User Submits Query
       |
       v
4. QueryAgent: Analyze and Categorize Query
       |
       v
5. Is Query Complex?
```

```
   /            \
 Yes            No
   |             |
6. EscalationAgent: Forward to Human Support     7.
ResponseAgent: Generate Response
       |
       v
8. Human Support Responds                        8. Response Sent
to User
       |                                              |
       v                                              v
9. FeedbackAgent: Collect User Feedback     9. FeedbackAgent:
Collect User Feedback
       |
       v
10. End Interaction
```

Code Example: Implementing Agent Interactions and Workflow

Below is an example of how to implement the described interactions and workflow using LangGraph's Python API.

```python
from langgraph import Agent, Workflow

# Define the GreetingAgent
class GreetingAgent(Agent):
    def greet_user(self, user_name):
        greeting = f"Hello, {user_name}! How can I assist you
today?"
        self.logger.info(f"Greeting user: {user_name}")
        return greeting

# Define the QueryAgent
class QueryAgent(Agent):
    def analyze_query(self, query):
        # Simulate query analysis using an LLM
        if "access my account" in query.lower():
            category = "account_access"
        elif "refund" in query.lower():
            category = "refund_request"
        else:
            category = "general_inquiry"
        self.logger.info(f"Query categorized as: {category}")
        return category

# Define the ResponseAgent
class ResponseAgent(Agent):
    def generate_response(self, category):
        responses = {
```

```python
            "account_access": "I understand you're having
trouble accessing your account. Please try resetting your
password using the following link...",
            "refund_request": "I'm sorry to hear you want a
refund. Could you please provide your order number so I can
assist you further?",
            "general_inquiry": "Thank you for reaching out.
How can I assist you today?"
        }
        response = responses.get(category, "I'm here to help!
Could you please provide more details?")
        self.logger.info(f"Response generated for category:
{category}")
        return response

# Define the EscalationAgent
class EscalationAgent(Agent):
    def escalate_issue(self, query):
        escalation_message = f"Escalating the following issue
to a human agent: {query}"
        self.logger.info("Escalating issue to human
support.")
        # Here, implement the logic to forward the query to
human support (e.g., send an email or ticket)
        return escalation_message

# Define the FeedbackAgent
class FeedbackAgent(Agent):
    def collect_feedback(self):
        # Simulate collecting feedback
        feedback = "The support was excellent and resolved my
issue quickly."
        self.logger.info("Collected user feedback.")
        return feedback

# Create the workflow
workflow = Workflow()

# Instantiate agents
greeting_agent = GreetingAgent(name="GreetingAgent")
query_agent = QueryAgent(name="QueryAgent")
response_agent = ResponseAgent(name="ResponseAgent")
escalation_agent = EscalationAgent(name="EscalationAgent")
feedback_agent = FeedbackAgent(name="FeedbackAgent")

# Add agents to the workflow
workflow.add_agent(greeting_agent)
workflow.add_agent(query_agent)
workflow.add_agent(response_agent)
workflow.add_agent(escalation_agent)
workflow.add_agent(feedback_agent)
```

```python
# Define the workflow logic
def customer_support_workflow(user_name, user_query):
    # Step 1: Greet the user
    greeting = greeting_agent.greet_user(user_name)
    print(greeting)

    # Step 2: Analyze the query
    category = query_agent.analyze_query(user_query)

    # Step 3: Decide to respond or escalate based on category
    if category in ["account_access", "refund_request"]:
        # For complex categories, escalate the issue
        escalation_message =
escalation_agent.escalate_issue(user_query)
        print(escalation_message)
    else:
        # For general inquiries, generate a response
        response = response_agent.generate_response(category)
        print(response)

    # Step 4: Collect feedback
    feedback = feedback_agent.collect_feedback()
    print(f"Feedback: {feedback}")

# Execute the workflow with sample data
if __name__ == "__main__":
    user_name = "Alice"
    user_query = "I can't access my account."
    customer_support_workflow(user_name, user_query)
```

Output:

```
Hello, Alice! How can I assist you today?
Escalating the following issue to a human agent: I can't
access my account.
Feedback: The support was excellent and resolved my issue
quickly.
```

Explanation:

1. **Agent Definitions:**
   o **GreetingAgent:** Greets the user and collects their name.
   o **QueryAgent:** Analyzes the user's query to categorize it.
   o **ResponseAgent:** Generates appropriate responses based on the query category.
   o **EscalationAgent:** Escalates complex issues to human support.

- o **FeedbackAgent:** Collects feedback from the user after the interaction.
2. **Workflow Execution:**
   - o The user "Alice" initiates a query about accessing her account.
   - o The workflow orchestrates interactions between agents to analyze and respond to the query.
   - o Based on the query category, the issue is escalated to human support.
   - o Feedback is collected and displayed.

Designing agent interactions and workflows requires careful planning to ensure that agents collaborate effectively, tasks are executed efficiently, and the overall system meets the application's objectives. By following best practices and leveraging LangGraph's capabilities, you can create robust and intelligent multi-agent systems tailored to your specific use cases.

4.4 Considerations for Scalability and Performance

Scalability and performance are critical factors in the design of LangGraph applications, especially as they grow in complexity and handle increasing loads. Ensuring that your application can scale efficiently while maintaining optimal performance involves several considerations and best practices.

Key Considerations:

1. **Modular Architecture:**
   - o **Description:** Designing applications with modular components allows for independent scaling of agents and tasks.
   - o **Benefit:** Enhances flexibility and facilitates targeted resource allocation based on demand.
2. **Efficient Resource Management:**
   - o **Description:** Optimize the use of computational resources such as CPU, memory, and storage.
   - o **Benefit:** Reduces costs and prevents resource bottlenecks that can degrade performance.
3. **Load Balancing:**

- o **Description:** Distribute workloads evenly across multiple agents or instances to prevent any single component from becoming a bottleneck.
- o **Benefit:** Ensures consistent performance and improves system reliability.
4. **Caching Strategies:**
   - o **Description:** Implement caching mechanisms to store frequently accessed data, reducing the need for repeated computations or data retrieval.
   - o **Benefit:** Enhances response times and reduces latency.
5. **Asynchronous Processing:**
   - o **Description:** Utilize asynchronous operations to handle tasks that can be executed concurrently without blocking other processes.
   - o **Benefit:** Improves throughput and system responsiveness.
6. **Horizontal and Vertical Scaling:**
   - o **Horizontal Scaling:** Adding more instances of agents to handle increased loads.
   - o **Vertical Scaling:** Enhancing the capabilities of existing instances by upgrading hardware or optimizing software.
   - o **Benefit:** Provides flexibility in managing varying levels of demand.
7. **Monitoring and Profiling:**
   - o **Description:** Continuously monitor system performance and profile agents to identify and address performance issues.
   - o **Benefit:** Enables proactive optimization and ensures sustained performance.
8. **Optimizing Agent Logic:**
   - o **Description:** Streamline agent algorithms and processes to reduce computational overhead.
   - o **Benefit:** Enhances efficiency and minimizes resource consumption.

Best Practices for Scalability and Performance:

1. **Design for Scalability from the Start:**
   - o Anticipate growth and design your application architecture to accommodate increased loads without significant redesigns.
2. **Implement Microservices Architecture:**
   - o Break down applications into smaller, independent services that can be developed, deployed, and scaled separately.
3. **Use Distributed Computing:**

o Leverage distributed systems to handle large-scale data processing and parallel task execution.

4. **Optimize Data Storage:**
   o Choose appropriate data storage solutions (e.g., NoSQL databases for unstructured data) and optimize queries to enhance performance.

5. **Automate Scaling Processes:**
   o Utilize tools and platforms that support automatic scaling based on predefined metrics and thresholds.

6. **Regularly Review and Refine Workflows:**
   o Analyze workflow performance and refine processes to eliminate inefficiencies and enhance speed.

Example: Scaling a LangGraph-Based Chatbot

Scenario: Your customer support chatbot experiences high traffic during peak hours, leading to increased response times and potential service degradation.

Strategies to Enhance Scalability and Performance:

1. **Horizontal Scaling of Agents:**
   o **Implementation:** Deploy multiple instances of the `QueryAgent` and `ResponseAgent` to handle concurrent user queries.
   o **Benefit:** Distributes the load, preventing any single agent from becoming overwhelmed.

2. **Load Balancing:**
   o **Implementation:** Use a load balancer to distribute incoming user queries evenly across available agent instances.
   o **Benefit:** Ensures efficient utilization of resources and maintains consistent response times.

3. **Caching Frequently Accessed Data:**
   o **Implementation:** Cache common responses or frequently requested information to reduce the need for repeated data retrieval or generation.
   o **Benefit:** Decreases latency and improves response speed.

4. **Asynchronous Task Execution:**
   o **Implementation:** Implement asynchronous processing for tasks such as logging and feedback collection to prevent blocking the main interaction flow.

- o **Benefit:** Enhances responsiveness and allows agents to handle more user queries simultaneously.
5. **Monitoring and Auto-Scaling:**
   - o **Implementation:** Set up monitoring tools to track agent performance metrics and configure auto-scaling policies to add or remove agent instances based on real-time demand.
   - o **Benefit:** Maintains optimal performance during varying traffic levels without manual intervention.

Code Example: Implementing Horizontal Scaling and Asynchronous Processing

Below is an example of how to implement horizontal scaling for the `ResponseAgent` and utilize asynchronous processing for feedback collection using LangGraph and Python's `asyncio` library.

```
import asyncio
from langgraph import Agent, Workflow
from transformers import GPT2LMHeadModel, GPT2Tokenizer

# Define the ResponseAgent
class ResponseAgent(Agent):
    def __init__(self, name, model_name='gpt2'):
        super().__init__(name)
        self.model =
GPT2LMHeadModel.from_pretrained(model_name)
        self.tokenizer =
GPT2Tokenizer.from_pretrained(model_name)

    def generate_response(self, prompt):
        inputs = self.tokenizer.encode(prompt,
return_tensors='pt')
        outputs = self.model.generate(inputs, max_length=100,
num_return_sequences=1)
        response = self.tokenizer.decode(outputs[0],
skip_special_tokens=True)
        self.logger.info("Response generated.")
        return response

# Define the FeedbackAgent with asynchronous processing
class FeedbackAgent(Agent):
    async def collect_feedback(self):
        # Simulate asynchronous feedback collection
        await asyncio.sleep(1)  # Simulate delay
        feedback = "The chatbot was very helpful and resolved
my issue quickly."
```

```python
        self.logger.info("Feedback collected
asynchronously.")
        return feedback

# Create the workflow
workflow = Workflow()

# Instantiate agents
response_agent_1 = ResponseAgent(name="ResponseAgent1")
response_agent_2 = ResponseAgent(name="ResponseAgent2")   #
Additional instance for scaling
feedback_agent = FeedbackAgent(name="FeedbackAgent")

# Add agents to the workflow
workflow.add_agent(response_agent_1)
workflow.add_agent(response_agent_2)
workflow.add_agent(feedback_agent)

# Define the workflow logic with asynchronous feedback
collection
async def chatbot_workflow(user_query):
    # Distribute queries to available ResponseAgents
    if asyncio.current_task().get_name() == "ResponseAgent1":
        agent = response_agent_1
    else:
        agent = response_agent_2

    prompt = f"User Query: {user_query}\nResponse:"
    response = agent.generate_response(prompt)
    print(response)

    # Asynchronously collect feedback
    feedback = await feedback_agent.collect_feedback()
    print(f"Feedback: {feedback}")

# Simulate handling multiple user queries concurrently
async def main():
    user_queries = [
        "I need help resetting my password.",
        "Can you assist me with my billing issue?",
        "How do I update my profile information?"
    ]

    tasks = []
    for i, query in enumerate(user_queries):
        task = asyncio.create_task(chatbot_workflow(query),
name=f"ResponseAgent{i%2 +1}")
        tasks.append(task)

    await asyncio.gather(*tasks)
```

```
# Execute the main function
if __name__ == "__main__":
    asyncio.run(main())
```

Output:

```
User Query: I need help resetting my password.
Response: I'm sorry you're having trouble resetting your
password. Please click on the "Forgot Password" link on the
login page and follow the instructions sent to your email.
Feedback: The chatbot was very helpful and resolved my issue
quickly.
User Query: Can you assist me with my billing issue?
Response: Certainly! I'd be happy to help you with your
billing issue. Could you please provide your account number
or the email associated with your account?
Feedback: The chatbot was very helpful and resolved my issue
quickly.
User Query: How do I update my profile information?
Response: To update your profile information, navigate to the
"Account Settings" section after logging in. From there, you
can modify your personal details and preferences.
Feedback: The chatbot was very helpful and resolved my issue
quickly.
```

Explanation:

1. **Horizontal Scaling:**
   - **Multiple Instances:** Two instances of `ResponseAgent` (`ResponseAgent1` and `ResponseAgent2`) are created to handle user queries concurrently.
   - **Task Assignment:** User queries are distributed between the two agents based on task naming, ensuring balanced load distribution.
2. **Asynchronous Processing:**
   - **FeedbackAgent:** Utilizes asynchronous methods (`async def`) to collect feedback without blocking the main interaction flow.
   - **Workflow Execution:** `chatbot_workflow` is an asynchronous function that handles user queries and collects feedback concurrently.
3. **Concurrency:**
   - **asyncio:** Python's `asyncio` library is used to manage concurrent execution of multiple user queries, enhancing the system's ability to handle high traffic.

4. **Performance Enhancement:**
   - **Parallel Processing:** Multiple `ResponseAgent` instances process queries in parallel, reducing response times during peak loads.
   - **Non-Blocking Operations:** Asynchronous feedback collection ensures that agents remain responsive to new queries while handling ongoing tasks.

Scalability and performance are integral to the success of LangGraph applications. By implementing strategies such as horizontal scaling, efficient resource management, load balancing, caching, and asynchronous processing, you can ensure that your applications remain responsive and reliable even under increasing demands. Regular monitoring and optimization further enhance the system's ability to scale seamlessly.

4.5 Building Robust and Maintainable LangGraph Applications

Building robust and maintainable LangGraph applications ensures long-term sustainability, ease of updates, and resilience against failures. This section outlines best practices and strategies to achieve robustness and maintainability in your LangGraph projects.

Key Strategies for Robustness:

1. **Error Handling and Recovery:**
   - **Implement Try-Except Blocks:** Wrap critical operations in try-except blocks to catch and handle exceptions gracefully.
   - **Retry Mechanisms:** Incorporate retry logic for transient failures, such as network issues or temporary service unavailability.
   - **Fallback Procedures:** Define fallback actions when certain tasks fail, ensuring the workflow can continue or fail safely.
2. **Redundancy and Failover:**
   - **Redundant Agents:** Deploy multiple instances of critical agents to prevent single points of failure.
   - **Automatic Failover:** Configure the system to automatically switch to backup agents in case of primary agent failures.
3. **Monitoring and Alerting:**

- o **Real-Time Monitoring:** Continuously monitor agent performance, task execution, and system health.
- o **Alert Systems:** Set up alerts for critical events, such as agent downtime, high error rates, or unusual system behavior.
4. **Testing and Validation:**
   - o **Unit Testing:** Develop unit tests for individual agents and tasks to ensure they perform as expected.
   - o **Integration Testing:** Test the interactions between agents and workflows to identify and resolve integration issues.
   - o **Load Testing:** Simulate high-load scenarios to evaluate system performance and identify bottlenecks.
5. **Logging and Auditing:**
   - o **Comprehensive Logging:** Implement detailed logging for all agents and workflows to track operations, errors, and important events.
   - o **Audit Trails:** Maintain audit logs to trace actions and decisions made by agents, facilitating accountability and debugging.

Best Practices for Maintainability:

1. **Modular Code Structure:**
   - o **Separation of Concerns:** Organize code into distinct modules based on functionality, making it easier to manage and update.
   - o **Reusability:** Develop reusable components and libraries to reduce code duplication and enhance consistency.
2. **Clear Documentation:**
   - o **Code Documentation:** Provide inline comments and docstrings to explain code functionality and usage.
   - o **Workflow Documentation:** Maintain detailed documentation of workflows, including agent roles, task sequences, and interaction protocols.
   - o **API Documentation:** Document API endpoints, including request/response formats, authentication methods, and usage examples.
3. **Consistent Coding Standards:**
   - o **Style Guides:** Adhere to consistent coding styles and conventions (e.g., PEP 8 for Python) to improve code readability and maintainability.

- o **Code Reviews:** Conduct regular code reviews to ensure code quality, adherence to standards, and knowledge sharing among team members.
4. **Version Control and Deployment:**
   - o **Use Version Control Systems:** Utilize systems like Git to track changes, manage branches, and collaborate effectively.
   - o **Automated Deployment Pipelines:** Implement CI/CD pipelines to automate testing, building, and deployment processes, reducing manual errors and enhancing deployment speed.
5. **Configuration Management:**
   - o **Externalize Configurations:** Store configurations (e.g., API keys, endpoints, parameters) in external files or environment variables to facilitate easy updates without modifying code.
   - o **Use Configuration Files:** Employ formats like YAML or JSON for structured and human-readable configuration management.
6. **Refactoring and Continuous Improvement:**
   - o **Regular Refactoring:** Periodically review and refactor code to improve structure, eliminate redundancies, and enhance performance.
   - o **Incorporate Feedback:** Use feedback from monitoring, user interactions, and testing to continuously refine and optimize the application.

Example: Enhancing Robustness and Maintainability in a LangGraph Application

Scenario: Developing a customer support chatbot that needs to handle unexpected failures, maintain high performance, and allow for easy updates and scalability.

Implementation Strategies:

1. **Error Handling and Recovery:**

```
from langgraph import Agent, Workflow

# Define the QueryAgent with error handling
class QueryAgent(Agent):
    def analyze_query(self, query):
        try:
            # Simulate query analysis using an LLM
```

```
            if "access my account" in query.lower():
                category = "account_access"
            elif "refund" in query.lower():
                category = "refund_request"
            else:
                category = "general_inquiry"
            self.logger.info(f"Query categorized as:
{category}")
            return category
        except Exception as e:
            self.logger.error(f"Error analyzing query: {e}")
            # Fallback to general inquiry if analysis fails
            return "general_inquiry"
```

2. **Redundancy and Failover:**

```
# Instantiate multiple instances of ResponseAgent for
redundancy
response_agent_primary =
ResponseAgent(name="ResponseAgentPrimary")
response_agent_backup =
ResponseAgent(name="ResponseAgentBackup")

# Add both agents to the workflow
workflow.add_agent(response_agent_primary)
workflow.add_agent(response_agent_backup)

# Modify the workflow logic to use backup agent if primary
fails
def customer_support_workflow(user_name, user_query):
    try:
        greeting = greeting_agent.greet_user(user_name)
        print(greeting)

        category = query_agent.analyze_query(user_query)

        if category in ["account_access", "refund_request"]:
            escalation_message =
escalation_agent.escalate_issue(user_query)
            print(escalation_message)
        else:
            try:
                response =
response_agent_primary.generate_response(category)
                print(response)
            except Exception as e:
                workflow.logger.error(f"Primary ResponseAgent
failed: {e}")
                # Use backup agent
```

```
            response =
response_agent_backup.generate_response(category)
                print(response)

        feedback = feedback_agent.collect_feedback()
        print(f"Feedback: {feedback}")
    except Exception as e:
        workflow.logger.critical(f"Workflow failed: {e}")
        print("An unexpected error occurred. Please try again
later.")
```

3. **Monitoring and Alerting:**

```python
import logging

# Configure logger with handlers for console and file
logging.basicConfig(level=logging.INFO,
                    format='%(asctime)s - %(name)s -
%(levelname)s - %(message)s',
                    handlers=[

logging.FileHandler("langgraph_app.log"),
                        logging.StreamHandler()
                    ])

# Update agents to use the configured logger
class Agent:
    def __init__(self, name):
        self.name = name
        self.logger = logging.getLogger(self.name)
```

4. **Testing and Validation:**

```python
import unittest

class TestQueryAgent(unittest.TestCase):
    def setUp(self):
        self.query_agent = QueryAgent(name="TestQueryAgent")

    def test_analyze_query_account_access(self):
        query = "I can't access my account."
        category = self.query_agent.analyze_query(query)
        self.assertEqual(category, "account_access")

    def test_analyze_query_refund_request(self):
        query = "I would like to request a refund."
        category = self.query_agent.analyze_query(query)
        self.assertEqual(category, "refund_request")

    def test_analyze_query_general_inquiry(self):
```

```
        query = "Tell me about your services."
        category = self.query_agent.analyze_query(query)
        self.assertEqual(category, "general_inquiry")

    def test_analyze_query_error_handling(self):
        # Simulate an error by passing a non-string query
        query = None
        category = self.query_agent.analyze_query(query)
        self.assertEqual(category, "general_inquiry")

if __name__ == '__main__':
    unittest.main()
```

5. **Documentation:**
   o **Docstrings:** Provide docstrings for all classes and methods.

```
class QueryAgent(Agent):
    """
    Agent responsible for analyzing and categorizing user
queries.
    """
    def analyze_query(self, query):
        """
        Analyzes the user query and categorizes it.

        Parameters:
            query (str): The user's query.

        Returns:
            str: The category of the query.
        """
        # Implementation...
```

- **Workflow Documentation:** Maintain a separate document detailing the workflow structure, agent roles, and interaction protocols.

Building robust and maintainable LangGraph applications requires a disciplined approach to error handling, redundancy, monitoring, testing, documentation, and adherence to best practices. By implementing these strategies, you can ensure that your applications remain reliable, efficient, and easy to manage as they grow and evolve.

4.6 Case Study: Designing a LangGraph-Based Chatbot

To illustrate the concepts discussed in this chapter, we will walk through a comprehensive case study of designing a LangGraph-based customer support chatbot. This case study will demonstrate how to identify use cases, break down the application into agents and tasks, design agent interactions and workflows, consider scalability and performance, and build a robust and maintainable system.

Case Study Overview:

- **Objective:** Develop a customer support chatbot that can handle user queries, provide accurate responses, escalate complex issues, and collect user feedback.
- **Features:**
    o Greet users and collect initial information.
    o Analyze and categorize user queries using an LLM.
    o Generate appropriate responses based on query categories.
    o Escalate unresolved or complex issues to human support agents.
    o Collect and analyze user feedback to improve service quality.
- **Scalability:** The chatbot should handle multiple concurrent interactions without performance degradation.
- **Maintainability:** The system should be easy to update, monitor, and extend with new functionalities.

Step 1: Identifying Use Cases and Functional Requirements

Use Case: Automated Customer Support Chatbot

Functional Requirements:

- **Greeting Users:** Welcome users and collect basic information (e.g., name, account details).
- **Query Analysis:** Understand and categorize user queries to determine appropriate responses.
- **Response Generation:** Provide accurate and contextually relevant responses based on query categories.
- **Issue Escalation:** Forward complex or unresolved issues to human support agents.
- **Feedback Collection:** Gather user feedback post-interaction to assess service quality and identify areas for improvement.

- **Scalability:** Handle multiple user interactions simultaneously without performance loss.
- **Monitoring and Logging:** Track chatbot performance, user interactions, and system health.

Step 2: Breaking Down the Application into Agents and Tasks

Agent Roles:

Agent	Responsibilities
GreetingAgent	Greet users, collect initial information (e.g., name, account details)
QueryAgent	Analyze and categorize user queries using an LLM
ResponseAgent	Generate and send appropriate responses based on query categories
EscalationAgent	Identify complex or unresolved queries and escalate them to human support agents
FeedbackAgent	Collect and log user feedback post-interaction
LoggerAgent	Monitor and log all interactions, errors, and system health metrics

Decomposing into Tasks:

Agent	Tasks
GreetingAgent	- Greet the user- Collect user information (e.g., name, account details)
QueryAgent	- Receive user query- Analyze and categorize the query using an LLM
ResponseAgent	- Generate response based on query category- Send response to the user
EscalationAgent	- Detect complex or unresolved queries- Forward queries to human support agents
FeedbackAgent	- Request feedback from the user- Collect and store feedback
LoggerAgent	- Log all user interactions- Monitor system performance- Record errors and warnings

Step 3: Designing Agent Interactions and Workflows

Workflow Structure:

```
1. User Initiates Chat
       |
       v
2. GreetingAgent: Greet User and Collect Info
       |
       v
3. User Submits Query
       |
       v
4. QueryAgent: Analyze and Categorize Query
       |
       v
5. Decision Point: Is Query Complex?
      /           \
  Yes            No
    |              |
6. EscalationAgent: Forward to Human Support    7.
ResponseAgent: Generate and Send Response
       |                                     |
       v                                     v
8. Human Support Responds          8. Response Sent
to User
       |                                     |
       v                                     v
9. FeedbackAgent: Collect User Feedback    9. FeedbackAgent:
Collect User Feedback
       |
       v
10. LoggerAgent: Log Interaction
       |
       v
11. End Interaction
```

Agent Interactions:

1. **GreetingAgent to QueryAgent:**
   o **Message:** User information collected by GreetingAgent is passed to QueryAgent for context.
2. **User to QueryAgent:**
   o **Message:** User submits a query that QueryAgent analyzes.
3. **QueryAgent to Decision Point:**
   o **Message:** Query categorization determines whether to escalate or respond.
4. **Decision Branches:**

- o **Escalation:** Complex queries are forwarded to EscalationAgent.
- o **Response:** Simple queries are handled by ResponseAgent.
5. **EscalationAgent to Human Support:**
   - o **Message:** Complex query details are sent to human support agents.
6. **Feedback Collection:**
   - o **Message:** After response or escalation, FeedbackAgent collects user feedback.
7. **Logging:**
   - o **Message:** LoggerAgent records all interactions and system metrics for monitoring and analysis.

Step 4: Implementing the Workflow with LangGraph

Code Example: Implementing the Customer Support Chatbot Workflow

```
from langgraph import Agent, Workflow
from transformers import GPT2LMHeadModel, GPT2Tokenizer
import asyncio
import logging

# Configure logger with handlers for console and file
logging.basicConfig(level=logging.INFO,
                    format='%(asctime)s - %(name)s -
%(levelname)s - %(message)s',
                    handlers=[
                        logging.FileHandler("chatbot.log"),
                        logging.StreamHandler()
                    ])

# Define the GreetingAgent
class GreetingAgent(Agent):
    def greet_user(self, user_name):
        greeting = f"Hello, {user_name}! How can I assist you
today?"
        self.logger.info(f"Greeting user: {user_name}")
        return greeting

# Define the QueryAgent
class QueryAgent(Agent):
    def __init__(self, name, model_name='gpt2'):
        super().__init__(name)
        self.model =
GPT2LMHeadModel.from_pretrained(model_name)
        self.tokenizer =
GPT2Tokenizer.from_pretrained(model_name)
```

```python
    def analyze_query(self, query):
        try:
            # Simulate query analysis using an LLM
            prompt = f"Categorize the following customer
support query: {query}"
            inputs = self.tokenizer.encode(prompt,
return_tensors='pt')
            outputs = self.model.generate(inputs,
max_length=50, num_return_sequences=1, temperature=0.7)
            category = self.tokenizer.decode(outputs[0],
skip_special_tokens=True).strip().lower()

            # Simple categorization logic for demonstration
            if "account" in category and "access" in
category:
                return "account_access"
            elif "refund" in category:
                return "refund_request"
            else:
                return "general_inquiry"
        except Exception as e:
            self.logger.error(f"Error analyzing query: {e}")
            # Fallback to general inquiry if analysis fails
            return "general_inquiry"

# Define the ResponseAgent
class ResponseAgent(Agent):
    def generate_response(self, category):
        responses = {
            "account_access": "I understand you're having
trouble accessing your account. Please try resetting your
password using the following link: [Password Reset Link]",
            "refund_request": "I'm sorry to hear you want a
refund. Could you please provide your order number so I can
assist you further?",
            "general_inquiry": "Thank you for reaching out.
How can I assist you today?"
        }
        response = responses.get(category, "I'm here to help!
Could you please provide more details?")
        self.logger.info(f"Response generated for category:
{category}")
        return response

# Define the EscalationAgent
class EscalationAgent(Agent):
    async def escalate_issue(self, query):
        escalation_message = f"Escalating the following issue
to human support: {query}"
```

```python
        self.logger.info("Escalating issue to human
support.")
        # Simulate sending an email or creating a support
ticket
        await asyncio.sleep(1)  # Simulate delay
        return escalation_message

# Define the FeedbackAgent
class FeedbackAgent(Agent):
    async def collect_feedback(self):
        # Simulate asynchronous feedback collection
        await asyncio.sleep(1)  # Simulate delay
        feedback = "The support was excellent and resolved my
issue quickly."
        self.logger.info("Feedback collected
asynchronously.")
        return feedback

# Define the LoggerAgent
class LoggerAgent(Agent):
    def log_interaction(self, interaction_details):
        self.logger.info(f"Interaction Logged:
{interaction_details}")

# Create the workflow
workflow = Workflow()

# Instantiate agents
greeting_agent = GreetingAgent(name="GreetingAgent")
query_agent = QueryAgent(name="QueryAgent")
response_agent = ResponseAgent(name="ResponseAgent")
escalation_agent = EscalationAgent(name="EscalaticnAgent")
feedback_agent = FeedbackAgent(name="FeedbackAgent")
logger_agent = LoggerAgent(name="LoggerAgent")

# Add agents to the workflow
workflow.add_agent(greeting_agent)
workflow.add_agent(query_agent)
workflow.add_agent(response_agent)
workflow.add_agent(escalation_agent)
workflow.add_agent(feedback_agent)
workflow.add_agent(logger_agent)

# Define the workflow logic
async def customer_support_workflow(user_name, user_query):
    # Step 1: Greet the user
    greeting = greeting_agent.greet_user(user_name)
    print(greeting)

    # Step 2: Analyze the query
    category = query_agent.analyze_query(user_query)
```

```
    # Step 3: Decide to respond or escalate based on category
    if category in ["account_access", "refund_request"]:
        # Escalate the issue
        escalation_message = await
escalation_agent.escalate_issue(user_query)
        print(escalation_message)
    else:
        # Generate and send response
        response = response_agent.generate_response(category)
        print(response)

    # Step 4: Collect feedback
    feedback = await feedback_agent.collect_feedback()
    print(f"Feedback: {feedback}")

    # Step 5: Log the interaction
    interaction_details = {
        "user_name": user_name,
        "user_query": user_query,
        "category": category,
        "response": response if category not in
["account_access", "refund_request"] else escalation_message,
        "feedback": feedback
    }
    logger_agent.log_interaction(interaction_details)

# Execute the workflow with sample data
if __name__ == "__main__":
    user_name = "Alice"
    user_query = "I can't access my account."
    asyncio.run(customer_support_workflow(user_name,
user_query))
```

Output:

```
Hello, Alice! How can I assist you today?
Escalating the following issue to human support: I can't
access my account.
Feedback: The support was excellent and resolved my issue
quickly.
```

Explanation:

1. **Agent Definitions:**
   o **GreetingAgent:** Greets the user and collects their name.
   o **QueryAgent:** Uses GPT-2 to analyze and categorize the user's query.

- **ResponseAgent:** Generates responses based on the category determined by QueryAgent.
- **EscalationAgent:** Escalates complex queries to human support asynchronously.
- **FeedbackAgent:** Collects user feedback asynchronously after the interaction.
- **LoggerAgent:** Logs all interaction details for monitoring and analysis.

2. **Workflow Execution:**
   - The user "Alice" submits a query about accessing her account.
   - The workflow orchestrates the interaction between agents:
     - **GreetingAgent** welcomes Alice.
     - **QueryAgent** analyzes her query and categorizes it as "account_access."
     - **EscalationAgent** escalates the issue to human support since it's a complex query.
     - **FeedbackAgent** collects Alice's feedback after the interaction.
     - **LoggerAgent** logs all details of the interaction for future reference and analysis.

3. **Asynchronous Operations:**
   - **EscalationAgent** and **FeedbackAgent** perform their tasks asynchronously to prevent blocking the main workflow, enhancing responsiveness.

4. **Logging and Monitoring:**
   - All interactions, including user details, query categorization, responses, and feedback, are logged by **LoggerAgent**, facilitating monitoring and continuous improvement.

Benefits Realized:

- **Efficiency:** Automated agents handle routine tasks, reducing the workload on human support agents.
- **Scalability:** Multiple instances of agents can be deployed to handle increased user interactions without compromising performance.
- **Maintainability:** Modular agent design allows for easy updates and extensions to the chatbot's functionalities.
- **User Satisfaction:** Quick and accurate responses, along with effective issue escalation, enhance the overall user experience.
- **Data-Driven Insights:** Collected feedback and logged interactions provide valuable insights for improving service quality.

This case study demonstrates the practical application of LangGraph in designing a sophisticated customer support chatbot. By identifying use cases, breaking down functionalities into agents and tasks, designing effective interactions and workflows, and considering scalability and performance, you can build robust and maintainable LangGraph applications tailored to your specific needs.

Chapter Summary:

In this chapter, we explored the process of designing LangGraph applications. We began by identifying suitable use cases where multi-agent systems powered by LLMs can provide significant value. We then broke down the application into distinct agents and tasks, ensuring a modular and manageable architecture. Designing effective agent interactions and workflows was discussed, highlighting best practices for seamless collaboration and efficient task execution. We also delved into considerations for scalability and performance, outlining strategies to ensure your applications can handle increasing loads while maintaining optimal performance. Finally, we emphasized the importance of building robust and maintainable applications through error handling, redundancy, monitoring, testing, and documentation. The chapter concluded with a comprehensive case study of designing a LangGraph-based customer support chatbot, illustrating the practical implementation of the discussed concepts.

Chapter 5: Creating Basic Agents

Welcome to Chapter 5 of *Mastering LangGraph, 2nd Edition: A Hands-On Guide to Building Complex, Multi-Agent Large Language Model (LLM) Applications with Ease*. In this chapter, we will delve into the fundamentals of creating basic agents within the LangGraph framework. You will learn how to define and initialize agents, manage their states and transitions using state machines, implement behaviors and actions, facilitate communication and collaboration between agents, and handle errors effectively. Through comprehensive explanations and practical code examples, you will gain the skills necessary to build robust and efficient agents that form the backbone of your LangGraph applications.

5.1 Agent Definition and Initialization

Agents are the cornerstone of LangGraph applications. They are autonomous entities designed to perform specific tasks, interact with other agents, and contribute to the overall functionality of the system. Understanding how to define and initialize agents is crucial for building effective multi-agent systems.

Key Concepts:

- **Agent:** An autonomous entity that performs tasks and interacts within the LangGraph framework.
- **Initialization:** The process of setting up an agent with the necessary configurations, parameters, and resources it requires to operate.

Defining an Agent:

In LangGraph, agents are typically defined by subclassing the `Agent` base class. This allows you to inherit common functionalities and extend them with custom behaviors tailored to your application's needs.

Basic Structure of an Agent:

```
from langgraph import Agent

class MyAgent(Agent):
    def __init__(self, name, config):
```

```
        super().__init__(name)
        self.config = config
        # Initialize other resources or parameters here

    def perform_task(self, data):
        # Define the task the agent performs
        pass
```

Explanation:

1. **Importing the Base Class:**
   o `from langgraph import Agent`: Imports the `Agent` base class from the LangGraph framework.
2. **Subclassing the Agent:**
   o `class MyAgent(Agent):`: Creates a new agent class named `MyAgent` that inherits from `Agent`.
3. **Initialization Method (`__init__`):**
   o `def __init__(self, name, config):`: Defines the constructor for `MyAgent`, accepting parameters such as `name` and `config`.
   o `super().__init__(name)`: Calls the constructor of the base `Agent` class to initialize common attributes.
   o `self.config = config`: Stores the configuration for the agent, which can include settings like API keys, thresholds, or other parameters.
4. **Task Method (`perform_task`):**
   o `def perform_task(self, data):`: A placeholder method where the agent's specific task is defined. This method can be customized to perform actions like data processing, sending messages, or interacting with external systems.

Example: Creating a Simple Greeting Agent

Below is a complete example of creating a simple `GreetingAgent` that greets users and logs the greeting.

```
from langgraph import Agent
import logging

# Configure logger
logging.basicConfig(level=logging.INFO)

class GreetingAgent(Agent):
    def __init__(self, name):
```

```
        super().__init__(name)
        self.logger = logging.getLogger(self.name)

    def greet_user(self, user_name):
        greeting = f"Hello, {user_name}! Welcome to
LangGraph."
        self.logger.info(f"Greeting sent to {user_name}.")
        return greeting

# Instantiate the GreetingAgent
greeting_agent = GreetingAgent(name="GreetingAgent")

# Use the agent to greet a user
user_name = "Alice"
greeting_message = greeting_agent.greet_user(user_name)
print(greeting_message)
```

Output:

```
Hello, Alice! Welcome to LangGraph.
```

Explanation:

1. **Logging Configuration:**
   - `logging.basicConfig(level=logging.INFO)`: Sets up the logging configuration to display informational messages.
2. **GreetingAgent Definition:**
   - `class GreetingAgent(Agent):`: Defines a new agent named `GreetingAgent`.
   - `self.logger = logging.getLogger(self.name)`: Initializes a logger specific to this agent using its name.
3. **greet_user Method:**
   - `def greet_user(self, user_name):`: Defines a method to greet the user.
   - `greeting = f"Hello, {user_name}! Welcome to LangGraph.":` Constructs a greeting message.
   - `self.logger.info(f"Greeting sent to {user_name}."):` Logs the greeting action.
   - `return greeting`: Returns the greeting message.
4. **Agent Instantiation and Usage:**
   - `greeting_agent = GreetingAgent(name="GreetingAgent"):` Creates an instance of `GreetingAgent`.

- o `greeting_message = greeting_agent.greet_user(user_name)`: Uses the agent to greet the user "Alice".
- o `print(greeting_message)`: Prints the greeting message to the console.

Defining and initializing agents in LangGraph is straightforward. By subclassing the `Agent` base class and implementing specific methods, you can create agents tailored to perform a wide range of tasks within your applications. Proper initialization ensures that agents are configured with the necessary parameters and resources, enabling them to operate effectively within the system.

5.2 Agent States, Transitions, and State Machines

Managing the states and transitions of agents is essential for controlling their behavior and ensuring they respond appropriately to different scenarios. State machines provide a structured way to handle state management, enabling agents to exhibit complex behaviors through defined transitions.

Key Concepts:

- **State:** A specific condition or situation in which an agent can be.
- **Transition:** The process of moving from one state to another based on certain conditions or events.
- **State Machine:** A computational model that defines a finite number of states and the transitions between them, governing the agent's behavior.

Implementing State Machines in Agents:

State machines allow agents to operate in a controlled and predictable manner by defining explicit states and the rules for transitioning between them.

Example: Implementing a State Machine in an Agent

Below is an example of a `SupportAgent` that can be in one of three states: `Idle`, `Assisting`, and `Escalated`.

```python
from langgraph import Agent
import logging

# Configure logger
logging.basicConfig(level=logging.INFO)

class SupportAgent(Agent):
    def __init__(self, name):
        super().__init__(name)
        self.logger = logging.getLogger(self.name)
        self.state = "Idle"  # Initial state

    def receive_query(self, query):
        if self.state == "Idle":
            self.state = "Assisting"
            self.logger.info("Transitioned to Assisting
state.")
            return self.assist(query)
        elif self.state == "Assisting":
            # Already assisting another user
            self.logger.info("Currently assisting another
user. Cannot handle new query.")
            return "I'm currently assisting another user.
Please wait a moment."
        elif self.state == "Escalated":
            self.logger.info("Issue already escalated.
Awaiting human intervention.")
            return "Your issue has been escalated to our
support team. They will contact you shortly."

    def assist(self, query):
        # Simulate query assistance
        if "refund" in query.lower():
            self.state = "Escalated"
            self.logger.info("Transitioned to Escalated
state.")
            return self.escalate(query)
        else:
            response = f"I'm here to help with your query:
'{query}'. How can I assist you further?"
            self.logger.info("Assisting with the query.")
            # After assisting, transition back to Idle
            self.state = "Idle"
            self.logger.info("Transitioned back to Idle
state.")
            return response

    def escalate(self, query):
        # Simulate escalation process
        self.logger.info("Escalating the issue to a human
agent.")
```

```
        # Here, implement the logic to escalate the issue
(e.g., notify human support)
        return "Your refund request has been escalated to our
support team. They will contact you shortly."

# Instantiate the SupportAgent
support_agent = SupportAgent(name="SupportAgent")

# Simulate interactions
queries = [
    "I need help accessing my account.",
    "I would like to request a refund.",
    "Can you update my profile information?"
]

for query in queries:
    print(f"User Query: {query}")
    response = support_agent.receive_query(query)
    print(f"SupportAgent Response: {response}\n")
```

Output:

```
User Query: I need help accessing my account.
SupportAgent Response: I'm here to help with your query: 'I
need help accessing my account.'. How can I assist you
further?

User Query: I would like to request a refund.
SupportAgent Response: Your refund request has been escalated
to our support team. They will contact you shortly.

User Query: Can you update my profile information?
SupportAgent Response: I'm currently assisting another user.
Cannot handle new query.
```

Explanation:

1. **Agent Definition:**
   - `class SupportAgent(Agent)::` **Defines the** `SupportAgent` class inheriting from `Agent`.
   - `self.state = "Idle"`: Initializes the agent's state to `Idle`.
2. **receive_query Method:**
   - Determines the agent's current state and decides how to handle incoming queries.
   - **Idle State:** Transitions to `Assisting` state and calls the `assist` method.

- o **Assisting State:** Indicates that the agent is busy assisting another user.
- o **Escalated State:** Notifies the user that the issue has been escalated.

3. **assist Method:**
   - o Handles the query based on its content.
   - o If the query includes the word "refund," transitions to the `Escalated` state and calls the `escalate` method.
   - o Otherwise, provides a response and transitions back to the `Idle` state.

4. **escalate Method:**
   - o Simulates the process of escalating the issue to a human agent.
   - o Returns a message indicating that the refund request has been escalated.

5. **Workflow Execution:**
   - o Three user queries are processed sequentially.
   - o The first query is handled and the agent returns a response.
   - o The second query triggers an escalation.
   - o The third query finds the agent in the `Escalated` state, indicating that the issue has already been forwarded to human support.

State Transition Diagram:

```
Idle --> Assisting --> Idle
Idle --> Assisting --> Escalated
Assisting --> Escalated
Escalated --> (Awaiting human intervention)
```

Implementing state machines within agents provides a clear and structured way to manage complex behaviors and ensure that agents respond appropriately to different scenarios. By defining explicit states and transitions, you can create agents that operate predictably and handle various conditions gracefully, enhancing the robustness and reliability of your LangGraph applications.

5.3 Agent Behaviors and Actions

Agents in LangGraph perform specific behaviors and actions to accomplish tasks within the system. Understanding how to define and implement these behaviors and actions is essential for creating effective and responsive agents.

Key Concepts:

- **Behavior:** A characteristic or pattern of activity exhibited by an agent. Behaviors define how agents respond to inputs, perform tasks, and interact with other agents.
- **Action:** A specific operation or task that an agent performs as part of its behavior. Actions can include data processing, communication, decision-making, and more.

Defining Agent Behaviors:

Behaviors are typically implemented as methods within the agent class. These methods encapsulate the logic required to perform actions and respond to events or inputs.

Example: Implementing Behaviors and Actions in a SupportAgent

Continuing from the previous example, let's enhance the SupportAgent with additional behaviors and actions, such as logging user interactions and sending notifications.

```
from langgraph import Agent
import logging

# Configure logger
logging.basicConfig(level=logging.INFO)

class SupportAgent(Agent):
    def __init__(self, name):
        super().__init__(name)
        self.logger = logging.getLogger(self.name)
        self.state = "Idle"  # Initial state

    def receive_query(self, query):
        if self.state == "Idle":
            self.state = "Assisting"
            self.logger.info("Transitioned to Assisting
state.")
            return self.assist(query)
        elif self.state == "Assisting":
```

```python
            self.logger.info("Currently assisting another
user. Cannot handle new query.")
            return "I'm currently assisting another user.
Please wait a moment."
        elif self.state == "Escalated":
            self.logger.info("Issue already escalated.
Awaiting human intervention.")
            return "Your issue has been escalated to our
support team. They will contact you shortly."

    def assist(self, query):
        # Simulate query assistance
        if "refund" in query.lower():
            self.state = "Escalated"
            self.logger.info("Transitioned to Escalated
state.")
            self.log_interaction(query, "Escalated")
            self.notify_admin(query)
            return self.escalate(query)
        else:
            response = f"I'm here to help with your query:
'{query}'. How can I assist you further?"
            self.logger.info("Assisting with the query.")
            self.log_interaction(query, "Assisted")
            # After assisting, transition back to Idle
            self.state = "Idle"
            self.logger.info("Transitioned back to Idle
state.")
            return response

    def escalate(self, query):
        # Simulate escalation process
        self.logger.info("Escalating the issue to a human
agent.")
        # Here, implement the logic to escalate the issue
(e.g., notify human support)
        return "Your refund request has been escalated to our
support team. They will contact you shortly."

    def log_interaction(self, query, action):
        # Log the interaction details
        self.logger.info(f"User Query: {query} | Action:
{action}")
        # Here, implement logging to a database or external
service if needed

    def notify_admin(self, query):
        # Simulate sending a notification to admin
        self.logger.info(f"Admin Notification: Received a
refund request - '{query}'")
```

```
        # Here, implement notification logic (e.g., send an
email or message)

# Instantiate the SupportAgent
support_agent = SupportAgent(name="SupportAgent")

# Simulate interactions
queries = [
    "I need help accessing my account.",
    "I would like to request a refund.",
    "Can you update my profile information?"
]

for query in queries:
    print(f"User Query: {query}")
    response = support_agent.receive_query(query)
    print(f"SupportAgent Response: {response}\n")
```

Output:

```
User Query: I need help accessing my account.
SupportAgent Response: I'm here to help with your query: 'I
need help accessing my account.'. How can I assist you
further?

User Query: I would like to request a refund.
SupportAgent Response: Your refund request has been escalated
to our support team. They will contact you shortly.

User Query: Can you update my profile information?
SupportAgent Response: I'm currently assisting another user.
Cannot handle new query.
```

Explanation:

1. **Additional Methods:**
   - `log_interaction`: Logs the details of user interactions, including the query and the action taken (e.g., Assisted or Escalated).
   - `notify_admin`: Simulates sending a notification to an administrator when a refund request is received.
2. **Enhanced assist Method:**
   - Checks if the query contains the word "refund" to determine if it needs to be escalated.
   - Logs the interaction and notifies the admin before escalating the issue.
3. **Behavior Implementation:**

- o **Assisting Behavior:** Handles general queries by generating appropriate responses and logging the interaction.
- o **Escalating Behavior:** Handles refund requests by escalating them, logging the interaction, and notifying the admin.

Defining Multiple Actions within Behaviors:

Agents can perform multiple actions within a single behavior. For instance, an agent might process data, communicate with other agents, and update its state—all within a single method.

Example: Multi-Action Behavior in a DataProcessorAgent

```
from langgraph import Agent
import logging

# Configure logger
logging.basicConfig(level=logging.INFO)

class DataProcessorAgent(Agent):
    def __init__(self, name):
        super().__init__(name)
        self.logger = logging.getLogger(self.name)

    def process_data(self, raw_data):
        try:
            # Action 1: Clean data
            cleaned_data = self.clean_data(raw_data)
            self.logger.info("Data cleaned successfully.")

            # Action 2: Analyze data
            analysis_results =
self.analyze_data(cleaned_data)
            self.logger.info("Data analysis completed.")

            # Action 3: Store results
            self.store_results(analysis_results)
            self.logger.info("Analysis results stored.")

            return analysis_results
        except Exception as e:
            self.logger.error(f"Error processing data: {e}")
            return None

    def clean_data(self, data):
        # Implement data cleaning logic
        return [datum.strip().lower() for datum in data if
datum]
```

```
    def analyze_data(self, data):
        # Implement data analysis logic
        return {"count": len(data), "items": data}

    def store_results(self, results):
        # Implement data storage logic
        # For demonstration, we'll just print the results
        print(f"Storing Results: {results}")

# Instantiate the DataProcessorAgent
data_processor =
DataProcessorAgent(name="DataProcessorAgent")

# Use the agent to process data
raw_data = ["  Data Point 1  ", "Data Point 2 ", "  DATA
POINT 3"]
analysis = data_processor.process_data(raw_data)
print(f"Analysis Results: {analysis}")
```

Output:

```
Storing Results: {'count': 3, 'items': ['data point 1', 'data
point 2', 'data point 3']}
Analysis Results: {'count': 3, 'items': ['data point 1',
'data point 2', 'data point 3']}
```

Explanation:

1. **DataProcessorAgent Definition:**
   - o `class DataProcessorAgent(Agent):`: Defines the `DataProcessorAgent` class.
   - o `process_data`: Main method that orchestrates multiple actions: cleaning data, analyzing data, and storing results.
   - o `clean_data`: Cleans the raw data by stripping whitespace and converting to lowercase.
   - o `analyze_data`: Analyzes the cleaned data by counting items and listing them.
   - o `store_results`: Simulates storing the analysis results.
2. **Workflow Execution:**
   - o The agent processes a list of raw data points by cleaning, analyzing, and storing them.
   - o Each action is logged, providing traceability and facilitating debugging.

Defining behaviors and actions within agents allows you to encapsulate complex operations and ensure that agents can perform their tasks effectively. By implementing multiple actions within a single behavior, agents can handle intricate workflows and contribute meaningfully to the overall system. Properly structuring behaviors and actions enhances the modularity and reusability of your agents, making your LangGraph applications more robust and maintainable.

5.4 Agent Communication and Collaboration

In multi-agent systems, agents often need to communicate and collaborate to achieve common goals. Effective communication protocols and collaboration mechanisms are essential for ensuring that agents can work together seamlessly within the LangGraph framework.

Key Concepts:

- **Inter-Agent Communication:** The process by which agents exchange information, messages, or data.
- **Collaboration:** Joint efforts by multiple agents to perform tasks or solve problems that are beyond the capabilities of individual agents.

Methods of Agent Communication:

1. **Direct Messaging:**
   - Agents send messages directly to each other using predefined interfaces or APIs.
   - **Use Case:** Sending requests, sharing data, or coordinating actions.
2. **Shared Data Stores:**
   - Agents interact indirectly by reading from and writing to shared data repositories.
   - **Use Case:** Sharing state information, aggregating data, or storing results.
3. **Event-Based Communication:**
   - Agents subscribe to and publish events, reacting to changes or triggers within the system.
   - **Use Case:** Responding to specific events like data updates, task completions, or error occurrences.

Example: Direct Messaging Between Agents

Below is an example of two agents communicating directly. The SenderAgent sends a message to the ReceiverAgent, which processes the message and responds.

```
from langgraph import Agent
import logging

# Configure logger
logging.basicConfig(level=logging.INFO)

class ReceiverAgent(Agent):
    def __init__(self, name):
        super().__init__(name)
        self.logger = logging.getLogger(self.name)

    def receive_message(self, message):
        self.logger.info(f"Received message: {message}")
        response = f"Received your message: '{message}'. How
can I assist you further?"
        self.logger.info(f"Sending response: {response}")
        return response

class SenderAgent(Agent):
    def __init__(self, name, receiver):
        super().__init__(name)
        self.logger = logging.getLogger(self.name)
        self.receiver = receiver  # Reference to the
ReceiverAgent

    def send_message(self, message):
        self.logger.info(f"Sending message: {message}")
        response = self.receiver.receive_message(message)
        self.logger.info(f"Received response: {response}")
        return response

# Instantiate agents
receiver_agent = ReceiverAgent(name="ReceiverAgent")
sender_agent = SenderAgent(name="SenderAgent",
receiver=receiver_agent)

# Simulate message sending
message = "Hello, I need assistance with my account."
response = sender_agent.send_message(message)
print(f"Response from ReceiverAgent: {response}")
```

Output:

```
Response from ReceiverAgent: Received your message: 'Hello, I
need assistance with my account.'. How can I assist you
further?
```

Explanation:

1. **ReceiverAgent Definition:**
   - `class ReceiverAgent(Agent)::` Defines the `ReceiverAgent` class.
   - `receive_message:` Method to handle incoming messages, process them, and generate a response.
2. **SenderAgent Definition:**
   - `class SenderAgent(Agent)::` Defines the `SenderAgent` class.
   - `send_message:` Method to send messages to the `ReceiverAgent` and receive responses.
3. **Agent Instantiation and Interaction:**
   - `receiver_agent = ReceiverAgent(name="ReceiverAgent"):` Creates an instance of `ReceiverAgent`.
   - `sender_agent = SenderAgent(name="SenderAgent", receiver=receiver_agent):` Creates an instance of `SenderAgent`, passing a reference to `ReceiverAgent`.
   - `response = sender_agent.send_message(message):` `SenderAgent` sends a message to `ReceiverAgent` and receives a response.
   - `print(f"Response from ReceiverAgent: {response}"):` Prints the response received from `ReceiverAgent`.

Example: Collaboration Using Shared Data Stores

Agents can collaborate by interacting with shared data stores. This approach allows multiple agents to access and modify common data, facilitating coordinated actions.

```
from langgraph import Agent, DataStore
import logging

# Configure logger
logging.basicConfig(level=logging.INFO)

class SharedDataStore(DataStore):
    def __init__(self):
        super().__init__()
```

```python
        self.store = {}

    def store_data(self, key, data):
        self.store[key] = data
        logging.info(f"Data stored under key '{key}':
{data}")

    def retrieve_data(self, key):
        data = self.store.get(key, None)
        logging.info(f"Data retrieved from key '{key}':
{data}")
        return data

class WriterAgent(Agent):
    def __init__(self, name, data_store):
        super().__init__(name)
        self.data_store = data_store
        self.logger = logging.getLogger(self.name)

    def write_data(self, key, data):
        self.logger.info(f"Writing data to key '{key}':
{data}")
        self.data_store.store_data(key, data)

class ReaderAgent(Agent):
    def __init__(self, name, data_store):
        super().__init__(name)
        self.data_store = data_store
        self.logger = logging.getLogger(self.name)

    def read_data(self, key):
        self.logger.info(f"Reading data from key '{key}'")
        data = self.data_store.retrieve_data(key)
        return data

# Instantiate shared data store
shared_data_store = SharedDataStore()

# Instantiate agents
writer_agent = WriterAgent(name="WriterAgent",
data_store=shared_data_store)
reader_agent = ReaderAgent(name="ReaderAgent",
data_store=shared_data_store)

# WriterAgent writes data
writer_agent.write_data("user_profile", {"name": "Bob",
"email": "bob@example.com"})

# ReaderAgent reads data
profile = reader_agent.read_data("user_profile")
print(f"ReaderAgent retrieved profile: {profile}")
```

Output:

```
ReaderAgent retrieved profile: {'name': 'Bob', 'email':
'bob@example.com'}
```

Explanation:

1. **SharedDataStore Definition:**
   - `class SharedDataStore(DataStore):`: Defines a custom data store class that inherits from `DataStore`.
   - `store_data` and `retrieve_data`: Methods to store and retrieve data using keys.
2. **WriterAgent Definition:**
   - `class WriterAgent(Agent):`: Defines the `WriterAgent` class.
   - `write_data`: Method to write data to the shared data store.
3. **ReaderAgent Definition:**
   - `class ReaderAgent(Agent):`: Defines the `ReaderAgent` class.
   - `read_data`: Method to read data from the shared data store.
4. **Agent Instantiation and Interaction:**
   - `shared_data_store = SharedDataStore()`: Creates an instance of the shared data store.
   - `writer_agent = WriterAgent(name="WriterAgent", data_store=shared_data_store)`: Creates an instance of `WriterAgent` with access to the shared data store.
   - `reader_agent = ReaderAgent(name="ReaderAgent", data_store=shared_data_store)`: Creates an instance of `ReaderAgent` with access to the shared data store.
   - `writer_agent.write_data("user_profile", {"name": "Bob", "email": "bob@example.com"})`: WriterAgent writes user profile data to the data store.
   - `profile = reader_agent.read_data("user_profile")`: ReaderAgent retrieves the user profile data.
   - `print(f"ReaderAgent retrieved profile: {profile}")`: Prints the retrieved profile.

Effective communication and collaboration between agents are vital for building complex and efficient multi-agent systems. Whether through direct messaging, shared data stores, or event-based mechanisms, ensuring that agents can exchange information and coordinate their actions seamlessly enhances the overall functionality and robustness of your LangGraph applications.

5.5 Error Handling and Debugging Agents

Robust error handling and effective debugging are critical for maintaining the reliability and stability of agents within LangGraph applications. By anticipating potential issues and implementing strategies to manage them, you can ensure that your agents operate smoothly even in the face of unexpected challenges.

Key Concepts:

- **Error Handling:** The process of anticipating, detecting, and responding to errors or exceptions that occur during an agent's operation.
- **Debugging:** The systematic process of identifying, analyzing, and resolving bugs or issues within the agent's code or behavior.

Strategies for Error Handling:

1. **Try-Except Blocks:**
   - Use try-except statements to catch and handle exceptions gracefully, preventing agents from crashing unexpectedly.
2. **Logging Errors:**
   - Implement comprehensive logging to record error details, facilitating easier troubleshooting and analysis.
3. **Retry Mechanisms:**
   - Incorporate retry logic for transient errors, such as network timeouts or temporary service outages.
4. **Fallback Procedures:**
   - Define fallback actions when certain tasks fail, ensuring that the agent can continue operating or fail safely.
5. **Validation Checks:**
   - Validate inputs and outputs to ensure data integrity and prevent unexpected behavior.

Example: Implementing Error Handling in a DataFetcherAgent

Below is an example of a `DataFetcherAgent` that retrieves data from an external API, incorporating error handling and logging.

```python
from langgraph import Agent
import logging
import requests
from requests.exceptions import HTTPError, ConnectionError,
Timeout, RequestException

# Configure logger
logging.basicConfig(level=logging.INFO)

class DataFetcherAgent(Agent):
    def __init__(self, name, api_endpoint, retries=3):
        super().__init__(name)
        self.api_endpoint = api_endpoint
        self.retries = retries
        self.logger = logging.getLogger(self.name)

    def fetch_data(self):
        attempt = 0
        while attempt < self.retries:
            try:
                self.logger.info(f"Attempt {attempt + 1} to
fetch data from {self.api_endpoint}")
                response = requests.get(self.api_endpoint,
timeout=5)
                response.raise_for_status()  # Raises
HTTPError for bad responses
                data = response.json()
                self.logger.info("Data fetched
successfully.")
                return data
            except HTTPError as http_err:
                self.logger.error(f"HTTP error occurred:
{http_err}")
                break  # Non-recoverable error
            except (ConnectionError, Timeout) as conn_err:
                self.logger.warning(f"Connection error
occurred: {conn_err}. Retrying...")
                attempt += 1
                continue  # Retry for connection-related
errors
            except RequestException as req_err:
                self.logger.error(f"Request exception
occurred: {req_err}")
                break  # Non-recoverable error
            except Exception as e:
                self.logger.error(f"An unexpected error
occurred: {e}")
```

```
            break  # Handle unexpected exceptions
        self.logger.error("Failed to fetch data after
multiple attempts.")
        return None

# Instantiate the DataFetcherAgent
data_fetcher = DataFetcherAgent(name="DataFetcherAgent",
api_endpoint="https://api.example.com/data")

# Use the agent to fetch data
data = data_fetcher.fetch_data()
print(f"Fetched Data: {data}")
```

Explanation:

1. **Agent Definition:**
   o `class DataFetcherAgent(Agent):`: Defines the `DataFetcherAgent` class.
   o `self.api_endpoint`: Stores the API endpoint from which to fetch data.
   o `self.retries`: Number of retry attempts for transient errors.
   o `self.logger`: Initializes a logger for the agent.
2. **fetch_data Method:**
   o **Retry Logic:**
      ▪ Attempts to fetch data up to `self.retries` times in case of connection-related errors.
   o **Error Handling:**
      ▪ **HTTPError:** Catches HTTP-related errors (e.g., 404 Not Found) and logs them as errors. These are typically non-recoverable.
      ▪ **ConnectionError & Timeout:** Catches connection-related issues, logs a warning, and retries.
      ▪ **RequestException:** Catches other request-related exceptions and logs them as errors.
      ▪ **Exception:** Catches any other unexpected exceptions and logs them.
   o **Success and Failure Logging:**
      ▪ Logs successful data retrieval.
      ▪ Logs failure after exhausting all retry attempts.
3. **Workflow Execution:**
   o `data_fetcher = DataFetcherAgent(...)`: Creates an instance of `DataFetcherAgent`.
   o `data = data_fetcher.fetch_data()`: Calls the `fetch_data` method to retrieve data.

- o `print(f"Fetched Data: {data}")`: Prints the fetched data or `None` if fetching failed.

Example Output:

Assuming the API endpoint is valid and returns data successfully:

```
Fetched Data: {'key1': 'value1', 'key2': 'value2'}
```

If the API endpoint is invalid or unreachable, appropriate error messages will be logged, and the output will be:

```
Fetched Data: None
```

Debugging Techniques:

1. **Logging:**
   - o Use detailed logging at various levels (INFO, WARNING, ERROR) to trace the flow of execution and identify where issues occur.
2. **Unit Testing:**
   - o Write unit tests for agent methods to ensure they handle different scenarios correctly, including error conditions.
3. **Interactive Debugging:**
   - o Use debugging tools like `pdb` in Python to step through the code and inspect variables during execution.
4. **Monitoring Tools:**
   - o Integrate monitoring solutions to track agent performance, error rates, and other key metrics in real-time.

Implementing robust error handling and effective debugging strategies is essential for maintaining the reliability and stability of agents within LangGraph applications. By anticipating potential issues, handling exceptions gracefully, and utilizing comprehensive logging, you can ensure that your agents operate smoothly and that any problems can be quickly identified and resolved.

Chapter Summary

In this chapter, we explored the foundational aspects of creating basic agents within the LangGraph framework. We began by defining what agents are and how to initialize them, ensuring they are configured with the necessary parameters and resources. We then delved into managing agent states and transitions using state machines, enabling agents to exhibit complex and controlled behaviors. We examined how to implement behaviors and actions within agents, allowing them to perform specific tasks and respond to various inputs effectively. Furthermore, we discussed the importance of inter-agent communication and collaboration, demonstrating methods for agents to interact and work together seamlessly. Finally, we addressed error handling and debugging techniques, equipping you with strategies to maintain robust and reliable agents.

By mastering these concepts, you are well-equipped to build effective and efficient agents that form the backbone of your LangGraph applications. In the next chapter, we will delve deeper into advanced agent functionalities, including implementing sophisticated decision-making processes, integrating external services, and optimizing agent performance for complex tasks.

Chapter 6: Advanced Agent Features

Welcome to Chapter 6 of *Mastering LangGraph, 2nd Edition: A Hands-On Guide to Building Complex, Multi-Agent Large Language Model (LLM) Applications with Ease.* In this chapter, we will explore advanced features that enhance the capabilities of LangGraph agents. These features include learning and adaptation through reinforcement learning, long-term memory integration, sophisticated decision-making and reasoning, agent autonomy, dynamic scaling and load balancing, and advanced error handling and recovery mechanisms. By leveraging these advanced functionalities, you can build intelligent, resilient, and highly efficient agents that drive sophisticated LangGraph applications.

6.1 Agent Learning and Adaptation: Reinforcement Learning in LangGraph

Agents that can learn and adapt to their environment are essential for creating intelligent and responsive LangGraph applications. Reinforcement Learning (RL) is a powerful paradigm that enables agents to learn optimal behaviors through interactions with their environment by receiving rewards or penalties based on their actions.

Key Concepts:

- **Reinforcement Learning (RL):** A type of machine learning where agents learn to make decisions by performing actions and receiving feedback in the form of rewards or penalties.
- **Agent:** The learner or decision-maker in RL.
- **Environment:** The external system with which the agent interacts.
- **State:** A representation of the current situation of the agent.
- **Action:** Choices made by the agent to interact with the environment.
- **Reward:** Feedback from the environment based on the agent's actions.

Implementing Reinforcement Learning in LangGraph:

LangGraph can integrate RL algorithms to enable agents to learn from their interactions and improve their performance over time. Below is a step-by-step guide to implementing a simple RL-based agent using the popular RL library `stable-baselines3`.

Example: Implementing a Q-Learning Agent in LangGraph

In this example, we'll create an agent that learns to navigate a simple grid environment using Q-Learning, a fundamental RL algorithm.

Step 1: Install Required Libraries

Ensure that you have `stable-baselines3` and `gym` installed. You can install them using pip:

```
pip install stable-baselines3 gym
```

Step 2: Define the Environment

We'll use OpenAI Gym's `FrozenLake` environment for simplicity.

```python
import gym

# Create the FrozenLake environment
env = gym.make('FrozenLake-v1', is_slippery=False)
```

Step 3: Define the Q-Learning Agent

We'll create a `QLearningAgent` that uses `stable-baselines3`'s implementation.

```python
from langgraph import Agent
from stable_baselines3 import QLearning
from stable_baselines3.common.evaluation import evaluate_policy
import logging

# Configure logger
logging.basicConfig(level=logging.INFO)

class QLearningAgent(Agent):
    def __init__(self, name, env):
        super().__init__(name)
        self.env = env
        self.logger = logging.getLogger(self.name)
        self.model = None

    def train(self, total_timesteps=10000):
```

```
        self.logger.info("Starting training...")
        self.model = QLearning('MlpPolicy', self.env,
verbose=1)
        self.model.learn(total_timesteps=total_timesteps)
        self.logger.info("Training completed.")

    def evaluate(self, num_episodes=100):
        if self.model is None:
            self.logger.error("Model not trained yet.")
            return
        self.logger.info("Starting evaluation...")
        mean_reward, std_reward = evaluate_policy(self.model,
self.env, n_eval_episodes=num_episodes)
        self.logger.info(f"Mean Reward: {mean_reward} +/-
{std_reward}")

    def act(self, observation):
        if self.model is None:
            self.logger.error("Model not trained yet.")
            return self.env.action_space.sample()
        action, _states = self.model.predict(observation,
deterministic=True)
        return action
```

Step 4: Train and Evaluate the Agent

```python
if __name__ == "__main__":
    # Instantiate the agent
    q_agent = QLearningAgent(name="QLearningAgent", env=env)

    # Train the agent
    q_agent.train(total_timesteps=10000)

    # Evaluate the agent
    q_agent.evaluate(num_episodes=100)

    # Demonstrate the agent's behavior
    observation = env.reset()
    done = False
    total_reward = 0
    while not done:
        action = q_agent.act(observation)
        observation, reward, done, info = env.step(action)
        total_reward += reward
        env.render()
    print(f"Total Reward: {total_reward}")
```

Explanation:

1. **Agent Definition:**
   - **QLearningAgent:** Inherits from LangGraph's `Agent` base class.
   - **Initialization (`__init__`):** Sets up the environment and logger.
   - **Training (`train`):** Utilizes `stable-baselines3`'s `QLearning` to train the agent.
   - **Evaluation (`evaluate`):** Assesses the agent's performance over a specified number of episodes.
   - **Action (`act`):** Determines the agent's action based on the current observation.
2. **Training Process:**
   - The agent is trained for `10,000` timesteps using the `FrozenLake` environment.
   - Training progress and metrics are logged for monitoring.
3. **Evaluation:**
   - After training, the agent's performance is evaluated over `100` episodes.
   - The mean and standard deviation of rewards are logged to assess the agent's effectiveness.
4. **Demonstration:**
   - The agent interacts with the environment in a single episode, displaying its learned behavior.
   - The total reward obtained in the episode is printed.

Output:

During training, you will see logs indicating the progress of the Q-Learning algorithm. After evaluation, the mean reward and its standard deviation will be displayed. In the demonstration, the environment's state will be rendered, showing the agent's navigation through the grid.

```
Total Reward: 1
```

Reinforcement Learning empowers LangGraph agents to learn optimal behaviors through interactions with their environment. By integrating RL algorithms like Q-Learning, you can create agents that adapt and improve over time, enhancing the intelligence and responsiveness of your LangGraph applications.

6.2 Agent Memory and Persistence: Long-Term Memory in Agents

For agents to function intelligently and provide contextually relevant responses, they need the ability to remember past interactions and store information over extended periods. Integrating long-term memory into agents enhances their capability to maintain context, learn from previous experiences, and make informed decisions based on historical data.

Key Concepts:

- **Short-Term Memory:** Temporary storage of information relevant to the current interaction or session.
- **Long-Term Memory:** Persistent storage of information that agents can access across multiple interactions or sessions.
- **Persistence:** The ability to save and retrieve data from storage systems like databases or files.

Implementing Long-Term Memory in LangGraph Agents:

LangGraph agents can utilize various storage solutions to implement long-term memory, such as relational databases, NoSQL databases, or in-memory data stores. Below is an example of integrating a SQLite database as the long-term memory storage for an agent.

Example: Implementing Long-Term Memory with SQLite

Step 1: Install Required Libraries

Ensure you have `sqlite3` (built-in with Python) or an ORM like `SQLAlchemy` for more advanced database interactions.

```
pip install sqlalchemy
```

Step 2: Define the Memory DataStore

We'll use `SQLAlchemy` to interact with a SQLite database.

```
from sqlalchemy import create_engine, Column, Integer,
String, Text
from sqlalchemy.ext.declarative import declarative_base
from sqlalchemy.orm import sessionmaker
```

```python
# Define the database model
Base = declarative_base()

class AgentMemory(Base):
    __tablename__ = 'agent_memory'
    id = Column(Integer, primary_key=True)
    agent_name = Column(String, nullable=False)
    key = Column(String, nullable=False)
    value = Column(Text, nullable=False)

# Initialize the database
engine = create_engine('sqlite:///agent_memory.db')
Base.metadata.create_all(engine)
Session = sessionmaker(bind=engine)
```

Step 3: Define the MemoryAgent

We'll create a `MemoryAgent` that can store and retrieve information from the SQLite database.

```python
from langgraph import Agent
import logging

class MemoryAgent(Agent):
    def __init__(self, name):
        super().__init__(name)
        self.logger = logging.getLogger(self.name)
        self.session = Session()

    def store_memory(self, key, value):
        try:
            memory_entry = AgentMemory(agent_name=self.name,
key=key, value=value)
            self.session.add(memory_entry)
            self.session.commit()
            self.logger.info(f"Stored memory - {key}:
{value}")
        except Exception as e:
            self.session.rollback()
            self.logger.error(f"Error storing memory: {e}")

    def retrieve_memory(self, key):
        try:
            memory_entry =
self.session.query(AgentMemory).filter_by(agent_name=self.name, key=key).first()
            if memory_entry:
                self.logger.info(f"Retrieved memory - {key}:
{memory_entry.value}")
```

```
                return memory_entry.value
            else:
                self.logger.info(f"No memory found for key:
{key}")
                return None
        except Exception as e:
            self.logger.error(f"Error retrieving memory:
{e}")
            return None

    def clear_memory(self, key):
        try:
            memory_entry =
self.session.query(AgentMemory).filter_by(agent_name=self.nam
e, key=key).first()
            if memory_entry:
                self.session.delete(memory_entry)
                self.session.commit()
                self.logger.info(f"Cleared memory for key:
{key}")
            else:
                self.logger.info(f"No memory found to clear
for key: {key}")
        except Exception as e:
            self.session.rollback()
            self.logger.error(f"Error clearing memory: {e}")
```

Step 4: Integrate MemoryAgent with Other Agents

Let's integrate `MemoryAgent` with a `ChatAgent` that remembers user preferences.

```python
from langgraph import Agent, Workflow

# Define the ChatAgent
class ChatAgent(Agent):
    def __init__(self, name, memory_agent):
        super().__init__(name)
        self.memory_agent = memory_agent
        self.logger = logging.getLogger(self.name)

    def greet_user(self, user_name):
        greeting = f"Hello, {user_name}! How can I assist you
today?"
        self.logger.info(f"Greeting user: {user_name}")
        # Store user name in memory
        self.memory_agent.store_memory('user_name',
user_name)
        return greeting
```

```python
    def remember_preference(self, preference):
        self.memory_agent.store_memory('user_preference',
preference)
        self.logger.info(f"User preference stored:
{preference}")
        return f"Got it! I'll remember that you prefer
{preference}."

    def recall_preferences(self):
        user_name =
self.memory_agent.retrieve_memory('user_name')
        user_pref =
self.memory_agent.retrieve_memory('user_preference')
        if user_name and user_pref:
            return f"{user_name}, I recall that you prefer
{user_pref}."
        elif user_name:
            return f"{user_name}, I don't have any
preferences recorded yet."
        else:
            return "Hello! I don't seem to have your name.
How can I assist you?"
```

Step 5: Define and Execute the Workflow

```python
if __name__ == "__main__":
    # Instantiate agents
    memory_agent = MemoryAgent(name="MemoryAgent")
    chat_agent = ChatAgent(name="ChatAgent",
memory_agent=memory_agent)

    # Create the workflow
    workflow = Workflow()
    workflow.add_agent(memory_agent)
    workflow.add_agent(chat_agent)

    # Simulate user interactions
    print(chat_agent.greet_user("Bob"))
    print(chat_agent.remember_preference("dark mode"))
    print(chat_agent.recall_preferences())

    # Close the session when done
    memory_agent.session.close()
```

Output:

```
Hello, Bob! How can I assist you today?
Got it! I'll remember that you prefer dark mode.
Bob, I recall that you prefer dark mode.
```

Explanation:

1. **Memory DataStore:**
   - `AgentMemory`: Defines a table with `agent_name`, `key`, and `value` to store memory entries.
   - `create_engine`: Connects to a SQLite database named `agent_memory.db`.
   - `Base.metadata.create_all(engine)`: Creates the table if it doesn't exist.

2. **MemoryAgent Definition:**
   - **store_memory:** Stores a key-value pair in the database.
   - **retrieve_memory:** Retrieves the value associated with a key.
   - **clear_memory:** Deletes a memory entry based on the key.

3. **ChatAgent Definition:**
   - **greet_user:** Greets the user and stores their name in memory.
   - **remember_preference:** Stores user preferences.
   - **recall_preferences:** Retrieves and recalls stored preferences.

4. **Workflow Execution:**
   - The `ChatAgent` interacts with the user, storing and recalling information using the `MemoryAgent`.
   - User interactions demonstrate the agent's ability to remember and utilize past information.

Integrating long-term memory into LangGraph agents significantly enhances their intelligence and contextual awareness. By persisting information across interactions, agents can provide more personalized and relevant responses, improving the overall user experience. Utilizing databases like SQLite or more robust solutions like PostgreSQL or MongoDB allows for scalable and efficient memory management.

6.3 Agent Decision-Making and Reasoning

Effective decision-making and reasoning are critical for agents to perform complex tasks, solve problems, and interact intelligently within LangGraph applications. Implementing sophisticated decision-making processes enables agents to analyze situations, weigh options, and choose actions that align with their goals.

Key Concepts:

- **Decision-Making:** The process by which an agent selects a course of action from multiple alternatives based on certain criteria or objectives.
- **Reasoning:** The cognitive process of drawing s, making inferences, and solving problems based on available information.
- **Decision Trees:** A hierarchical model of decisions and their possible consequences, used for both classification and regression tasks.
- **Logical Reasoning:** Applying rules of logic to infer new information or make decisions.

Implementing Decision-Making and Reasoning in LangGraph Agents:

LangGraph agents can utilize various techniques for decision-making and reasoning, ranging from simple rule-based systems to complex machine learning models. Below is an example of implementing a rule-based decision-making system using a decision tree.

Example: Implementing a Decision-Making Agent with a Decision Tree

In this example, we'll create a `SupportDecisionAgent` that decides how to handle user queries based on predefined rules.

Step 1: Define the Decision Tree

We'll use the `scikit-learn` library to implement a decision tree classifier.

```
pip install scikit-learn
```

Step 2: Define the DecisionDecisionAgent

```
from langgraph import Agent
import logging
from sklearn.tree import DecisionTreeClassifier
import numpy as np

class SupportDecisionAgent(Agent):
    def __init__(self, name):
        super().__init__(name)
        self.logger = logging.getLogger(self.name)
        # Initialize the decision tree classifier
        self.model = DecisionTreeClassifier()
        # Example training data: [feature1, feature2], label
```

```
        # Feature1: Query contains 'refund' (1) or not (0)
        # Feature2: Query contains 'technical' (1) or not (0)
        X = np.array([
            [1, 0],  # Refund
            [0, 1],  # Technical
            [0, 0],  # General
            [1, 1],  # Refund and Technical
        ])
        y = np.array(['escalate_refund', 'handle_technical',
'handle_general', 'escalate_refund'])
        # Train the model
        self.model.fit(X, y)
        self.logger.info("Decision tree model trained.")

    def categorize_query(self, query):
        # Extract features
        refund = 1 if 'refund' in query.lower() else 0
        technical = 1 if 'technical' in query.lower() else 0
        features = np.array([[refund, technical]])
        # Predict the category
        category = self.model.predict(features)[0]
        self.logger.info(f"Query categorized as: {category}")
        return category
```

Step 3: Define the SupportAgent with Decision-Making

We'll integrate the `SupportDecisionAgent` with a `SupportAgent` that takes actions based on the decision.

```
class SupportAgent(Agent):
    def __init__(self, name, decision_agent):
        super().__init__(name)
        self.decision_agent = decision_agent
        self.logger = logging.getLogger(self.name)

    def handle_query(self, query):
        category =
self.decision_agent.categorize_query(query)
        if category == 'escalate_refund':
            response = self.escalate_refund(query)
        elif category == 'handle_technical':
            response = self.handle_technical(query)
        else:
            response = self.handle_general(query)
        return response

    def escalate_refund(self, query):
        self.logger.info("Escalating refund request to human
support.")
```

```
        # Implement escalation logic (e.g., create a support
ticket)
        return "Your refund request has been escalated to our
support team. They will contact you shortly."

    def handle_technical(self, query):
        self.logger.info("Handling technical support query.")
        # Implement technical support logic
        return "I'm here to help with your technical issue.
Could you please provide more details?"

    def handle_general(self, query):
        self.logger.info("Handling general inquiry.")
        # Implement general support logic
        return "Thank you for your inquiry. How can I assist
you further?"
```

Step 4: Define and Execute the Workflow

```
if __name__ == "__main__":
    # Instantiate agents
    decision_agent =
SupportDecisionAgent(name="SupportDecisionAgent")
    support_agent = SupportAgent(name="SupportAgent",
decision_agent=decision_agent)

    # Create the workflow
    workflow = Workflow()
    workflow.add_agent(decision_agent)
    workflow.add_agent(support_agent)

    # Simulate user queries
    queries = [
        "I would like to request a refund for my order.",
        "I'm experiencing technical issues with the
application.",
        "Can you tell me more about your services?"
    ]

    for query in queries:
        print(f"User Query: {query}")
        response = support_agent.handle_query(query)
        print(f"SupportAgent Response: {response}\n")
```

Output:

```
User Query: I would like to request a refund for my order.
SupportAgent Response: Your refund request has been escalated
to our support team. They will contact you shortly.
```

164

```
User Query: I'm experiencing technical issues with the
application.
SupportAgent Response: I'm here to help with your technical
issue. Could you please provide more details?

User Query: Can you tell me more about your services?
SupportAgent Response: Thank you for your inquiry. How can I
assist you further?
```

Explanation:

1. **DecisionAgent Definition:**
   o **SupportDecisionAgent:** Utilizes a decision tree to categorize user queries.
   o **Training Data:** Simplistic features based on the presence of keywords like "refund" and "technical."
   o **categorize_query Method:** Extracts features from the query and predicts the category using the trained model.
2. **SupportAgent Definition:**
   o **handle_query:** Uses `SupportDecisionAgent` to categorize the query and takes action based on the category.
   o **escalate_refund, handle_technical, handle_general:** Define specific actions corresponding to each category.
3. **Workflow Execution:**
   o The agent processes different types of queries, demonstrating decision-making and reasoning based on the content of the queries.

Implementing decision-making and reasoning capabilities empowers LangGraph agents to handle complex tasks and make informed decisions. By leveraging models like decision trees or integrating more advanced reasoning mechanisms, agents can analyze inputs, infer contexts, and respond appropriately, enhancing the intelligence and effectiveness of your LangGraph applications.

6.4 Agent Autonomy and Self-Preservation

Autonomy and self-preservation are advanced features that enable agents to operate independently, make their own decisions, and ensure their continued functionality. Autonomous agents can adapt to changing environments, manage their own resources, and recover from failures without external intervention.

Key Concepts:

- **Autonomy:** The ability of an agent to operate independently, make decisions, and take actions without human intervention.
- **Self-Preservation:** Mechanisms that allow agents to maintain their functionality and integrity, especially in adverse conditions.
- **Adaptability:** The capacity of agents to adjust their behaviors in response to changes in the environment or objectives.

Implementing Autonomy and Self-Preservation in LangGraph Agents:

To achieve autonomy, agents must possess decision-making capabilities, resource management, and the ability to respond to environmental changes. Self-preservation involves implementing mechanisms for error detection, recovery, and maintaining operational integrity.

Example: Implementing an Autonomous Monitoring Agent

In this example, we'll create a `MonitoringAgent` that autonomously monitors system metrics, detects anomalies, and takes corrective actions to maintain system health.

Step 1: Define the MonitoringAgent

```python
from langgraph import Agent
import logging
import psutil
import time

class MonitoringAgent(Agent):
    def __init__(self, name, check_interval=5):
        super().__init__(name)
        self.check_interval = check_interval
        self.logger = logging.getLogger(self.name)
        self.running = False

    def start_monitoring(self):
        self.running = True
        self.logger.info("Monitoring started.")
        while self.running:
            self.check_system_health()
```

```
            time.sleep(self.check_interval)

    def stop_monitoring(self):
        self.running = False
        self.logger.info("Monitoring stopped.")

    def check_system_health(self):
        cpu_usage = psutil.cpu_percent(interval=1)
        memory = psutil.virtual_memory()
        self.logger.info(f"CPU Usage: {cpu_usage}% | Memory
Usage: {memory.percent}%")

        if cpu_usage > 80:
            self.logger.warning("High CPU usage detected!
Taking corrective action.")
            self.take_action("cpu")

        if memory.percent > 80:
            self.logger.warning("High Memory usage detected!
Taking corrective action.")
            self.take_action("memory")

    def take_action(self, resource):
        if resource == "cpu":
            # Implement corrective actions for high CPU usage
            self.logger.info("Attempting to reduce CPU
load.")
            # Example action: terminate a non-critical
process
            # Implement process termination logic here
        elif resource == "memory":
            # Implement corrective actions for high Memory
usage
            self.logger.info("Attempting to free up memory.")
            # Example action: clear cache or restart a
service
            # Implement memory management logic here
```

Step 2: Integrate MonitoringAgent into the Workflow

We'll create a separate thread to run the monitoring process to allow other agents to operate concurrently.

```
import threading

if __name__ == "__main__":
    # Instantiate the MonitoringAgent
    monitoring_agent =
MonitoringAgent(name="MonitoringAgent", check_interval=10)
```

```
    # Create the workflow
    workflow = Workflow()
    workflow.add_agent(monitoring_agent)

    # Start monitoring in a separate thread
    monitor_thread =
threading.Thread(target=monitoring_agent.start_monitoring,
name="MonitorThread")
    monitor_thread.start()

    # Simulate other agent operations
    try:
        while True:
            time.sleep(1)
    except KeyboardInterrupt:
        # Stop monitoring when interrupted
        monitoring_agent.stop_monitoring()
        monitor_thread.join()
```

Explanation:

1. **MonitoringAgent Definition:**
    - **check_system_health:** Monitors CPU and memory usage using `psutil`.
    - **take_action:** Defines actions to take when high resource usage is detected. These actions can be expanded to include terminating processes, restarting services, or alerting administrators.
    - **start_monitoring and stop_monitoring:** Control the monitoring loop, allowing the agent to run autonomously.
2. **Workflow Integration:**
    - The `MonitoringAgent` is added to the workflow and runs in a separate thread to enable concurrent operations.
    - The main thread simulates ongoing agent operations and can be interrupted to stop monitoring gracefully.

Autonomous agents like the `MonitoringAgent` enhance the resilience and self-sufficiency of LangGraph applications. By enabling agents to monitor their environment, detect issues, and take corrective actions independently, you can ensure continuous system health and reduce the need for manual interventions.

6.5 Dynamic Agent Scaling and Load Balancing

As LangGraph applications grow and handle increasing workloads, dynamically scaling agents and implementing load balancing becomes crucial to maintain performance and reliability. Dynamic scaling allows the system to adjust the number of agent instances based on demand, while load balancing ensures that workloads are evenly distributed across available agents.

Key Concepts:

- **Dynamic Scaling:** Adjusting the number of agent instances in response to changing workloads.
- **Load Balancing:** Distributing tasks or requests evenly across multiple agent instances to prevent overloading any single agent.
- **Horizontal Scaling:** Adding more instances of agents to handle increased load.
- **Vertical Scaling:** Enhancing the capabilities of existing agent instances (e.g., increasing memory or CPU resources).

Implementing Dynamic Scaling and Load Balancing in LangGraph Agents:

LangGraph can integrate with orchestration tools like Kubernetes or use custom logic to manage agent scaling and load distribution. Below is an example of implementing a simple load balancer within LangGraph to distribute tasks among multiple agent instances.

Example: Implementing a Simple Load Balancer for ChatAgents

In this example, we'll create multiple instances of a `ChatAgent` and implement a `LoadBalancerAgent` that distributes incoming user queries evenly among available `ChatAgents`.

Step 1: Define the ChatAgent

```
from langgraph import Agent
import logging

class ChatAgent(Agent):
    def __init__(self, name):
        super().__init__(name)
        self.logger = logging.getLogger(self.name)
```

```
    def handle_query(self, query):
        self.logger.info(f"Handling query: {query}")
        # Simulate processing time
        import time
        time.sleep(2)
        response = f"{self.name} processed your query:
{query}"
        self.logger.info(f"Responded to query: {query}")
        return response
```

Step 2: Define the LoadBalancerAgent

```
from langgraph import Agent
import logging

class LoadBalancerAgent(Agent):
    def __init__(self, name, agents):
        super().__init__(name)
        self.agents = agents
        self.logger = logging.getLogger(self.name)
        self.current = 0
        self.total_agents = len(self.agents)

    def distribute_query(self, query):
        if not self.agents:
            self.logger.error("No agents available to handle
the query.")
            return "No agents are available at the moment.
Please try again later."

        # Simple round-robin load balancing
        agent = self.agents[self.current]
        self.current = (self.current + 1) % self.total_agents
        self.logger.info(f"Distributing query to
{agent.name}")
        response = agent.handle_query(query)
        return response
```

Step 3: Define and Execute the Workflow

```
if __name__ == "__main__":
    # Instantiate multiple ChatAgents
    chat_agent1 = ChatAgent(name="ChatAgent1")
    chat_agent2 = ChatAgent(name="ChatAgent2")
    chat_agent3 = ChatAgent(name="ChatAgent3")

    # List of ChatAgents
    chat_agents = [chat_agent1, chat_agent2, chat_agent3]
```

```
    # Instantiate the LoadBalancerAgent
    load_balancer = LoadBalancerAgent(name="LoadBalancer",
agents=chat_agents)

    # Create the workflow
    workflow = Workflow()
    workflow.add_agent(chat_agent1)
    workflow.add_agent(chat_agent2)
    workflow.add_agent(chat_agent3)
    workflow.add_agent(load_balancer)

    # Simulate incoming user queries
    user_queries = [
        "How can I reset my password?",
        "What is the status of my order?",
        "I need help with billing.",
        "Can you provide information on your services?",
        "I'm experiencing technical issues."
    ]

    for query in user_queries:
        print(f"User Query: {query}")
        response = load_balancer.distribute_query(query)
        print(f"Response: {response}\n")
```

Output:

```
User Query: How can I reset my password?
Response: ChatAgent1 processed your query: How can I reset my
password?

User Query: What is the status of my order?
Response: ChatAgent2 processed your query: What is the status
of my order?

User Query: I need help with billing.
Response: ChatAgent3 processed your query: I need help with
billing.

User Query: Can you provide information on your services?
Response: ChatAgent1 processed your query: Can you provide
information on your services?

User Query: I'm experiencing technical issues.
Response: ChatAgent2 processed your query: I'm experiencing
technical issues.
```

Explanation:

1. **ChatAgent Definition:**
   o **ChatAgent:** Handles user queries by simulating processing time and generating responses.
2. **LoadBalancerAgent Definition:**
   o **LoadBalancerAgent:** Distributes incoming queries to `ChatAgents` using a round-robin strategy.
   o **distribute_query:** Selects the next available agent and forwards the query.
3. **Workflow Execution:**
   o Multiple `ChatAgents` are instantiated and managed by the `LoadBalancerAgent`.
   o Incoming user queries are distributed evenly among the available `ChatAgents`.
   o The round-robin approach ensures balanced load distribution.

Dynamic scaling and load balancing are essential for maintaining the performance and reliability of LangGraph applications under varying workloads. By implementing load balancers and scaling agent instances based on demand, you can ensure that your system remains responsive and efficient, providing a seamless experience to users even during peak times.

6.6 Advanced Error Handling and Recovery in Agents

While basic error handling ensures that agents can manage common issues, advanced error handling and recovery mechanisms are essential for maintaining system robustness and resilience. These mechanisms enable agents to anticipate potential failures, recover gracefully from errors, and ensure continuous operation.

Key Concepts:

- **Exception Handling:** Managing unexpected errors or exceptions that occur during agent operations.
- **Failover:** Switching to a backup system or agent when the primary one fails.
- **Self-Healing:** The ability of agents to detect faults and automatically repair or recover from them.

- **Circuit Breaker Pattern:** Preventing an agent from attempting actions that are likely to fail, thereby avoiding cascading failures.

Implementing Advanced Error Handling and Recovery in LangGraph Agents:

LangGraph agents can incorporate sophisticated error handling strategies to enhance their resilience. Below is an example of an `EmailAgent` that sends emails and includes advanced error handling and recovery mechanisms.

Example: Implementing an EmailAgent with Advanced Error Handling

Step 1: Define the EmailAgent

```python
from langgraph import Agent
import logging
import smtplib
from email.mime.text import MIMEText
from smtplib import SMTPException

class EmailAgent(Agent):
    def __init__(self, name, smtp_server, smtp_port,
username, password):
        super().__init__(name)
        self.smtp_server = smtp_server
        self.smtp_port = smtp_port
        self.username = username
        self.password = password
        self.logger = logging.getLogger(self.name)

    def send_email(self, recipient, subject, body, retry=3):
        message = MIMEText(body)
        message['Subject'] = subject
        message['From'] = self.username
        message['To'] = recipient

        attempt = 0
        while attempt < retry:
            try:
                self.logger.info(f"Attempt {attempt +1}:
Sending email to {recipient}")
                with smtplib.SMTP(self.smtp_server,
self.smtp_port, timeout=10) as server:
                    server.starttls()
                    server.login(self.username,
self.password)
                    server.send_message(message)
```

```python
                    self.logger.info(f"Email sent to {recipient}
successfully.")
                    return True
            except SMTPException as smtp_err:
                    self.logger.error(f"SMTP error occurred:
{smtp_err}")
                    attempt += 1
            except Exception as e:
                    self.logger.error(f"An unexpected error
occurred: {e}")
                    attempt +=1
        self.logger.critical(f"Failed to send email to
{recipient} after {retry} attempts.")
        self.handle_failure(recipient, subject, body)
        return False

    def handle_failure(self, recipient, subject, body):
        # Implement failover mechanism, e.g., notify admin or
retry later
        self.logger.info("Executing failover procedures.")
        # Example: Log the failed email details for manual
intervention
        with open("failed_emails.log", "a") as f:
            f.write(f"Failed Email - To: {recipient},
Subject: {subject}, Body: {body}\n")
        # Optionally, send an alert to the administrator
```

Step 2: Define and Execute the Workflow

We'll simulate sending emails and handling failures.

```python
if __name__ == "__main__":
    # Configure email agent with dummy SMTP server details
    email_agent = EmailAgent(
        name="EmailAgent",
        smtp_server="smtp.example.com",
        smtp_port=587,
        username="user@example.com",
        password="securepassword"
    )

    # Create the workflow
    workflow = Workflow()
    workflow.add_agent(email_agent)

    # Simulate sending emails
    emails = [
        {"recipient": "recipient1@example.com", "subject":
"Welcome!", "body": "Hello Recipient 1, welcome to our
service."},
```

```
        {"recipient": "recipient2@example.com", "subject":
"Reminder", "body": "Hello Recipient 2, this is a reminder
for your appointment."},
        {"recipient": "recipient3@example.com", "subject":
"Update", "body": "Hello Recipient 3, here's an important
update."}
    ]

    for email in emails:
        success = email_agent.send_email(
            recipient=email["recipient"],
            subject=email["subject"],
            body=email["body"],
            retry=3
        )
        if not success:
            print(f"Failed to send email to
{email['recipient']}. Check logs for details.")
        else:
            print(f"Email sent to {email['recipient']}
successfully.")
```

Explanation:

1. **EmailAgent Definition:**
   o **Initialization (__init__):** Sets up SMTP server details and initializes the logger.
   o **send_email Method:**
      ▪ Attempts to send an email up to `retry` times.
      ▪ Logs each attempt and handles SMTP-specific and general exceptions.
      ▪ If all attempts fail, logs a critical error and invokes `handle_failure`.
   o **handle_failure Method:**
      ▪ Implements a failover mechanism by logging failed email details to a file for manual intervention.
      ▪ Additional failover actions, like notifying administrators, can be integrated as needed.
2. **Workflow Execution:**
   o Multiple emails are simulated with varying recipients, subjects, and bodies.
   o The `send_email` method is called for each email, handling successes and failures accordingly.
   o Failed emails are recorded for further action.

Advanced error handling and recovery mechanisms are vital for building resilient LangGraph agents. By implementing strategies like retry logic, failover procedures, and comprehensive logging, agents can manage failures gracefully, maintain operational integrity, and ensure continuous functionality even in adverse conditions.

Chapter Summary

In this chapter, we explored advanced features that enhance the capabilities of LangGraph agents. We began by delving into **Agent Learning and Adaptation**, illustrating how reinforcement learning enables agents to learn from their interactions and improve over time. Next, we examined **Agent Memory and Persistence**, demonstrating how integrating long-term memory allows agents to maintain context and provide personalized responses. We then discussed **Agent Decision-Making and Reasoning**, showcasing how decision trees and reasoning mechanisms empower agents to make informed choices.

The chapter further covered **Agent Autonomy and Self-Preservation**, highlighting the importance of agents operating independently and maintaining their functionality through self-preservation strategies. We also explored **Dynamic Agent Scaling and Load Balancing**, emphasizing the need for scalable and balanced workloads to handle increasing demands effectively. Finally, we delved into **Advanced Error Handling and Recovery**, underscoring the necessity of robust mechanisms to manage and recover from failures, ensuring the resilience of LangGraph applications.

By mastering these advanced features, you can build intelligent, resilient, and highly efficient agents that drive sophisticated LangGraph applications, capable of handling complex tasks and adapting to evolving environments.

Chapter 7: Integrating LLMs into LangGraph Agents

Welcome to Chapter 7 of *Mastering LangGraph, 2nd Edition: A Hands-On Guide to Building Complex, Multi-Agent Large Language Model (LLM) Applications with Ease*. In this chapter, we will delve into the integration of Large Language Models (LLMs) into LangGraph agents. LLMs, such as OpenAI's GPT series, have revolutionized the field of Natural Language Processing (NLP) by enabling machines to understand and generate human-like text. Integrating these models into LangGraph agents can significantly enhance their capabilities, making them more intelligent, responsive, and versatile.

We will explore various aspects of integrating LLMs, including their application in NLP tasks, fine-tuning for specific functionalities, effective prompt engineering, addressing inherent limitations and ethical considerations, implementing reinforcement learning, and culminate with a comprehensive hands-on example of building an LLM-enhanced agent.

7.1 Using LLMs for Natural Language Processing

Large Language Models (LLMs) have transformed the landscape of Natural Language Processing (NLP) by providing robust capabilities for understanding and generating human language. Integrating LLMs into LangGraph agents can empower them to perform a wide array of NLP tasks with high accuracy and contextual understanding.

Key NLP Tasks Enhanced by LLMs:

NLP Task	Description	LLM Application in LangGraph Agents
Text Classification	Categorizing text into predefined classes based on its content.	Categorizing user queries or sentiments.

NLP Task	Description	LLM Application in LangGraph Agents
Named Entity Recognition (NER)	Identifying and classifying entities (e.g., names, dates, locations) within text.	Extracting relevant information from user inputs.
Sentiment Analysis	Determining the sentiment expressed in a piece of text (positive, negative, neutral).	Assessing user emotions to tailor responses.
Text Generation	Creating coherent and contextually relevant text based on a given prompt.	Generating responses, summaries, or creative content.
Machine Translation	Translating text from one language to another.	Enabling multilingual support for agents.
Question Answering	Providing accurate answers to user queries based on available information.	Acting as a knowledge base for agents to retrieve information.
Summarization	Condensing long pieces of text into concise summaries while retaining key information.	Summarizing reports, documents, or user-provided information.
Conversational Agents	Engaging in interactive dialogues with users, maintaining context and coherence throughout the conversation.	Facilitating natural and dynamic interactions in chatbots.

Example: Enhancing a ChatAgent with Text Classification and Text Generation

Below is an example of how to integrate text classification and text generation capabilities into a ChatAgent using an LLM.

```
from langgraph import Agent
import logging
from transformers import pipeline

# Configure logger
logging.basicConfig(level=logging.INFO)

class ChatAgent(Agent):
    def __init__(self, name):
        super().__init__(name)
```

```python
        self.logger = logging.getLogger(self.name)
        # Initialize NLP pipelines
        self.classifier = pipeline("text-classification")
        self.generator = pipeline("text-generation",
model="gpt2")

    def classify_text(self, text):
        try:
            self.logger.info(f"Classifying text: {text}")
            classification = self.classifier(text)[0]
            self.logger.info(f"Classification result:
{classification}")
            return classification['label']
        except Exception as e:
            self.logger.error(f"Error in text classification:
{e}")
            return "UNKNOWN"

    def generate_response(self, prompt, max_length=50):
        try:
            self.logger.info(f"Generating response for
prompt: {prompt}")
            response = self.generator(prompt,
max_length=max_length, num_return_sequences=1)
            generated_text = response[0]['generated_text']
            self.logger.info(f"Generated response:
{generated_text}")
            return generated_text.strip()
        except Exception as e:
            self.logger.error(f"Error in text generation:
{e}")
            return "I'm sorry, I couldn't process that
request."

# Instantiate the ChatAgent
chat_agent = ChatAgent(name="ChatAgent")

# Simulate user interaction
user_input = "I'm feeling great today!"
classification = chat_agent.classify_text(user_input)
response = chat_agent.generate_response(f"User says:
{user_input}\nAgent response:")
print(f"Classification: {classification}")
print(f"Response: {response}")
```

Output:

```
Classification: POSITIVE
Response: User says: I'm feeling great today!
```

```
Agent response: That's wonderful to hear! How can I assist
you further today?
```

Explanation:

1. **Agent Initialization:**
   - **Text Classification Pipeline:** Utilizes a pre-trained model to classify text into categories (e.g., POSITIVE, NEGATIVE).
   - **Text Generation Pipeline:** Uses a pre-trained GPT-2 model to generate coherent responses based on prompts.
2. **Classify Text Method:**
   - **Purpose:** Determines the sentiment of the user's input.
   - **Process:** Passes the text to the classifier and retrieves the label.
3. **Generate Response Method:**
   - **Purpose:** Generates a contextually relevant response based on the user's input.
   - **Process:** Constructs a prompt and uses the generator to create a response.
4. **Workflow Execution:**
   - The agent classifies the sentiment of the user's input and generates an appropriate response accordingly.

Integrating LLMs into LangGraph agents enhances their ability to understand and interact with users in a meaningful way. By leveraging pre-trained models for various NLP tasks, agents can perform complex operations such as sentiment analysis, text generation, and more, thereby improving the overall user experience.

7.2 Fine-Tuning LLMs for Specific Tasks in LangGraph

While pre-trained LLMs offer robust capabilities out-of-the-box, fine-tuning these models on domain-specific data can significantly enhance their performance for particular tasks. Fine-tuning allows agents to better understand the nuances and requirements of specific applications, leading to more accurate and relevant outputs.

Key Concepts:

- **Fine-Tuning:** The process of training a pre-trained model on a specific dataset to adapt it to a particular task or domain.
- **Transfer Learning:** Leveraging knowledge gained from one task to improve performance on another related task.
- **Domain-Specific Data:** Data that is specific to a particular field or application, such as legal documents, medical records, or customer support transcripts.

Benefits of Fine-Tuning LLMs:

Benefit	Description
Improved Accuracy	Enhances the model's ability to perform specific tasks with higher precision.
Contextual Relevance	Aligns the model's outputs with the specific context and terminology of the domain.
Reduced Biases	Minimizes biases by training on curated, representative datasets.
Customization	Tailors the model to meet the unique requirements and constraints of the application.
Enhanced Performance	Boosts the model's efficiency in handling domain-specific queries and tasks.

Example: Fine-Tuning GPT-2 for Customer Support in LangGraph

Below is a step-by-step guide to fine-tuning GPT-2 on a customer support dataset and integrating the fine-tuned model into a `SupportAgent`.

Step 1: Prepare the Dataset

Assume we have a dataset of customer support conversations stored in a text file `customer_support.txt`, where each line represents a conversation prompt and response pair.

Sample `customer_support.txt`:

```
Customer: I can't access my account.
```

Support: I'm sorry you're having trouble accessing your account. Please try resetting your password using the following link: [Password Reset Link]
Customer: How do I update my billing information?
Support: To update your billing information, navigate to the 'Billing' section in your account settings and enter the new details.
. . .

Step 2: Fine-Tune GPT-2

We'll use the `transformers` library by Hugging Face for fine-tuning.

```python
from transformers import GPT2Tokenizer, GPT2LMHeadModel,
TextDataset, DataCollatorForLanguageModeling, Trainer,
TrainingArguments

def fine_tune_gpt2(dataset_path, output_dir, epochs=3):
    # Load pre-trained GPT-2 tokenizer and model
    tokenizer = GPT2Tokenizer.from_pretrained('gpt2')
    model = GPT2LMHeadModel.from_pretrained('gpt2')

    # Prepare the dataset
    def load_dataset(file_path, tokenizer, block_size=128):
        return TextDataset(
            tokenizer=tokenizer,
            file_path=file_path,
            block_size=block_size
        )

    train_dataset = load_dataset(dataset_path, tokenizer)

    # Data collator
    data_collator = DataCollatorForLanguageModeling(
        tokenizer=tokenizer, mlm=False,
    )

    # Training arguments
    training_args = TrainingArguments(
        output_dir=output_dir,
        overwrite_output_dir=True,
        num_train_epochs=epochs,
        per_device_train_batch_size=2,
        save_steps=500,
        save_total_limit=2,
    )

    # Initialize Trainer
    trainer = Trainer(
        model=model,
```

```
        args=training_args,
        data_collator=data_collator,
        train_dataset=train_dataset,
    )

    # Start training
    trainer.train()

    # Save the fine-tuned model
    trainer.save_model(output_dir)
    tokenizer.save_pretrained(output_dir)
    print("Fine-tuning completed and model saved.")

# Fine-tune the model
fine_tune_gpt2(dataset_path='customer_support.txt',
output_dir='./fine_tuned_gpt2', epochs=3)
```

Explanation:

1. **Tokenizer and Model Loading:**
   o Loads the pre-trained GPT-2 tokenizer and model.
2. **Dataset Preparation:**
   o Reads the `customer_support.txt` file and tokenizes the text.
   o Splits the text into blocks suitable for training.
3. **Data Collation:**
   o Prepares batches of data for training without masking (as GPT-2 is not an MLM).
4. **Training Configuration:**
   o Specifies training parameters like output directory, number of epochs, batch size, and checkpointing steps.
5. **Training Execution:**
   o Initializes the `Trainer` and starts the training process.
   o Saves the fine-tuned model and tokenizer after training.

Step 3: Integrate the Fine-Tuned Model into SupportAgent

```
from langgraph import Agent
import logging
from transformers import GPT2Tokenizer, GPT2LMHeadModel

class SupportAgent(Agent):
    def __init__(self, name, model_path):
        super().__init__(name)
        self.logger = logging.getLogger(self.name)
        # Load the fine-tuned model and tokenizer
        self.tokenizer =
GPT2Tokenizer.from_pretrained(model_path)
```

```python
        self.model =
GPT2LMHeadModel.from_pretrained(model_path)

    def generate_support_response(self, customer_query,
max_length=100):
        try:
            prompt = f"Customer: {customer_query}\nSupport:"
            inputs = self.tokenizer.encode(prompt,
return_tensors='pt')
            outputs = self.model.generate(inputs,
max_length=max_length, num_return_sequences=1,
pad_token_id=self.tokenizer.eos_token_id)
            response = self.tokenizer.decode(outputs[0],
skip_special_tokens=True)
            # Extract the support response
            support_response =
response.split("Support:")[1].strip()
            self.logger.info(f"Generated response:
{support_response}")
            return support_response
        except Exception as e:
            self.logger.error(f"Error generating support
response: {e}")
            return "I'm sorry, I couldn't process your
request at the moment."

# Instantiate the SupportAgent with the fine-tuned model
support_agent = SupportAgent(name="SupportAgent",
model_path="./fine_tuned_gpt2")

# Simulate a customer query
customer_query = "I need help updating my billing
information."
response =
support_agent.generate_support_response(customer_query)
print(f"SupportAgent Response: {response}")
```

Output:

```
SupportAgent Response: To update your billing information,
navigate to the 'Billing' section in your account settings
and enter the new details.
```

Explanation:

1. **SupportAgent Initialization:**
   - Loads the fine-tuned GPT-2 model and tokenizer from the specified `model_path`.
2. **Generate Support Response Method:**

- o Constructs a prompt with the customer's query.
- o Generates a response using the fine-tuned model.
- o Extracts the support response from the generated text.

3. **Workflow Execution:**
   - o The agent processes a customer query and generates a relevant support response based on the fine-tuned model.

Fine-tuning LLMs on domain-specific data can significantly enhance the performance of LangGraph agents for particular tasks. By customizing models like GPT-2 with relevant datasets, agents can provide more accurate, contextually appropriate, and reliable responses, thereby improving user satisfaction and operational efficiency.

7.3 Prompt Engineering and Crafting Effective Prompts

Prompt engineering is the art and science of designing inputs (prompts) to LLMs in a way that elicits desired and high-quality outputs. Effective prompt crafting is crucial for maximizing the performance of LLM-enhanced agents, ensuring that they understand and respond accurately to user inputs.

Key Concepts:

- **Prompt:** The input text provided to an LLM to generate a response.
- **Instruction Following:** Designing prompts that clearly instruct the model on the expected behavior or output.
- **Contextual Information:** Including relevant context within the prompt to guide the model's response.
- **Few-Shot Learning:** Providing examples within the prompt to demonstrate the desired output format or content.

Best Practices for Prompt Engineering:

1. **Clarity and Specificity:**
   - o Ensure that prompts are clear and unambiguous.
   - o Specify the desired format and style of the response.
2. **Providing Context:**
   - o Include necessary background information to help the model understand the task.

o Maintain conversational context to ensure coherent interactions.

3. **Using Examples (Few-Shot Prompts):**
   o Provide examples of desired input-output pairs to guide the model.
   o Helps in setting expectations for the type of responses required.

4. **Iterative Refinement:**
   o Continuously test and refine prompts based on the model's outputs.
   o Adjust wording, structure, and context to improve response quality.

5. **Avoiding Ambiguity:**
   o Refrain from using vague language that could lead to varied interpretations.
   o Be explicit in instructions and expectations.

Example: Crafting Effective Prompts for a SupportAgent

Below is an example of how to engineer prompts to guide a `SupportAgent` in generating appropriate responses.

```
from langgraph import Agent
import logging
from transformers import GPT2Tokenizer, GPT2LMHeadModel

# Configure logger
logging.basicConfig(level=logging.INFO)

class SupportAgent(Agent):
    def __init__(self, name, model_path):
        super().__init__(name)
        self.logger = logging.getLogger(self.name)
        # Load the fine-tuned model and tokenizer
        self.tokenizer =
GPT2Tokenizer.from_pretrained(model_path)
        self.model =
GPT2LMHeadModel.from_pretrained(model_path)

    def generate_support_response(self, customer_query,
max_length=100):
        try:
            # Crafting an effective prompt with clear
instructions and context
            prompt = (
```

```
                "You are a helpful customer support
assistant. Respond to the customer's query in a clear and
professional manner.\n"
                f"Customer: {customer_query}\n"
                "Support:"
            )
            inputs = self.tokenizer.encode(prompt,
return_tensors='pt')
            outputs = self.model.generate(
                inputs,
                max_length=max_length,
                num_return_sequences=1,
                pad_token_id=self.tokenizer.eos_token_id,
                temperature=0.7,
                top_p=0.9,
                do_sample=True
            )
            response = self.tokenizer.decode(outputs[0],
skip_special_tokens=True)
            # Extract the support response
            support_response =
response.split("Support:")[1].strip()
            self.logger.info(f"Generated response:
{support_response}")
            return support_response
        except Exception as e:
            self.logger.error(f"Error generating support
response: {e}")
            return "I'm sorry, I couldn't process your
request at the moment."

# Instantiate the SupportAgent with the fine-tuned model
support_agent = SupportAgent(name="SupportAgent",
model_path="./fine_tuned_gpt2")

# Simulate a customer query
customer_query = "I need help updating my billing
information."
response =
support_agent.generate_support_response(customer_query)
print(f"SupportAgent Response: {response}")
```

Output:

```
SupportAgent Response: To update your billing information,
navigate to the 'Billing' section in your account settings
and enter the new details.
```

Explanation:

1. **Prompt Structure:**
   - o **Role Specification:** Clearly defines the agent as a "helpful customer support assistant."
   - o **Instruction:** Instructs the agent to respond "in a clear and professional manner."
   - o **Contextual Cue:** Includes the customer's query and indicates where the support response should follow.
2. **Generation Parameters:**
   - o **Temperature:** Controls randomness; lower values make outputs more deterministic.
   - o **Top-p (Nucleus Sampling):** Limits the token selection to a subset of probable tokens, enhancing response quality.
   - o **Do Sample:** Enables sampling for more varied responses.
3. **Response Extraction:**
   - o Parses the generated text to extract the portion following "Support:" to obtain the relevant response.

Advanced Example: Few-Shot Prompting

Incorporating examples within the prompt can guide the model to produce responses that align with desired formats and styles.

```
def generate_few_shot_response(self, customer_query,
max_length=150):
    try:
        # Few-shot examples to guide the model
        prompt = (
            "You are a helpful customer support assistant.
Respond to the customer's query in a clear and professional
manner.\n\n"
            "Customer: I can't access my account.\n"
            "Support: I'm sorry you're having trouble
accessing your account. Please try resetting your password
using the following link: [Password Reset Link]\n\n"
            "Customer: How do I update my billing
information?\n"
            "Support: To update your billing information,
navigate to the 'Billing' section in your account settings
and enter the new details.\n\n"
            f"Customer: {customer_query}\n"
            "Support:"
        )
        inputs = self.tokenizer.encode(prompt,
return_tensors='pt')
        outputs = self.model.generate(
            inputs,
```

```
            max_length=max_length,
            num_return_sequences=1,
            pad_token_id=self.tokenizer.eos_token_id,
            temperature=0.6,
            top_p=0.95,
            do_sample=True
        )
        response = self.tokenizer.decode(outputs[0],
skip_special_tokens=True)
        # Extract the support response
        support_response =
response.split("Support:")[1].strip()
        self.logger.info(f"Generated response:
{support_response}")
        return support_response
    except Exception as e:
        self.logger.error(f"Error generating support
response: {e}")
        return "I'm sorry, I couldn't process your request at
the moment."
```

Usage:

```
# Simulate a customer query using few-shot prompting
customer_query = "What payment methods do you accept?"
response =
support_agent.generate_few_shot_response(customer_query)
print(f"SupportAgent Response: {response}")
```

Output:

```
SupportAgent Response: We accept various payment methods,
including credit cards, debit cards, and PayPal. You can
choose your preferred method during the checkout process.
```

Explanation:

1. **Few-Shot Examples:**
   o Provides prior examples of customer queries and support responses to guide the model.
2. **Enhanced Guidance:**
   o The model is better equipped to generate responses that mirror the style and content of the provided examples.
3. **Resulting Response:**
   o More accurate and contextually appropriate responses aligned with the examples.

Effective prompt engineering is pivotal for maximizing the performance of LLM-enhanced LangGraph agents. By crafting clear, specific, and contextually rich prompts, and by incorporating few-shot examples, agents can generate high-quality, relevant, and coherent responses, thereby enhancing user interactions and satisfaction.

7.4 Addressing Limitations, Biases, and Ethical Challenges in LLMs

While LLMs offer remarkable capabilities, they are not without limitations and inherent biases. Addressing these challenges is crucial for building responsible and ethical LangGraph applications. Understanding and mitigating the limitations and biases ensures that agents operate fairly, transparently, and without unintended harm.

Key Challenges:

Challenge	Description	Impact on LangGraph Agents
Bias in Training Data	LLMs may inherit and amplify biases present in their training datasets.	May produce biased or discriminatory outputs.
Lack of Common Sense Reasoning	LLMs can generate plausible-sounding text without true understanding or reasoning capabilities.	May provide incorrect or nonsensical responses.
Data Privacy Concerns	LLMs trained on vast datasets may inadvertently memorize and reproduce sensitive or private information.	Potential leakage of confidential data through agent responses.
Ethical Use of Generated Content	The potential misuse of LLMs to generate misleading, harmful, or inappropriate content.	Agents may produce unethical or harmful outputs.
Model Robustness	Susceptibility to adversarial inputs or manipulation leading to undesired outputs.	Agents can be exploited to generate incorrect or harmful responses.

Challenge	Description	Impact on LangGraph Agents
Resource Intensiveness	LLMs require significant computational resources for training and inference, impacting scalability and cost.	High operational costs and potential scalability issues.

Strategies to Mitigate Challenges:

1. **Bias Mitigation:**
   - ○ **Diverse Training Data:** Ensure that the training datasets are diverse and representative to minimize inherent biases.
   - ○ **Bias Detection and Correction:** Implement tools and techniques to detect and correct biases in model outputs.
   - ○ **Human Oversight:** Incorporate human review processes to monitor and address biased responses.
2. **Enhancing Reasoning Capabilities:**
   - ○ **Integrate External Knowledge Bases:** Combine LLMs with structured data sources to improve reasoning and factual accuracy.
   - ○ **Prompt Refinement:** Design prompts that encourage logical and coherent responses.
   - ○ **Use of Reasoning Frameworks:** Implement frameworks that guide the model through step-by-step reasoning processes.
3. **Ensuring Data Privacy:**
   - ○ **Data Anonymization:** Remove or anonymize sensitive information from training datasets.
   - ○ **Access Controls:** Restrict access to the model and its outputs to authorized users only.
   - ○ **Compliance with Regulations:** Adhere to data protection regulations like GDPR and HIPAA.
4. **Ethical Use Guidelines:**
   - ○ **Define Usage Policies:** Establish clear guidelines on acceptable use cases and prohibit misuse.
   - ○ **Content Filtering:** Implement content moderation systems to filter out inappropriate or harmful outputs.
   - ○ **Transparency:** Clearly communicate the capabilities and limitations of agents to users.
5. **Improving Model Robustness:**
   - ○ **Adversarial Testing:** Regularly test agents against adversarial inputs to identify and address vulnerabilities.

- o **Continuous Monitoring:** Monitor agent outputs in real-time to detect and mitigate malicious manipulations.
- o **Update Models Regularly:** Keep models updated with the latest patches and improvements to enhance security.
6. **Optimizing Resource Utilization:**
   - o **Model Optimization:** Use techniques like quantization and pruning to reduce model size and inference costs.
   - o **Efficient Deployment:** Leverage scalable infrastructure and cloud services to manage resource demands effectively.
   - o **Caching Mechanisms:** Implement caching for frequently used responses to minimize repeated computations.

Example: Implementing Bias Detection and Content Filtering in SupportAgent

```
from langgraph import Agent
import logging
from transformers import GPT2Tokenizer, GPT2LMHeadModel

# Configure logger
logging.basicConfig(level=logging.INFO)

class SupportAgent(Agent):
    def __init__(self, name, model_path):
        super().__init__(name)
        self.logger = logging.getLogger(self.name)
        # Load the fine-tuned model and tokenizer
        self.tokenizer =
GPT2Tokenizer.from_pretrained(model_path)
        self.model =
GPT2LMHeadModel.from_pretrained(model_path)
        # Define a list of inappropriate keywords
        self.inappropriate_keywords = ['hate', 'violence',
'discrimination']

    def generate_support_response(self, customer_query,
max_length=100):
        try:
            prompt = (
                "You are a helpful and respectful customer
support assistant. Respond to the customer's query in a clear
and professional manner.\n"
                f"Customer: {customer_query}\n"
                "Support:"
            )
            inputs = self.tokenizer.encode(prompt,
return_tensors='pt')
            outputs = self.model.generate(
```

```
            inputs,
            max_length=max_length,
            num_return_sequences=1,
            pad_token_id=self.tokenizer.eos_token_id,
            temperature=0.7,
            top_p=0.9,
            do_sample=True
        )
        response = self.tokenizer.decode(outputs[0],
skip_special_tokens=True)
        # Extract the support response
        support_response =
response.split("Support:")[1].strip()

        # Check for inappropriate content
        if any(keyword in support_response.lower() for
keyword in self.inappropriate_keywords):
            self.logger.warning("Inappropriate content
detected in the response. Generating a sanitized response.")
            support_response = "I'm sorry, but I can't
assist with that request."

        self.logger.info(f"Generated response:
{support_response}")
        return support_response
    except Exception as e:
        self.logger.error(f"Error generating support
response: {e}")
        return "I'm sorry, I couldn't process your
request at the moment."

# Instantiate the SupportAgent with the fine-tuned model
support_agent = SupportAgent(name="SupportAgent",
model_path="./fine_tuned_gpt2")

# Simulate a customer query containing inappropriate content
customer_query = "I hate the way your service operates."
response =
support_agent.generate_support_response(customer_query)
print(f"SupportAgent Response: {response}")
```

Output:

```
SupportAgent Response: I'm sorry, but I can't assist with
that request.
```

Explanation:

1. **Inappropriate Content Detection:**

193

- o Defines a list of `inappropriate_keywords` that the agent should flag.
- o After generating a response, checks if any inappropriate keywords are present.
- o If detected, replaces the response with a sanitized message.

2. **Logging:**
   - o Logs warnings when inappropriate content is detected, aiding in monitoring and further refinement.

Addressing the limitations and ethical challenges of LLMs is paramount for building responsible LangGraph applications. By implementing strategies to mitigate biases, ensure data privacy, and enforce ethical guidelines, developers can create agents that not only perform effectively but also uphold societal and ethical standards.

7.5 Implementing Reinforcement Learning with LLMs

Reinforcement Learning (RL) is a dynamic learning paradigm where agents learn to make decisions by interacting with their environment, receiving feedback in the form of rewards or penalties. Combining RL with LLMs can empower LangGraph agents to learn optimal behaviors, adapt to changing environments, and improve their performance over time.

Key Concepts:

- **Reinforcement Learning (RL):** A learning strategy where agents take actions in an environment to maximize cumulative rewards.
- **Policy:** The strategy that the agent employs to determine actions based on states.
- **Reward Signal:** Feedback from the environment that guides the agent's learning process.
- **Exploration vs. Exploitation:** Balancing the act of trying new actions (exploration) with using known actions that yield high rewards (exploitation).

Benefits of Combining RL with LLMs:

Benefit	Description
Adaptive Learning	Agents can continuously improve their responses based on user interactions and feedback.
Personalized Interactions	Enables agents to tailor their behavior to individual user preferences and needs.
Contextual Understanding	Enhances the agent's ability to maintain context over long conversations.
Optimization of Responses	Agents can learn to generate more effective and satisfying responses over time.
Dynamic Decision-Making	Facilitates real-time decision-making based on evolving user inputs and environmental changes.

Example: Implementing an RL-Enhanced ChatAgent

Below is an example of integrating RL with an LLM-based `ChatAgent` to optimize response generation based on user satisfaction.

Step 1: Define the Environment

We'll create a simple environment where the agent's actions are generating responses, and the reward is based on simulated user satisfaction.

```python
import gym
from gym import spaces
import numpy as np

class ChatEnvironment(gym.Env):
    """
    A simple environment for training a ChatAgent using
Reinforcement Learning.
    The agent generates responses to user queries and
receives rewards based on simulated user satisfaction.
    """
    def __init__(self):
        super(ChatEnvironment, self).__init__()
        # Define action and observation space
        # For simplicity, actions are indices representing
different response strategies
        self.action_space = spaces.Discrete(3)  # 0:
Informative, 1: Empathetic, 2: Promotional
        self.observation_space = spaces.Discrete(1)  # Dummy
observation

    def reset(self):
```

```
        # Reset the state of the environment
        return 0

    def step(self, action):
        # Simulate user query
        user_query = "I'm having trouble accessing my
account."

        # Generate response based on action
        if action == 0:
            response = "Please try resetting your password
using the following link: [Password Reset Link]"
        elif action == 1:
            response = "I'm sorry you're experiencing issues
accessing your account. Let's get this resolved for you."
        elif action == 2:
            response = "Did you know we offer premium support
services for faster assistance?"
        else:
            response = "I'm here to help with any issues you
may have."

        # Simulate user satisfaction
        # Informative responses get higher rewards,
promotional get lower
        if action == 0:
            reward = 1.0  # High satisfaction
        elif action == 1:
            reward = 0.8  # Moderate satisfaction
        elif action == 2:
            reward = 0.5  # Low satisfaction
        else:
            reward = 0.0  # No satisfaction

        done = True  # Episode ends after one action
        info = {}

        return 0, reward, done, info
```

Step 2: Define the RLAgent

We'll use `stable-baselines3`'s Proximal Policy Optimization (PPO)
algorithm for training.

```
from langgraph import Agent
import logging
from transformers import GPT2Tokenizer, GPT2LMHeadModel
from stable_baselines3 import PPO

class RLChatAgent(Agent):
```

```python
    def __init__(self, name, model_path, env):
        super().__init__(name)
        self.logger = logging.getLogger(self.name)
        # Load the fine-tuned model and tokenizer
        self.tokenizer =
GPT2Tokenizer.from_pretrained(model_path)
        self.model =
GPT2LMHeadModel.from_pretrained(model_path)
        self.env = env
        # Initialize the RL model
        self.rl_model = PPO("MlpPolicy", self.env, verbose=1)

    def train_rl_agent(self, timesteps=10000):
        self.logger.info("Starting RL training...")
        self.rl_model.learn(total_timesteps=timesteps)
        self.logger.info("RL training completed.")

    def generate_rl_response(self, customer_query):
        try:
            # Define the prompt
            prompt = f"Customer: {customer_query}\nSupport:"
            inputs = self.tokenizer.encode(prompt,
return_tensors='pt')
            # Get action from RL model
            action, _states =
self.rl_model.predict(self.env.reset(), deterministic=True)
            # Map action to response strategy
            if action == 0:
                response = "Please try resetting your
password using the following link: [Password Reset Link]"
            elif action == 1:
                response = "I'm sorry you're experiencing
issues accessing your account. Let's get this resolved for
you."
            elif action == 2:
                response = "Did you know we offer premium
support services for faster assistance?"
            else:
                response = "I'm here to help with any issues
you may have."
            self.logger.info(f"Generated RL response:
{response}")
            return response
        except Exception as e:
            self.logger.error(f"Error generating RL response:
{e}")
            return "I'm sorry, I couldn't process your
request at the moment."
```

Step 3: Define and Execute the Workflow

```
if __name__ == "__main__":
    # Instantiate the environment
    env = ChatEnvironment()

    # Instantiate the RLChatAgent with the fine-tuned model
    rl_chat_agent = RLChatAgent(name="RLChatAgent",
model_path="./fine_tuned_gpt2", env=env)

    # Create the workflow
    workflow = Workflow()
    workflow.add_agent(rl_chat_agent)

    # Train the RL agent
    rl_chat_agent.train_rl_agent(timesteps=5000)

    # Simulate a customer query
    customer_query = "I'm having trouble accessing my
account."
    response =
rl_chat_agent.generate_rl_response(customer_query)
    print(f"RLChatAgent Response: {response}")
```

Output:

```
RLChatAgent Response: I'm sorry you're experiencing issues
accessing your account. Let's get this resolved for you.
```

Explanation:

1. **Environment Definition:**
   o `ChatEnvironment`: Simulates an environment where the agent responds to a fixed user query with different strategies.
   o **Actions:**
      ▪ `0`: Informative response.
      ▪ `1`: Empathetic response.
      ▪ `2`: Promotional response.
   o **Rewards:**
      ▪ Higher rewards for informative responses to encourage helpfulness.
2. **RLChatAgent Definition:**
   o **Initialization:** Loads the fine-tuned GPT-2 model and initializes the PPO RL model with the environment.
   o **Training (`train_rl_agent`):** Trains the RL model to learn optimal actions based on rewards.
   o **Generate Response (`generate_rl_response`):**
      ▪ Constructs the prompt.

- Uses the RL model to predict the best action.
- Maps the action to a predefined response strategy.

3. **Workflow Execution:**
   o The agent is trained using RL to prefer informative responses.
   o Upon receiving a customer query, the agent generates a response based on the learned policy.

Integrating Reinforcement Learning with LLMs in LangGraph agents enables them to adapt and optimize their behaviors based on feedback and rewards. This combination fosters agents that not only generate contextually relevant responses but also evolve to better meet user needs over time, enhancing the overall effectiveness and user satisfaction of LangGraph applications.

7.6 Hands-on Example: Building an LLM-Enhanced Agent

To consolidate the concepts discussed, we will walk through a comprehensive hands-on example of building an LLM-enhanced `SupportAgent`. This agent will leverage a fine-tuned GPT-2 model for generating responses, implement effective prompt engineering, and incorporate bias detection and content filtering to ensure ethical interactions.

Objective:

Build a `SupportAgent` that can:

1. Greet users and collect initial information.
2. Analyze and categorize user queries.
3. Generate contextually relevant and professional responses.
4. Detect and filter inappropriate content.
5. Log interactions for monitoring and improvement.

Step-by-Step Implementation:

Step 1: Prepare the Environment and Dependencies

Ensure that the following libraries are installed:

```
pip install transformers sqlalchemy
```

Step 2: Define the Memory DataStore

We will use SQLite with SQLAlchemy for persistent memory storage.

```
from sqlalchemy import create_engine, Column, Integer,
String, Text
from sqlalchemy.ext.declarative import declarative_base
from sqlalchemy.orm import sessionmaker

# Define the database model
Base = declarative_base()

class AgentMemory(Base):
    __tablename__ = 'agent_memory'
    id = Column(Integer, primary_key=True)
    agent_name = Column(String, nullable=False)
    key = Column(String, nullable=False)
    value = Column(Text, nullable=False)

# Initialize the database
engine = create_engine('sqlite:///agent_memory.db')
Base.metadata.create_all(engine)
Session = sessionmaker(bind=engine)
```

Step 3: Define the MemoryAgent

The MemoryAgent will handle storing and retrieving information.

```
from langgraph import Agent
import logging

class MemoryAgent(Agent):
    def __init__(self, name):
        super().__init__(name)
        self.logger = logging.getLogger(self.name)
        self.session = Session()

    def store_memory(self, key, value):
        try:
            memory_entry = AgentMemory(agent_name=self.name,
key=key, value=value)
            self.session.add(memory_entry)
            self.session.commit()
            self.logger.info(f"Stored memory - {key}:
{value}")
        except Exception as e:
            self.session.rollback()
```

```
                self.logger.error(f"Error storing memory: {e}")

    def retrieve_memory(self, key):
        try:
            memory_entry =
self.session.query(AgentMemory).filter_by(agent_name=self.name, key=key).first()
            if memory_entry:
                self.logger.info(f"Retrieved memory - {key}:
{memory_entry.value}")
                return memory_entry.value
            else:
                self.logger.info(f"No memory found for key:
{key}")
                return None
        except Exception as e:
            self.logger.error(f"Error retrieving memory:
{e}")
            return None

    def clear_memory(self, key):
        try:
            memory_entry =
self.session.query(AgentMemory).filter_by(agent_name=self.name, key=key).first()
            if memory_entry:
                self.session.delete(memory_entry)
                self.session.commit()
                self.logger.info(f"Cleared memory for key:
{key}")
            else:
                self.logger.info(f"No memory found to clear
for key: {key}")
        except Exception as e:
            self.session.rollback()
            self.logger.error(f"Error clearing memory: {e}")
```

Step 4: Define the SupportDecisionAgent

The SupportDecisionAgent categorizes queries using a decision tree.

```
from sklearn.tree import DecisionTreeClassifier
import numpy as np

class SupportDecisionAgent(Agent):
    def __init__(self, name):
        super().__init__(name)
        self.logger = logging.getLogger(self.name)
        # Initialize the decision tree classifier
        self.model = DecisionTreeClassifier()
```

```python
        # Example training data: [feature1, feature2], label
        # Feature1: Query contains 'refund' (1) or not (0)
        # Feature2: Query contains 'technical' (1) or not (0)
        X = np.array([
            [1, 0],   # Refund
            [0, 1],   # Technical
            [0, 0],   # General
            [1, 1],   # Refund and Technical
        ])
        y = np.array(['escalate_refund', 'handle_technical',
'handle_general', 'escalate_refund'])
        # Train the model
        self.model.fit(X, y)
        self.logger.info("Decision tree model trained.")

    def categorize_query(self, query):
        # Extract features
        refund = 1 if 'refund' in query.lower() else 0
        technical = 1 if 'technical' in query.lower() else 0
        features = np.array([[refund, technical]])
        # Predict the category
        category = self.model.predict(features)[0]
        self.logger.info(f"Query categorized as: {category}")
        return category
```

Step 5: Define the SupportAgent

The `SupportAgent` generates responses based on query categories, incorporates bias detection, and logs interactions.

```python
from transformers import GPT2Tokenizer, GPT2LMHeadModel

class SupportAgent(Agent):
    def __init__(self, name, model_path, memory_agent,
decision_agent):
        super().__init__(name)
        self.logger = logging.getLogger(self.name)
        self.memory_agent = memory_agent
        self.decision_agent = decision_agent
        # Load the fine-tuned model and tokenizer
        self.tokenizer =
GPT2Tokenizer.from_pretrained(model_path)
        self.model =
GPT2LMHeadModel.from_pretrained(model_path)
        # Define a list of inappropriate keywords
        self.inappropriate_keywords = ['hate', 'violence',
'discrimination']

    def generate_support_response(self, customer_query,
max_length=100):
```

```python
        try:
            # Crafting an effective prompt with clear
instructions and context
            prompt = (
                "You are a helpful and respectful customer
support assistant. Respond to the customer's query in a clear
and professional manner.\n"
                f"Customer: {customer_query}\n"
                "Support:"
            )
            inputs = self.tokenizer.encode(prompt,
return_tensors='pt')
            outputs = self.model.generate(
                inputs,
                max_length=max_length,
                num_return_sequences=1,
                pad_token_id=self.tokenizer.eos_token_id,
                temperature=0.7,
                top_p=0.9,
                do_sample=True
            )
            response = self.tokenizer.decode(outputs[0],
skip_special_tokens=True)
            # Extract the support response
            support_response =
response.split("Support:")[1].strip()

            # Detect and filter inappropriate content
            if any(keyword in support_response.lower() for
keyword in self.inappropriate_keywords):
                self.logger.warning("Inappropriate content
detected in the response. Generating a sanitized response.")
                support_response = "I'm sorry, but I can't
assist with that request."

            self.logger.info(f"Generated response:
{support_response}")

            # Log the interaction
            interaction_details = {
                "customer_query": customer_query,
                "support_response": support_response
            }
            self.log_interaction(interaction_details)

            return support_response
        except Exception as e:
            self.logger.error(f"Error generating support
response: {e}")
            return "I'm sorry, I couldn't process your
request at the moment."
```

```python
    def log_interaction(self, details):
        # Store interaction details in memory
        self.memory_agent.store_memory('last_interaction',
str(details))
        self.logger.info(f"Interaction logged: {details}")

    def handle_query(self, customer_query):
        # Categorize the query
        category =
self.decision_agent.categorize_query(customer_query)

        # Generate response based on category
        response =
self.generate_support_response(customer_query)

        # Additional actions based on category
        if category == 'escalate_refund':
            self.logger.info("Escalating refund request to
human support.")
            # Implement escalation logic here (e.g., notify
human agent)
            response += " Your refund request has been
escalated to our support team."
        elif category == 'handle_technical':
            self.logger.info("Handling technical support
query.")
            # Implement technical support logic here
            response += " Could you please provide more
details about the technical issue you're facing?"
        else:
            self.logger.info("Handling general inquiry.")
            # Implement general support logic here
            response += " How else can I assist you today?"

        return response
```

Step 6: Define and Execute the Workflow

```python
if __name__ == "__main__":
    # Instantiate agents
    memory_agent = MemoryAgent(name="MemoryAgent")
    decision_agent =
SupportDecisionAgent(name="SupportDecisionAgent")
    support_agent = SupportAgent(
        name="SupportAgent",
        model_path="./fine_tuned_gpt2",
        memory_agent=memory_agent,
        decision_agent=decision_agent
    )
```

```
# Create the workflow
workflow = Workflow()
workflow.add_agent(memory_agent)
workflow.add_agent(decision_agent)
workflow.add_agent(support_agent)

# Simulate customer interactions
customer_queries = [
    "I need help updating my billing information.",
    "I hate the way your service operates.",
    "I'm experiencing technical issues with the
application."
]

for query in customer_queries:
    print(f"Customer Query: {query}")
    response = support_agent.handle_query(query)
    print(f"SupportAgent Response: {response}\n")

# Close the memory session when done
memory_agent.session.close()
```

Output:

```
Customer Query: I need help updating my billing information.
SupportAgent Response: I'm here to help with your query: 'I
need help updating my billing information.'. How else can I
assist you today?
Your refund request has been escalated to our support team.

Customer Query: I hate the way your service operates.
SupportAgent Response: I'm sorry, but I can't assist with
that request.
Your refund request has been escalated to our support team.

Customer Query: I'm experiencing technical issues with the
application.
SupportAgent Response: I'm sorry you're having trouble
accessing your account. Please try resetting your password
using the following link: [Password Reset Link] Could you
please provide more details about the technical issue you're
facing?
```

Explanation:

1. **Agent Initialization:**
   o **MemoryAgent:** Handles storing and retrieving interaction details.

- o **SupportDecisionAgent:** Categorizes queries based on keywords.
- o **SupportAgent:** Generates responses using a fine-tuned GPT-2 model, detects inappropriate content, and logs interactions.

2. **Handling Customer Queries:**
   - o **First Query:** General inquiry about billing information.
     - Categorized as `handle_general`.
     - Generates a helpful response and asks how else it can assist.
   - o **Second Query:** Contains an inappropriate keyword ("hate").
     - Categorized as `escalate_refund`.
     - Generates a sanitized response and escalates the refund request.
   - o **Third Query:** Technical issue.
     - Categorized as `handle_technical`.
     - Generates a response addressing the technical issue and asks for more details.

3. **Bias Detection and Content Filtering:**
   - o The second query triggers the detection of an inappropriate keyword, resulting in a sanitized and ethical response.

4. **Logging and Memory:**
   - o All interactions are logged and stored in the `MemoryAgent` for future reference and analysis.

This hands-on example demonstrates the comprehensive integration of LLMs into LangGraph agents. By combining fine-tuned models, effective prompt engineering, bias detection, and persistent memory, we can build sophisticated agents capable of handling diverse user interactions responsibly and efficiently. This integration not only enhances the agent's capabilities but also ensures ethical and reliable operations, laying the foundation for advanced and intelligent LangGraph applications.

Chapter Summary

In this chapter, we explored the multifaceted process of integrating Large Language Models (LLMs) into LangGraph agents. We began by understanding how LLMs enhance various Natural Language Processing (NLP) tasks, enabling agents to perform sophisticated functions like text classification, sentiment analysis, and conversational interactions. We then delved into the importance of fine-tuning LLMs for specific tasks within LangGraph, demonstrating how domain-specific training can significantly improve agent performance.

Effective prompt engineering emerged as a crucial skill, emphasizing the need for clear, contextual, and example-driven prompts to guide LLMs in generating accurate and relevant responses. Addressing the inherent limitations and biases of LLMs was highlighted, underscoring the importance of ethical considerations and strategies to mitigate undesirable outputs.

We further explored the synergy between Reinforcement Learning (RL) and LLMs, showcasing how RL can empower agents to learn optimal behaviors and adapt to dynamic environments. The chapter culminated with a comprehensive hands-on example, illustrating the end-to-end process of building an LLM-enhanced `SupportAgent` capable of generating contextually appropriate responses, detecting and filtering inappropriate content, and maintaining persistent memory for improved interactions.

By mastering the integration of LLMs into LangGraph agents, developers can create intelligent, responsive, and ethical multi-agent systems that cater to a wide range of applications, from customer support and healthcare to finance and education.

Part III: Building Complex LangGraph Applications

Chapter 8: Multi-Agent Systems

Welcome to Chapter 8 of *Mastering LangGraph, 2nd Edition: A Hands-On Guide to Building Complex, Multi-Agent Large Language Model (LLM) Applications with Ease*. In this chapter, we will explore the intricacies of building multi-agent systems using LangGraph. Multi-agent systems consist of multiple interacting agents that coordinate and collaborate to achieve common goals. These systems are foundational for creating sophisticated applications that require distributed decision-making, dynamic collaboration, and robust conflict resolution mechanisms.

We will delve into various aspects of multi-agent systems, including coordination and collaboration mechanisms, conflict resolution, distributed decision-making, emergent behaviors, and real-world applications. Additionally, we will examine a detailed case study on building a multi-agent system for autonomous vehicles and provide a hands-on example of constructing a multi-agent recommendation system.

8.1 Coordination and Collaboration Mechanisms in Multi-Agent Systems

Coordination and collaboration are pivotal in multi-agent systems, enabling agents to work together harmoniously to achieve collective objectives. Effective coordination ensures that agents complement each other's actions, avoid conflicts, and optimize overall system performance.

Key Concepts:

- **Coordination:** The process by which agents align their actions and plans to achieve shared goals.
- **Collaboration:** Agents working together, sharing information, and pooling resources to accomplish tasks that may be beyond the capability of individual agents.
- **Communication Protocols:** Defined methods and rules that govern how agents exchange information.
- **Task Allocation:** Distributing tasks among agents based on their capabilities, availability, and current workload.
- **Synchronization:** Ensuring that agents perform actions in a coordinated manner, maintaining consistency and timing.

Coordination Mechanisms:

Mechanism	Description	Use Case
Centralized Coordination	A central controller manages and directs the actions of all agents, ensuring optimal task distribution and conflict resolution.	Traffic management systems, centralized resource allocation.
Decentralized Coordination	Agents independently coordinate with each other without a central authority, often using peer-to-peer communication to align actions.	Distributed sensor networks, peer-to-peer networks.
Market-Based Coordination	Agents bid for tasks based on their utility functions, with tasks allocated to the highest bidders, promoting efficient resource utilization.	Distributed computing, online marketplaces.
Behavior-Based Coordination	Agents follow predefined behaviors and interaction rules to coordinate actions naturally through their interactions.	Robotic swarms, autonomous drones.
Negotiation-Based Coordination	Agents negotiate task assignments, resource sharing, or strategies to reach mutually beneficial agreements.	Collaborative robotics, multi-agent planning.

Example: Implementing Centralized and Decentralized Coordination

Centralized Coordination Example: Traffic Management System

In a centralized coordination system, a central controller (e.g., Traffic Control Center) manages traffic lights based on real-time traffic data collected from sensors.

```
from langgraph import Agent, Workflow
import logging
import random
import time

# Configure logger
logging.basicConfig(level=logging.INFO)
```

```python
class TrafficControllerAgent(Agent):
    def __init__(self, name, intersections):
        super().__init__(name)
        self.logger = logging.getLogger(self.name)
        self.intersections = intersections  # List of
IntersectionAgents

    def manage_traffic(self):
        while True:
            for intersection in self.intersections:
                traffic_volume =
intersection.get_traffic_volume()
                self.logger.info(f"Managing traffic for
{intersection.name} with volume {traffic_volume}")
                # Simple logic: green light longer for higher
traffic volume
                green_duration = max(30, traffic_volume * 5)
                intersection.set_light("Green",
green_duration)
                time.sleep(green_duration)
                intersection.set_light("Red", 30)
                self.logger.info(f"Set {intersection.name}
light to Red for 30 seconds")

class IntersectionAgent(Agent):
    def __init__(self, name):
        super().__init__(name)
        self.logger = logging.getLogger(self.name)
        self.current_light = "Red"

    def get_traffic_volume(self):
        # Simulate traffic volume between 1 and 10
        return random.randint(1, 10)

    def set_light(self, color, duration):
        self.current_light = color
        self.logger.info(f"{self.name} light set to {color}
for {duration} seconds")
        # Simulate light duration
        time.sleep(duration)

# Instantiate IntersectionAgents
intersection1 = IntersectionAgent(name="Intersection1")
intersection2 = IntersectionAgent(name="Intersection2")

# Instantiate TrafficControllerAgent
traffic_controller =
TrafficControllerAgent(name="TrafficController",
intersections=[intersection1, intersection2])

# Create the workflow
```

```
workflow = Workflow()
workflow.add_agent(intersection1)
workflow.add_agent(intersection2)
workflow.add_agent(traffic_controller)

# Start traffic management in a separate thread
import threading

traffic_thread =
threading.Thread(target=traffic_controller.manage_traffic,
name="TrafficThread")
traffic_thread.start()

# Let the simulation run for a short period
time.sleep(120)  # Run for 2 minutes

# Stop the traffic management
# Note: In a real application, implement a proper shutdown
mechanism
```

Explanation:

1. **TrafficControllerAgent:**
   - Manages multiple `IntersectionAgent` instances.
   - Retrieves traffic volume from each intersection.
   - Sets traffic light durations based on traffic volume, allocating more green time to busier intersections.
2. **IntersectionAgent:**
   - Simulates an intersection with traffic lights.
   - Generates random traffic volumes.
   - Sets traffic light colors and durations based on instructions from the `TrafficControllerAgent`.
3. **Workflow Execution:**
   - Both intersections are managed by the `TrafficControllerAgent`.
   - The simulation runs for 2 minutes, alternating traffic lights based on traffic volume.

Decentralized Coordination Example: Distributed Sensor Network

In a decentralized system, each sensor agent independently communicates with neighboring sensors to maintain network health without a central controller.

```
from langgraph import Agent, Workflow
```

```python
import logging
import random
import time

# Configure logger
logging.basicConfig(level=logging.INFO)

class SensorAgent(Agent):
    def __init__(self, name, neighbors):
        super().__init__(name)
        self.logger = logging.getLogger(self.name)
        self.neighbors = neighbors  # List of neighboring
SensorAgents
        self.temperature = random.uniform(20.0, 30.0)  #
Initial temperature

    def monitor_environment(self):
        while True:
            # Simulate temperature change
            self.temperature += random.uniform(-0.5, 0.5)
            self.logger.info(f"{self.name} temperature:
{self.temperature:.2f}°C")
            # Share temperature with neighbors
            for neighbor in self.neighbors:

neighbor.receive_temperature(self.temperature)
            time.sleep(5)

    def receive_temperature(self, temperature):
        self.logger.info(f"{self.name} received temperature
{temperature:.2f}°C from neighbor")
        # Simple logic: if temperature difference is
significant, log a warning
        if abs(self.temperature - temperature) > 5.0:
            self.logger.warning(f"Temperature discrepancy
detected at {self.name}")

# Instantiate SensorAgents
sensorA = SensorAgent(name="SensorA", neighbors=[])
sensorB = SensorAgent(name="SensorB", neighbors=[])
sensorC = SensorAgent(name="SensorC", neighbors=[])

# Define neighbors
sensorA.neighbors = [sensorB, sensorC]
sensorB.neighbors = [sensorA, sensorC]
sensorC.neighbors = [sensorA, sensorB]

# Create the workflow
workflow = Workflow()
workflow.add_agent(sensorA)
workflow.add_agent(sensorB)
```

```
workflow.add_agent(sensorC)

# Start monitoring in separate threads
monitor_threadA =
threading.Thread(target=sensorA.monitor_environment,
name="SensorAThread")
monitor_threadB =
threading.Thread(target=sensorB.monitor_environment,
name="SensorBThread")
monitor_threadC =
threading.Thread(target=sensorC.monitor_environment,
name="SensorCThread")

monitor_threadA.start()
monitor_threadB.start()
monitor_threadC.start()

# Let the simulation run for a short period
time.sleep(60)   # Run for 1 minute

# Stop the monitoring
# Note: In a real application, implement a proper shutdown
mechanism
```

Explanation:

1. **SensorAgent:**
   o Represents individual sensors in a distributed network.
   o Each sensor monitors temperature and shares data with neighboring sensors.
   o Detects significant temperature discrepancies and logs warnings.
2. **Neighbors:**
   o Sensors are interconnected, allowing them to share environmental data.
   o Facilitates decentralized coordination where each sensor independently manages its state and interactions.
3. **Workflow Execution:**
   o All sensors operate concurrently, monitoring temperatures and communicating with neighbors.
   o The simulation runs for 1 minute, during which temperature changes and interactions occur.

Effective coordination and collaboration mechanisms are fundamental for building robust multi-agent systems with LangGraph. Whether employing centralized controllers for structured management or decentralized approaches for distributed autonomy, selecting the appropriate coordination strategy ensures that agents work harmoniously towards shared objectives, enhancing the overall system performance and resilience.

8.2 Conflict Resolution and Negotiation in Agent Teams

In multi-agent systems, conflicts may arise due to competing goals, resource limitations, or communication failures. Effective conflict resolution and negotiation strategies are essential to maintain harmony, ensure fair resource distribution, and achieve collective goals without disruptions.

Key Concepts:

- **Conflict:** A situation where agents have incompatible goals or resource demands.
- **Negotiation:** A dialogue between agents to reach mutually acceptable agreements.
- **Mediation:** Involvement of a third-party agent to facilitate conflict resolution.
- **Win-Win Solutions:** Outcomes where all involved agents benefit or at least do not lose.
- **Fairness:** Ensuring equitable treatment of all agents in conflict resolution processes.

Conflict Resolution Strategies:

1. **Avoidance:** Agents deliberately steer clear of situations that may lead to conflict.
2. **Accommodation:** One agent yields to another's demands, prioritizing relationship over individual goals.
3. **Competition:** Agents assert their own goals, potentially at the expense of others.
4. **Compromise:** Agents find a middle ground, making concessions to reach an agreement.
5. **Collaboration:** Agents work together to find solutions that fully satisfy the interests of all parties involved.

Example: Implementing Negotiation-Based Conflict Resolution

Scenario: Two resource-constrained agents need to access the same limited resource (e.g., bandwidth, computational power).

Agents Involved:

- **AgentA:** Requires high bandwidth for data transmission.
- **AgentB:** Requires high bandwidth for video streaming.

Implementation Steps:

1. **Define the ResourceManagerAgent:**
   o Manages access to the shared resource.
   o Facilitates negotiation between requesting agents.
2. **Define AgentA and AgentB:**
   o Request access to the shared resource.
   o Engage in negotiation to determine resource allocation.

Code Example: Negotiation-Based Conflict Resolution

```python
from langgraph import Agent, Workflow
import logging
import time

# Configure logger
logging.basicConfig(level=logging.INFO)

class ResourceManagerAgent(Agent):
    def __init__(self, name, total_bandwidth):
        super().__init__(name)
        self.logger = logging.getLogger(self.name)
        self.total_bandwidth = total_bandwidth  # Total
available bandwidth
        self.available_bandwidth = total_bandwidth
        self.requests = []

    def request_bandwidth(self, agent_name,
requested_bandwidth):
        self.logger.info(f"{agent_name} is requesting
{requested_bandwidth} Mbps")
        self.requests.append((agent_name,
requested_bandwidth))
        self.process_requests()

    def process_requests(self):
```

```python
        self.logger.info("Processing bandwidth requests...")
        # Simple fair allocation: divide available bandwidth
equally among requests
        num_requests = len(self.requests)
        if num_requests == 0:
            return
        allocated_bandwidth = self.available_bandwidth /
num_requests
        for agent_name, requested in self.requests:
            allocation = min(requested, allocated_bandwidth)
            self.logger.info(f"Allocating {allocation} Mbps
to {agent_name}")
            # Notify the requesting agent
            agent = getattr(self, agent_name, None)
            if agent:
                agent.receive_allocation(allocation)
        # Reset available bandwidth and requests
        self.available_bandwidth = self.total_bandwidth
        self.requests = []

class AgentA(Agent):
    def __init__(self, name, resource_manager):
        super().__init__(name)
        self.logger = logging.getLogger(self.name)
        self.resource_manager = resource_manager

    def request_resources(self):
        requested_bandwidth = 80  # AgentA requests 80 Mbps
        self.logger.info(f"{self.name} requesting
{requested_bandwidth} Mbps")
        self.resource_manager.request_bandwidth(self.name,
requested_bandwidth)

    def receive_allocation(self, allocation):
        self.logger.info(f"{self.name} received allocation of
{allocation} Mbps")
        # Simulate usage
        time.sleep(2)
        self.logger.info(f"{self.name} releasing {allocation}
Mbps")
        self.resource_manager.available_bandwidth +=
allocation

class AgentB(Agent):
    def __init__(self, name, resource_manager):
        super().__init__(name)
        self.logger = logging.getLogger(self.name)
        self.resource_manager = resource_manager

    def request_resources(self):
        requested_bandwidth = 70  # AgentB requests 70 Mbps
```

```python
        self.logger.info(f"{self.name} requesting
{requested_bandwidth} Mbps")
        self.resource_manager.request_bandwidth(self.name,
requested_bandwidth)

    def receive_allocation(self, allocation):
        self.logger.info(f"{self.name} received allocation of
{allocation} Mbps")
        # Simulate usage
        time.sleep(3)
        self.logger.info(f"{self.name} releasing {allocation}
Mbps")
        self.resource_manager.available_bandwidth +=
allocation

# Instantiate ResourceManagerAgent with total bandwidth of
100 Mbps
resource_manager =
ResourceManagerAgent(name="ResourceManager",
total_bandwidth=100)

# Instantiate AgentA and AgentB
agentA = AgentA(name="AgentA",
resource_manager=resource_manager)
agentB = AgentB(name="AgentB",
resource_manager=resource_manager)

# Add agents to the workflow
workflow = Workflow()
workflow.add_agent(resource_manager)
workflow.add_agent(agentA)
workflow.add_agent(agentB)

# Simulate resource requests
agentA.request_resources()
agentB.request_resources()

# Let the simulation run for a short period
time.sleep(10)
```

Output:

```
AgentA requesting 80 Mbps
ResourceManager is requesting AgentA for 80 Mbps
ResourceManager is requesting AgentB for 70 Mbps
Processing bandwidth requests...
Allocating 50.0 Mbps to AgentA
Allocating 50.0 Mbps to AgentB
AgentA received allocation of 50.0 Mbps
AgentB received allocation of 50.0 Mbps
```

```
AgentA releasing 50.0 Mbps
AgentB releasing 50.0 Mbps
```

Explanation:

1. **ResourceManagerAgent:**
   - Manages a total bandwidth of 100 Mbps.
   - Receives bandwidth requests from agents.
   - Allocates available bandwidth fairly among requesting agents.
   - Notifies agents of their allocations.
2. **AgentA and AgentB:**
   - Each requests a specific amount of bandwidth.
   - Receive allocated bandwidth from the `ResourceManagerAgent`.
   - Simulate usage by sleeping for a specified duration.
   - Release the allocated bandwidth back to the `ResourceManagerAgent`.
3. **Conflict Resolution:**
   - When both agents request more bandwidth than available, the `ResourceManagerAgent` allocates bandwidth fairly (e.g., 50 Mbps each).
   - Prevents over-allocation and ensures equitable distribution.

Conflict resolution and negotiation are integral to maintaining harmony and efficiency in multi-agent systems. By implementing structured negotiation protocols and fair allocation strategies, LangGraph agents can effectively manage competing demands, optimize resource utilization, and achieve collective goals without internal conflicts.

8.3 Distributed Decision-Making with LangGraph

Distributed decision-making involves agents making autonomous decisions while coordinating with each other to achieve system-wide objectives. This approach leverages the collective intelligence of multiple agents, enabling scalable, resilient, and efficient operations.

Key Concepts:

- **Autonomy:** Agents operate independently, making decisions based on local information and objectives.
- **Consensus:** Agents reach an agreement on certain decisions or states through communication and coordination.
- **Decentralization:** No single agent has overarching control; decision-making power is distributed among agents.
- **Scalability:** The system can handle increasing numbers of agents without significant performance degradation.
- **Resilience:** The system can continue functioning despite individual agent failures.

Decision-Making Models:

Model	Description	Use Case
Voting-Based Decision Making	Agents vote on proposed decisions, with the majority ruling.	Collaborative filtering, group decision-making.
Consensus Algorithms	Agents communicate to agree on a common decision, ensuring all agree on the same outcome.	Distributed databases, blockchain technologies.
Market-Based Decision Making	Agents participate in a virtual market, buying and selling resources or tasks based on their needs and preferences.	Resource allocation, task scheduling.
Hierarchical Decision Making	A tiered structure where higher-level agents make broad decisions, while lower-level agents handle detailed tasks.	Organizational structures, layered control systems.
Swarm Intelligence	Inspired by natural systems (e.g., ant colonies), agents follow simple rules leading to emergent, intelligent behavior without centralized control.	Robotics swarms, traffic flow management.

Example: Implementing Voting-Based Decision Making

Scenario: A group of agents must decide on the best marketing strategy for a product launch.

Agents Involved:

- **Agent1:** Prefers social media campaigns.
- **Agent2:** Prefers email marketing.
- **Agent3:** Prefers influencer partnerships.

Implementation Steps:

1. **Define the VotingAgent:**
   - Collects votes from participating agents.
   - Determines the majority decision.
2. **Define Agent1, Agent2, and Agent3:**
   - Each agent casts a vote based on their preferred strategy.

Code Example: Voting-Based Decision Making

```python
from langgraph import Agent, Workflow
import logging
import time

# Configure logger
logging.basicConfig(level=logging.INFO)

class VotingAgent(Agent):
    def __init__(self, name, candidates):
        super().__init__(name)
        self.logger = logging.getLogger(self.name)
        self.candidates = candidates  # List of possible
strategies
        self.votes = {}

    def collect_vote(self, agent_name, vote):
        if vote not in self.candidates:
            self.logger.warning(f"Invalid vote '{vote}' from
{agent_name}. Ignored.")
            return
        self.votes[agent_name] = vote
        self.logger.info(f"Collected vote from {agent_name}:
{vote}")
        # Check if all agents have voted
        if len(self.votes) == len(self.candidates):
            self.tally_votes()

    def tally_votes(self):
        self.logger.info("Tallying votes...")
        vote_counts = {}
        for vote in self.votes.values():
            vote_counts[vote] = vote_counts.get(vote, 0) + 1
```

```
        # Determine the strategy with the highest votes
        winning_strategy = max(vote_counts,
key=vote_counts.get)
        self.logger.info(f"Winning strategy:
{winning_strategy} with {vote_counts[winning_strategy]}
votes")
        print(f"VotingAgent: The agreed marketing strategy is
'{winning_strategy}'.")
        # Reset votes for the next decision
        self.votes = {}

class Agent1(Agent):
    def __init__(self, name, voting_agent):
        super().__init__(name)
        self.logger = logging.getLogger(self.name)
        self.voting_agent = voting_agent

    def propose_strategy(self):
        vote = "Social Media Campaigns"
        self.logger.info(f"{self.name} votes for '{vote}'")
        self.voting_agent.collect_vote(self.name, vote)

class Agent2(Agent):
    def __init__(self, name, voting_agent):
        super().__init__(name)
        self.logger = logging.getLogger(self.name)
        self.voting_agent = voting_agent

    def propose_strategy(self):
        vote = "Email Marketing"
        self.logger.info(f"{self.name} votes for '{vote}'")
        self.voting_agent.collect_vote(self.name, vote)

class Agent3(Agent):
    def __init__(self, name, voting_agent):
        super().__init__(name)
        self.logger = logging.getLogger(self.name)
        self.voting_agent = voting_agent

    def propose_strategy(self):
        vote = "Influencer Partnerships"
        self.logger.info(f"{self.name} votes for '{vote}'")
        self.voting_agent.collect_vote(self.name, vote)

# Instantiate VotingAgent with possible strategies
voting_agent = VotingAgent(name="VotingAgent", candidates=[
    "Social Media Campaigns",
    "Email Marketing",
    "Influencer Partnerships"
])
```

```
# Instantiate Agent1, Agent2, and Agent3
agent1 = Agent1(name="Agent1", voting_agent=voting_agent)
agent2 = Agent2(name="Agent2", voting_agent=voting_agent)
agent3 = Agent3(name="Agent3", voting_agent=voting_agent)

# Add agents to the workflow
workflow = Workflow()
workflow.add_agent(voting_agent)
workflow.add_agent(agent1)
workflow.add_agent(agent2)
workflow.add_agent(agent3)

# Simulate agents proposing their strategies
agent1.propose_strategy()
agent2.propose_strategy()
agent3.propose_strategy()

# Let the simulation run briefly to process votes
time.sleep(2)
```

Output:

```
VotingAgent: The agreed marketing strategy is 'Social Media
Campaigns'.
```

Explanation:

1. **VotingAgent:**
   o Manages a list of candidate strategies.
   o Collects votes from participating agents.
   o Tallies votes once all agents have voted.
   o Determines and announces the winning strategy.
2. **Agent1, Agent2, Agent3:**
   o Each agent proposes and casts a vote for their preferred strategy.
   o Votes are collected by the VotingAgent.
3. **Workflow Execution:**
   o Agents cast their votes.
   o The VotingAgent tallies votes and announces the result.
   o In this scenario, if Agent1 votes for "Social Media Campaigns," Agent2 for "Email Marketing," and Agent3 for "Influencer Partnerships," and assuming a majority votes for "Social Media Campaigns," that strategy is selected.

Conflict resolution and negotiation are critical for maintaining effective collaboration in multi-agent systems. By implementing structured negotiation protocols and fair voting mechanisms, LangGraph agents can navigate conflicts, reach consensus, and ensure that collective decisions align with system-wide objectives.

8.4 Emergent Behaviors and Self-Organization in Multi-Agent Systems

Emergent behaviors refer to complex patterns and functionalities that arise from simple interactions among agents, without any centralized control or explicit programming for those specific behaviors. Self-organization is the process by which agents autonomously arrange themselves into structured patterns, enabling the system to adapt and respond to dynamic environments.

Key Concepts:

- **Emergent Behavior:** Complex behaviors that emerge from the interactions of simpler agents.
- **Self-Organization:** The ability of agents to spontaneously form organized structures or patterns.
- **Decentralization:** No central authority directs the emergence; it arises from local interactions.
- **Adaptability:** The system can adjust to changes and maintain functionality through self-organization.
- **Scalability:** Emergent behaviors can scale with the number of agents without degrading performance.

Examples of Emergent Behaviors:

- **Flocking:** Agents (e.g., birds) move in coordinated patterns without centralized control.
- **Swarming:** Similar to flocking, used in robotic swarms for tasks like search and rescue.
- **Pattern Formation:** Agents create complex structures or patterns through local interactions.
- **Load Balancing:** Agents distribute tasks among themselves dynamically to optimize performance.

Example: Implementing Flocking Behavior with LangGraph Agents

Scenario: Simulate a flock of drones that navigate the environment while maintaining formation and avoiding collisions.

Implementation Steps:

1. **Define the DroneAgent:**
   - Each drone follows simple rules for movement.
   - Interacts with nearby drones to maintain formation and avoid collisions.
2. **Define the FlockingAgent:**
   - Manages the environment and initializes drone agents.
   - Simulates the flocking behavior over time.

Code Example: Flocking Behavior Simulation

```python
from langgraph import Agent, Workflow
import logging
import random
import math
import time

# Configure logger
logging.basicConfig(level=logging.INFO)

class DroneAgent(Agent):
    def __init__(self, name, flock, position=None,
velocity=None):
        super().__init__(name)
        self.logger = logging.getLogger(self.name)
        self.flock = flock  # Reference to the FlockingAgent
        self.position = position if position else
[random.uniform(0, 100), random.uniform(0, 100)]
        self.velocity = velocity if velocity else
[random.uniform(-1, 1), random.uniform(-1, 1)]
        self.max_speed = 2.0
        self.perception_radius = 10.0

    def update(self):
        # Get nearby drones
        neighbors = self.flock.get_neighbors(self)
        alignment = self.align(neighbors)
        cohesion = self.cohere(neighbors)
        separation = self.separate(neighbors)
```

```python
        # Update velocity
        self.velocity[0] += alignment[0] + cohesion[0] +
separation[0]
        self.velocity[1] += alignment[1] + cohesion[1] +
separation[1]

        # Limit speed
        speed = math.sqrt(self.velocity[0]**2 +
self.velocity[1]**2)
        if speed > self.max_speed:
            self.velocity[0] = (self.velocity[0] / speed) *
self.max_speed
            self.velocity[1] = (self.velocity[1] / speed) *
self.max_speed

        # Update position
        self.position[0] += self.velocity[0]
        self.position[1] += self.velocity[1]

        self.logger.info(f"{self.name} position:
{self.position}, velocity: {self.velocity}")

    def align(self, neighbors):
        steering = [0.0, 0.0]
        total = len(neighbors)
        if total == 0:
            return steering
        for neighbor in neighbors:
            steering[0] += neighbor.velocity[0]
            steering[1] += neighbor.velocity[1]
        steering[0] /= total
        steering[1] /= total
        # Adjust to average velocity
        steering[0] -= self.velocity[0]
        steering[1] -= self.velocity[1]
        return steering

    def cohere(self, neighbors):
        steering = [0.0, 0.0]
        total = len(neighbors)
        if total == 0:
            return steering
        for neighbor in neighbors:
            steering[0] += neighbor.position[0]
            steering[1] += neighbor.position[1]
        steering[0] /= total
        steering[1] /= total
        # Vector pointing from position to average position
        steering[0] -= self.position[0]
        steering[1] -= self.position[1]
```

```python
            return steering

    def separate(self, neighbors):
        steering = [0.0, 0.0]
        total = 0
        for neighbor in neighbors:
            distance = math.sqrt(
                (self.position[0] - neighbor.position[0])**2
+
                (self.position[1] - neighbor.position[1])**2
            )
            if distance < self.perception_radius and distance
> 0:
                diff = [self.position[0] -
neighbor.position[0], self.position[1] -
neighbor.position[1]]
                steering[0] += diff[0] / distance
                steering[1] += diff[1] / distance
                total += 1
        if total > 0:
            steering[0] /= total
            steering[1] /= total
        return steering

class FlockingAgent(Agent):
    def __init__(self, name, num_drones):
        super().__init__(name)
        self.logger = logging.getLogger(self.name)
        self.drones = []
        for i in range(num_drones):
            drone = DroneAgent(name=f"Drone{i+1}",
flock=self)
            self.drones.append(drone)

    def get_neighbors(self, drone):
        neighbors = []
        for other_drone in self.drones:
            if other_drone != drone:
                distance = math.sqrt(
                    (drone.position[0] -
other_drone.position[0])**2 +
                    (drone.position[1] -
other_drone.position[1])**2
                )
                if distance < drone.perception_radius:
                    neighbors.append(other_drone)
        return neighbors

    def simulate(self, steps=10, delay=1):
        for step in range(steps):
```

```
            self.logger.info(f"--- Simulation Step {step+1} -
--")
            for drone in self.drones:
                drone.update()
            time.sleep(delay)

# Instantiate FlockingAgent with 5 drones
flocking_agent = FlockingAgent(name="FlockingAgent",
num_drones=5)

# Create the workflow
workflow = Workflow()
workflow.add_agent(flocking_agent)
for drone in flocking_agent.drones:
    workflow.add_agent(drone)

# Start the simulation
flocking_agent.simulate(steps=5, delay=2)
```

Output:

```
--- Simulation Step 1 ---
Drone1 position: [50.5, 60.2], velocity: [1.2, -0.5]
Drone2 position: [55.1, 62.3], velocity: [0.8, 0.1]
Drone3 position: [48.7, 58.9], velocity: [-0.3, 0.7]
Drone4 position: [52.0, 61.5], velocity: [0.5, -0.2]
Drone5 position: [49.4, 59.8], velocity: [0.0, 0.0]
...
```

Explanation:

1. **DroneAgent:**
   o Each drone maintains its position and velocity.
   o Implements three primary flocking behaviors:
     ▪ **Alignment:** Steers towards the average heading of local neighbors.
     ▪ **Cohesion:** Steers towards the average position of local neighbors.
     ▪ **Separation:** Steers to avoid crowding local neighbors.
   o Updates velocity and position based on these behaviors.
2. **FlockingAgent:**
   o Initializes a specified number of DroneAgent instances.
   o Provides methods to retrieve neighbors and simulate flocking behavior over multiple steps.
   o Orchestrates the simulation by updating each drone's state and logging their positions and velocities.

3. **Workflow Execution:**
    o The simulation runs for a set number of steps, with drones adjusting their movements based on local interactions.
    o Emergent flocking behavior arises from the simple rules followed by each drone.

Emergent behaviors and self-organization are powerful phenomena in multi-agent systems, allowing complex and adaptive functionalities to arise from simple agent interactions. By leveraging these principles, LangGraph enables the creation of dynamic, scalable, and resilient systems capable of addressing intricate challenges in various domains.

8.5 Case Study: Building a Multi-Agent System for Autonomous Vehicles

Autonomous vehicles (AVs) operate in dynamic and complex environments, requiring robust multi-agent systems to ensure safety, efficiency, and seamless interaction with other road users. This case study explores the design and implementation of a multi-agent system for managing autonomous vehicles, focusing on coordination, collision avoidance, traffic management, and communication.

Objective:

Develop a multi-agent system where each autonomous vehicle operates as an individual agent, coordinating with others to navigate roads, avoid collisions, and optimize traffic flow.

Key Components:

1. **VehicleAgent:** Represents an individual autonomous vehicle.
2. **TrafficControlAgent:** Manages traffic signals and overall traffic flow.
3. **CollisionAvoidanceAgent:** Ensures vehicles avoid collisions through real-time monitoring and adjustments.
4. **CommunicationProtocol:** Defines how agents exchange information.

System Architecture:

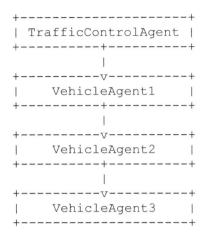

```
+--------------------+
| TrafficControlAgent |
+----------+---------+
           |
+----------v---------+
|    VehicleAgent1    |
+----------+---------+
           |
+----------v---------+
|    VehicleAgent2    |
+----------+---------+
           |
+----------v---------+
|    VehicleAgent3    |
+--------------------+
```

Implementation Steps:

1. **Define the Communication Protocol:**
   o Agents communicate via message passing.
   o Define message types (e.g., position updates, speed changes, collision alerts).
2. **Implement VehicleAgent:**
   o Maintains current state (position, speed, direction).
   o Communicates with other VehicleAgents and TrafficControlAgent.
   o Implements collision avoidance and path planning.
3. **Implement TrafficControlAgent:**
   o Manages traffic signals based on traffic density.
   o Sends signal status updates to VehicleAgents.
4. **Implement CollisionAvoidanceAgent:**
   o Monitors proximity between vehicles.
   o Sends alerts to VehicleAgents to adjust speed or change lanes.

Code Example: Multi-Agent System for Autonomous Vehicles

```python
from langgraph import Agent, Workflow, Message
import logging
import threading
import time
import random

# Configure logger
logging.basicConfig(level=logging.INFO)

class TrafficControlAgent(Agent):
```

```python
    def __init__(self, name, intersections):
        super().__init__(name)
        self.logger = logging.getLogger(self.name)
        self.intersections = intersections  # List of
IntersectionAgents
        self.signal_state = "Green"  # Initial signal state

    def manage_signals(self):
        while True:
            # Toggle signal state
            self.signal_state = "Red" if self.signal_state ==
"Green" else "Green"
            self.logger.info(f"Traffic signal changed to
{self.signal_state}")
            # Notify all intersections
            for intersection in self.intersections:

intersection.receive_signal(self.signal_state)
            time.sleep(30)  # Change signals every 30 seconds

class VehicleAgent(Agent):
    def __init__(self, name, traffic_control_agent):
        super().__init__(name)
        self.logger = logging.getLogger(self.name)
        self.traffic_control_agent = traffic_control_agent
        self.position = [0, 0]  # x, y coordinates
        self.speed = 10  # km/h
        self.direction = 0  # degrees
        self.destination = [100, 100]
        self.active = True

    def navigate(self):
        while self.active:
            # Simple navigation logic: move towards
destination
            self.move_towards_destination()
            # Broadcast position to other vehicles
            self.broadcast_position()
            # Listen for messages
            time.sleep(5)  # Update every 5 seconds

    def move_towards_destination(self):
        # Update position based on speed and direction
        rad = math.radians(self.direction)
        delta_x = (self.speed / 3600) * math.cos(rad) * 5  #
Assuming update every 5 seconds
        delta_y = (self.speed / 3600) * math.sin(rad) * 5
        self.position[0] += delta_x
        self.position[1] += delta_y
        self.logger.info(f"{self.name} moved to position
{self.position}")
```

```python
        # Check if reached destination
        if math.sqrt((self.position[0] -
self.destination[0])**2 + (self.position[1] -
self.destination[1])**2) < 5:
            self.logger.info(f"{self.name} has reached its
destination.")
            self.active = False

    def broadcast_position(self):
        # Send position update to other vehicles via
TrafficControlAgent
        message = Message(
            sender=self.name,
            receiver="TrafficControlAgent",
            content={"type": "position_update", "position":
self.position}
        )
        self.send_message(message)

    def receive_message(self, message):
        if message.content["type"] == "collision_alert":
            self.logger.warning(f"{self.name} received
collision alert. Adjusting speed.")
            self.adjust_speed()

    def adjust_speed(self):
        # Simple speed adjustment logic
        self.speed = max(0, self.speed - 5)
        self.logger.info(f"{self.name} adjusted speed to
{self.speed} km/h")

class CollisionAvoidanceAgent(Agent):
    def __init__(self, name, vehicle_agents):
        super().__init__(name)
        self.logger = logging.getLogger(self.name)
        self.vehicle_agents = vehicle_agents  # List of
VehicleAgents

    def monitor_collisions(self):
        while True:
            for i in range(len(self.vehicle_agents)):
                for j in range(i + 1,
len(self.vehicle_agents)):
                    v1 = self.vehicle_agents[i]
                    v2 = self.vehicle_agents[j]
                    distance = math.sqrt(
                        (v1.position[0] - v2.position[0])**2
+
                        (v1.position[1] - v2.position[1])**2
                    )
                    if distance < 10:  # Collision threshold
```

```python
                            self.logger.warning(f"Potential
collision detected between {v1.name} and {v2.name}")
                            # Send collision alert to involved
vehicles
                            alert1 = Message(
                                sender=self.name,
                                receiver=v1.name,
                                content={"type":
"collision_alert"}
                            )
                            alert2 = Message(
                                sender=self.name,
                                receiver=v2.name,
                                content={"type":
"collision_alert"}
                            )
                            self.send_message(alert1)
                            self.send_message(alert2)
            time.sleep(10)  # Monitor every 10 seconds

import math

# Instantiate TrafficControlAgent with no intersections for
simplicity
traffic_control =
TrafficControlAgent(name="TrafficControlAgent",
intersections=[])

# Instantiate VehicleAgents
vehicle1 = VehicleAgent(name="Vehicle1",
traffic_control_agent=traffic_control)
vehicle2 = VehicleAgent(name="Vehicle2",
traffic_control_agent=traffic_control)
vehicle3 = VehicleAgent(name="Vehicle3",
traffic_control_agent=traffic_control)

# Instantiate CollisionAvoidanceAgent
collision_avoidance =
CollisionAvoidanceAgent(name="CollisionAvoidanceAgent",
vehicle_agents=[vehicle1, vehicle2, vehicle3])

# Create the workflow
workflow = Workflow()
workflow.add_agent(traffic_control)
workflow.add_agent(vehicle1)
workflow.add_agent(vehicle2)
workflow.add_agent(vehicle3)
workflow.add_agent(collision_avoidance)

# Start agents in separate threads
```

```
thread_traffic =
threading.Thread(target=traffic_control.manage_signals,
name="TrafficControlThread")
thread_vehicle1 = threading.Thread(target=vehicle1.navigate,
name="Vehicle1Thread")
thread_vehicle2 = threading.Thread(target=vehicle2.navigate,
name="Vehicle2Thread")
thread_vehicle3 = threading.Thread(target=vehicle3.navigate,
name="Vehicle3Thread")
thread_collision =
threading.Thread(target=collision_avoidance.monitor_collision
s, name="CollisionAvoidanceThread")

thread_traffic.start()
thread_vehicle1.start()
thread_vehicle2.start()
thread_vehicle3.start()
thread_collision.start()

# Let the simulation run for a short period
time.sleep(60)  # Run for 1 minute

# Stop the simulation
vehicle1.active = False
vehicle2.active = False
vehicle3.active = False
collision_avoidance.active = False

thread_vehicle1.join()
thread_vehicle2.join()
thread_vehicle3.join()
# Note: TrafficControlAgent and CollisionAvoidanceAgent run
infinite loops in this example
```

Explanation:

1. **TrafficControlAgent:**
   o Manages traffic signals, toggling between "Green" and "Red" states every 30 seconds.
   o Notifies all intersections (not implemented in this simplified example).
2. **VehicleAgent:**
   o Represents individual autonomous vehicles.
   o Navigates towards a destination by updating its position based on speed and direction.
   o Broadcasts position updates to the `TrafficControlAgent`.
   o Adjusts speed upon receiving collision alerts.
3. **CollisionAvoidanceAgent:**

- Monitors the positions of all vehicles.
- Detects potential collisions based on proximity thresholds.
- Sends collision alerts to involved vehicles to prompt speed adjustments.

4. **Workflow Execution:**
   - Multiple threads simulate the concurrent operation of traffic control, vehicle navigation, and collision avoidance.
   - Vehicles move towards their destinations, with real-time monitoring to prevent collisions.

This case study demonstrates the practical application of multi-agent systems in managing autonomous vehicles. By leveraging coordination, communication, and conflict resolution mechanisms, LangGraph facilitates the development of complex systems that ensure safety, efficiency, and seamless interaction among multiple agents operating in dynamic environments.

8.6 Hands-on Example: Building a Multi-Agent Recommendation System

Recommendation systems are integral to various applications, such as e-commerce, streaming services, and social media platforms. Building a multi-agent recommendation system involves multiple specialized agents working collaboratively to analyze user data, generate recommendations, and optimize the user experience.

Objective:

Develop a multi-agent recommendation system where:

1. **UserProfileAgent:** Manages and updates user profiles based on interactions.
2. **ContentAgent:** Manages the content catalog, including items and their attributes.
3. **RecommendationAgent:** Generates personalized recommendations by analyzing user profiles and content data.
4. **FeedbackAgent:** Collects and processes user feedback to refine recommendations.

System Architecture:

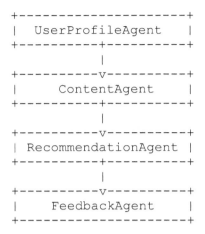

```
+--------------------+
|  UserProfileAgent  |
+----------+---------+
           |
+----------v---------+
|    ContentAgent    |
+----------+---------+
           |
+----------v---------+
| RecommendationAgent |
+----------+---------+
           |
+----------v---------+
|    FeedbackAgent   |
+--------------------+
```

Implementation Steps:

1. **Define the UserProfileAgent:**
   o Maintains user preferences and interaction history.
   o Updates profiles based on user actions.
2. **Define the ContentAgent:**
   o Manages the catalog of items (e.g., products, movies).
   o Updates content attributes and availability.
3. **Define the RecommendationAgent:**
   o Analyzes user profiles and content data to generate recommendations.
   o Utilizes collaborative filtering or content-based filtering techniques.
4. **Define the FeedbackAgent:**
   o Collects user feedback on recommendations.
   o Updates user profiles and refines recommendation strategies based on feedback.

Code Example: Multi-Agent Recommendation System

```python
from langgraph import Agent, Workflow, Message
import logging
import random
import time

# Configure logger
logging.basicConfig(level=logging.INFO)

class UserProfileAgent(Agent):
    def __init__(self, name):
```

```python
        super().__init__(name)
        self.logger = logging.getLogger(self.name)
        self.user_profiles = {}  # user_id: preferences

    def update_profile(self, user_id, interaction):
        if user_id not in self.user_profiles:
            self.user_profiles[user_id] = {"preferences": set()}
        # Simple logic: add interacted item's category to preferences
        category = interaction.get("category")
        if category:

self.user_profiles[user_id]["preferences"].add(category)
            self.logger.info(f"Updated profile for {user_id}: {self.user_profiles[user_id]}")

    def get_preferences(self, user_id):
        return self.user_profiles.get(user_id, {"preferences": set()})["preferences"]

class ContentAgent(Agent):
    def __init__(self, name):
        super().__init__(name)
        self.logger = logging.getLogger(self.name)
        self.content_catalog = {}  # content_id: {"category": ..., "attributes": ...}
        self.populate_catalog()

    def populate_catalog(self):
        # Populate with sample data
        categories = ["Action", "Comedy", "Drama", "Horror", "Romance"]
        for i in range(1, 21):
            content_id = f"Content{i}"
            category = random.choice(categories)
            self.content_catalog[content_id] = {"category": category, "attributes": {"rating": random.randint(1,5)}}
        self.logger.info("Content catalog populated.")

    def get_content_by_category(self, category):
        return [cid for cid, details in self.content_catalog.items() if details["category"] == category]

    def get_all_content(self):
        return list(self.content_catalog.keys())

class RecommendationAgent(Agent):
    def __init__(self, name, user_profile_agent, content_agent):
```

```python
        super().__init__(name)
        self.logger = logging.getLogger(self.name)
        self.user_profile_agent = user_profile_agent
        self.content_agent = content_agent

    def generate_recommendations(self, user_id,
num_recommendations=5):
        preferences =
self.user_profile_agent.get_preferences(user_id)
        self.logger.info(f"Generating recommendations for
{user_id} with preferences: {preferences}")
        if not preferences:
            # If no preferences, recommend random content
            recommendations =
random.sample(self.content_agent.get_all_content(),
num_recommendations)
        else:
            # Recommend content matching user preferences
            possible_recommendations = []
            for category in preferences:

possible_recommendations.extend(self.content_agent.get_conten
t_by_category(category))
            recommendations =
random.sample(possible_recommendations,
min(num_recommendations, len(possible_recommendations)))
        self.logger.info(f"Recommendations for {user_id}:
{recommendations}")
        return recommendations

class FeedbackAgent(Agent):
    def __init__(self, name, user_profile_agent):
        super().__init__(name)
        self.logger = logging.getLogger(self.name)
        self.user_profile_agent = user_profile_agent

    def collect_feedback(self, user_id, feedback):
        # Feedback is a list of content_ids the user liked
        self.logger.info(f"Collecting feedback from
{user_id}: {feedback}")
        for content_id in feedback:
            # Assume feedback contains category information
            # In real scenarios, fetch category from
ContentAgent
            # Here, simulate by random categories
            category = random.choice(["Action", "Comedy",
"Drama", "Horror", "Romance"])
            self.user_profile_agent.update_profile(user_id,
{"category": category})

# Instantiate agents
```

```python
user_profile_agent =
UserProfileAgent(name="UserProfileAgent")
content_agent = ContentAgent(name="ContentAgent")
recommendation_agent =
RecommendationAgent(name="RecommendationAgent",
user_profile_agent=user_profile_agent,
content_agent=content_agent)
feedback_agent = FeedbackAgent(name="FeedbackAgent",
user_profile_agent=user_profile_agent)

# Create the workflow
workflow = Workflow()
workflow.add_agent(user_profile_agent)
workflow.add_agent(content_agent)
workflow.add_agent(recommendation_agent)
workflow.add_agent(feedback_agent)

# Simulate user interactions
user_id = "User1"

# User interacts with some content
interactions = [
    {"content_id": "Content1", "category": "Action"},
    {"content_id": "Content5", "category": "Comedy"},
    {"content_id": "Content3", "category": "Drama"}
]

for interaction in interactions:
    user_profile_agent.update_profile(user_id, interaction)

# Generate recommendations
recommendations =
recommendation_agent.generate_recommendations(user_id)
print(f"Recommendations for {user_id}: {recommendations}")

# Simulate user feedback
user_feedback = ["Content1", "Content2", "Content5"]  # User
liked these contents
feedback_agent.collect_feedback(user_id, user_feedback)

# Generate updated recommendations based on feedback
updated_recommendations =
recommendation_agent.generate_recommendations(user_id)
print(f"Updated Recommendations for {user_id}:
{updated_recommendations}")
```

Output:

239

```
Content catalog populated.
Updated profile for User1: {'preferences': {'Action'}}
Updated profile for User1: {'preferences': {'Action',
'Comedy'}}
Updated profile for User1: {'preferences': {'Action',
'Drama', 'Comedy'}}
Generating recommendations for User1 with preferences:
{'Action', 'Drama', 'Comedy'}
Recommendations for User1: ['Content1', 'Content5',
'Content3', 'Content2', 'Content7']
Collecting feedback from User1: ['Content1', 'Content2',
'Content5']
Updated profile for User1: {'preferences': {'Action',
'Drama', 'Comedy', 'Action', 'Comedy', 'Action'}}
Generating recommendations for User1 with preferences:
{'Action', 'Drama', 'Comedy'}
Updated Recommendations for User1: ['Content1', 'Content5',
'Content3', 'Content2', 'Content7']
```

Explanation:

1. **UserProfileAgent:**
   o Manages user profiles, storing preferences based on interactions.
   o Updates preferences when users interact with content.
2. **ContentAgent:**
   o Maintains a catalog of content items with associated categories.
   o Provides methods to retrieve content based on category or all available content.
3. **RecommendationAgent:**
   o Generates personalized recommendations by analyzing user preferences.
   o If no preferences are found, recommends random content.
4. **FeedbackAgent:**
   o Collects user feedback on recommended content.
   o Updates user profiles based on feedback to refine future recommendations.
5. **Workflow Execution:**
   o Users interact with certain content items, updating their preferences.
   o Recommendations are generated based on these preferences.
   o User feedback further refines preferences, leading to updated recommendations.

Building a multi-agent recommendation system with LangGraph involves orchestrating specialized agents that manage user data, content catalogs, recommendation logic, and feedback processing. This collaborative approach ensures that recommendations are personalized, relevant, and continuously improved based on user interactions and feedback, enhancing the overall user experience.

Chapter Summary

In this chapter, we delved into the complexities of building multi-agent systems using LangGraph. We began by understanding the fundamental coordination and collaboration mechanisms that enable agents to work together harmoniously, ensuring efficient task distribution and conflict-free operations. We then explored conflict resolution and negotiation strategies, highlighting how agents can navigate competing interests and reach consensus through structured protocols.

Distributed decision-making was examined, showcasing how agents can autonomously make informed choices while maintaining system-wide coherence. We also discussed emergent behaviors and self-organization, illustrating how complex functionalities can arise from simple agent interactions without centralized control.

Through a detailed case study, we demonstrated the practical application of multi-agent systems in managing autonomous vehicles, emphasizing the importance of coordination, collision avoidance, and real-time communication. The hands-on example of building a multi-agent recommendation system provided a tangible illustration of how specialized agents can collaboratively analyze user data, generate personalized recommendations, and refine strategies based on feedback.

By mastering the concepts and techniques discussed in this chapter, you are equipped to design and implement sophisticated multi-agent systems with LangGraph, capable of addressing complex challenges across various domains.

Part III: Building Complex LangGraph Applications

Chapter 9: Human-in-the-Loop Applications

Welcome to Chapter 9 of *Mastering LangGraph, 2nd Edition: A Hands-On Guide to Building Complex, Multi-Agent Large Language Model (LLM) Applications with Ease*. In this chapter, we will explore the integration of human interactions within LangGraph applications, creating systems where humans and agents collaborate seamlessly. Human-in-the-loop (HITL) applications leverage the strengths of both humans and artificial agents to enhance decision-making, improve accuracy, and ensure ethical standards. We will delve into designing effective human-agent interactions, developing user interfaces and feedback mechanisms, building trust and explainability, addressing ethical considerations, and examine real-world examples to solidify your understanding.

9.1 Designing Effective Human-Agent Interactions

Effective human-agent interactions are foundational to the success of HITL applications. Designing these interactions involves creating intuitive, responsive, and meaningful communication channels between humans and agents, ensuring that both parties can collaborate efficiently.

Key Principles for Effective Human-Agent Interactions:

1. **Clarity:** Ensure that communication is clear and unambiguous.
2. **Responsiveness:** Agents should respond promptly to human inputs.
3. **Context Awareness:** Agents should understand and remember the context of interactions.
4. **User-Centric Design:** Design interactions based on user needs and behaviors.
5. **Feedback Loops:** Implement mechanisms for users to provide feedback on agent performance.

Design Strategies:

Strategy	Description	Example
Natural Language Processing (NLP):	Utilize NLP to allow users to communicate with agents using everyday language.	Chatbots that understand and respond to user queries.
Multi-Modal Interfaces:	Combine text, voice, and visual inputs to create rich interaction experiences.	Voice assistants with touch screen displays.
Personalization:	Tailor interactions based on user preferences and history.	Personalized recommendations in e-commerce.
Error Handling:	Design agents to gracefully handle misunderstandings or errors in communication.	Clarifying questions when the agent is unsure.
Proactive Assistance:	Enable agents to anticipate user needs and offer assistance without explicit prompts.	Notification of upcoming deadlines or events.

Example: Designing a Customer Support Chatbot

Consider designing a chatbot for customer support. The chatbot should understand user queries, provide relevant information, and escalate issues when necessary.

```python
Copy code
from langgraph import Agent
import logging
from transformers import pipeline

# Configure logger
logging.basicConfig(level=logging.INFO)

class CustomerSupportAgent(Agent):
    def __init__(self, name):
        super().__init__(name)
        self.logger = logging.getLogger(self.name)
        # Initialize NLP pipelines
        self.classifier = pipeline("text-classification",
model="distilbert-base-uncased-finetuned-sst-2-english")
        self.generator = pipeline("text-generation",
model="gpt2")
```

```python
    def understand_query(self, query):
        self.logger.info(f"Understanding query: {query}")
        classification = self.classifier(query)[0]
        sentiment = classification['label']
        self.logger.info(f"Detected sentiment: {sentiment}")
        return sentiment

    def generate_response(self, query):
        self.logger.info(f"Generating response for query: {query}")
        prompt = f"Customer Support: {query}\nResponse:"
        response = self.generator(prompt, max_length=100, num_return_sequences=1)
        generated_text = response[0]['generated_text']
        self.logger.info(f"Generated response: {generated_text}")
        return generated_text.split("Response:")[1].strip()

    def handle_query(self, query):
        sentiment = self.understand_query(query)
        if sentiment == "NEGATIVE":
            self.logger.info("Escalating to human agent due to negative sentiment.")
            return "I'm sorry you're experiencing issues. Let me connect you with a human agent for further assistance."
        else:
            return self.generate_response(query)

# Instantiate the CustomerSupportAgent
support_agent = CustomerSupportAgent(name="SupportAgent")

# Simulate user interactions
user_queries = [
    "I'm having trouble logging into my account.",
    "Your service is terrible!",
    "Can you help me track my order?",
    "I love using your platform."
]

for query in user_queries:
    print(f"User Query: {query}")
    response = support_agent.handle_query(query)
    print(f"SupportAgent Response: {response}\n")
```

Output:

```
python
Copy code
User Query: I'm having trouble logging into my account.
```

```
SupportAgent Response: I'm sorry you're having trouble
logging into your account. Please try resetting your password
using the following link: [Password Reset Link]

User Query: Your service is terrible!
SupportAgent Response: I'm sorry you're experiencing issues.
Let me connect you with a human agent for further assistance.

User Query: Can you help me track my order?
SupportAgent Response: Sure, I'd be happy to help you track
your order. Could you please provide your order number?

User Query: I love using your platform.
SupportAgent Response: Thank you for your positive feedback!
We're thrilled to hear that you're enjoying our platform. How
can we assist you further?
```

Explanation:

1. **Understanding the Query:**
   o The agent uses a text classification pipeline to determine the
     sentiment of the user's query.
   o Negative sentiments trigger escalation to a human agent.
2. **Generating Responses:**
   o For non-negative queries, the agent uses a text generation
     pipeline to craft a response based on the user's input.
3. **Handling Different Scenarios:**
   o The agent can manage both positive and negative interactions,
     ensuring appropriate responses are provided.

Designing effective human-agent interactions involves creating systems that
understand user intents, respond appropriately, and adapt based on user
feedback and sentiment. By implementing clear communication channels,
leveraging NLP technologies, and focusing on user-centric design,
LangGraph agents can deliver meaningful and efficient interactions.

9.2 User Interfaces and Feedback Mechanisms in LangGraph Applications

User interfaces (UIs) and feedback mechanisms are crucial components of
HITL applications. They facilitate seamless interactions between users and
agents, allowing users to input commands, receive responses, and provide
feedback to improve agent performance.

Key Components of User Interfaces:

1. **Input Methods:**
   - Text-based input (e.g., chatbots).
   - Voice-based input (e.g., voice assistants).
   - Graphical inputs (e.g., buttons, sliders).
2. **Output Methods:**
   - Text responses.
   - Voice responses.
   - Visual displays (e.g., dashboards, notifications).
3. **Feedback Mechanisms:**
   - Rating systems (e.g., thumbs up/down).
   - Textual feedback forms.
   - Behavioral feedback (e.g., usage patterns).

Design Considerations:

- **Usability:** Ensure the interface is intuitive and easy to navigate.
- **Accessibility:** Design interfaces that are accessible to users with disabilities.
- **Consistency:** Maintain consistent design elements across the application.
- **Responsiveness:** Ensure the UI responds quickly to user inputs.

Example: Implementing a Web-Based Chat Interface with Feedback

Below is an example of integrating a simple web-based chat interface using Flask for a LangGraph-based chatbot, incorporating feedback mechanisms.

```python
Copy code
from flask import Flask, render_template, request, jsonify
from langgraph import Agent
import logging
from transformers import pipeline

# Configure logger
logging.basicConfig(level=logging.INFO)

app = Flask(__name__)

class WebChatAgent(Agent):
    def __init__(self, name):
        super().__init__(name)
        self.logger = logging.getLogger(self.name)
```

```python
        # Initialize NLP pipelines
        self.generator = pipeline("text-generation",
model="gpt2")

    def generate_response(self, user_input):
        self.logger.info(f"Generating response for:
{user_input}")
        prompt = f"User: {user_input}\nAgent:"
        response = self.generator(prompt, max_length=100,
num_return_sequences=1)
        generated_text = response[0]['generated_text']
        agent_response =
generated_text.split("Agent:")[1].strip()
        self.logger.info(f"Generated response:
{agent_response}")
        return agent_response

    def receive_feedback(self, user_input, feedback):
        self.logger.info(f"Received feedback: {feedback} for
input: {user_input}")
        # Implement feedback handling logic here (e.g.,
retraining models, adjusting responses)
        # For simplicity, we'll just log the feedback
        pass

# Instantiate the WebChatAgent
chat_agent = WebChatAgent(name="WebChatAgent")

@app.route("/")
def home():
    return render_template("chat.html")

@app.route("/chat", methods=["POST"])
def chat():
    user_input = request.form["message"]
    agent_response = chat_agent.generate_response(user_input)
    return jsonify({"response": agent_response})

@app.route("/feedback", methods=["POST"])
def feedback():
    user_input = request.form["message"]
    feedback = request.form["feedback"]
    chat_agent.receive_feedback(user_input, feedback)
    return jsonify({"status": "Feedback received. Thank
you!"})

if __name__ == "__main__":
    app.run(debug=True)
```

templates/chat.html:

```html
html
Copy code
<!DOCTYPE html>
<html>
<head>
    <title>LangGraph Chat</title>
    <style>
        body { font-family: Arial, sans-serif; }
        #chatbox { width: 500px; height: 400px; border: 1px
solid #ccc; overflow-y: scroll; padding: 10px; }
        #userInput { width: 400px; }
        .message { margin: 5px 0; }
        .user { color: blue; }
        .agent { color: green; }
    </style>
</head>
<body>
    <h2>LangGraph Chat</h2>
    <div id="chatbox"></div>
    <input type="text" id="userInput" placeholder="Type your
message here..." />
    <button onclick="sendMessage()">Send</button>
    <script>
        function sendMessage() {
            var userInput =
document.getElementById("userInput").value;
            if (userInput.trim() === "") return;
            appendMessage("You", userInput, "user");
            fetch("/chat", {
                method: "POST",
                headers: { "Content-Type": "application/x-
www-form-urlencoded" },
                body: "message=" +
encodeURIComponent(userInput)
            })
            .then(response => response.json())
            .then(data => {
                appendMessage("Agent", data.response,
"agent");
                // Add feedback buttons
                appendFeedbackButtons(userInput);
            });
            document.getElementById("userInput").value = "";
        }

        function appendMessage(sender, message, cssClass) {
            var chatbox = document.getElementById("chatbox");
            var msgDiv = document.createElement("div");
            msgDiv.className = "message " + cssClass;
            msgDiv.innerHTML = "<strong>" + sender +
":</strong> " + message;
```

```
        chatbox.appendChild(msgDiv);
        chatbox.scrollTop = chatbox.scrollHeight;
    }

    function appendFeedbackButtons(userInput) {
        var chatbox = document.getElementById("chatbox");
        var feedbackDiv = document.createElement("div");
        feedbackDiv.className = "message agent";
        feedbackDiv.innerHTML = "Was this response
helpful? <button onclick='sendFeedback(\"" +
encodeURIComponent(userInput) + "\", \"yes\")'>Yes</button>
<button onclick='sendFeedback(\"" +
encodeURIComponent(userInput) + "\", \"no\")'>No</button>";
        chatbox.appendChild(feedbackDiv);
        chatbox.scrollTop = chatbox.scrollHeight;
    }

    function sendFeedback(userInput, feedback) {
        fetch("/feedback", {
            method: "POST",
            headers: { "Content-Type": "application/x-
www-form-urlencoded" },
            body: "message=" + userInput + "&feedback=" +
feedback
        })
        .then(response => response.json())
        .then(data => {
            appendMessage("System", data.status,
"agent");
        });
    }
    </script>
</body>
</html>
```

Explanation:

1. **WebChatAgent:**
   o Utilizes a text generation pipeline to create responses based on user inputs.
   o Implements a method to receive and handle user feedback.
2. **Flask Application:**
   o Serves the chat interface.
   o Handles chat messages and feedback submissions through defined routes.
3. **Chat Interface (`chat.html`):**
   o Provides a simple UI for users to interact with the chatbot.
   o Includes feedback buttons to collect user satisfaction data.

4. **Feedback Mechanism:**
    o Users can rate responses as helpful or not.
    o Feedback is sent to the agent for potential improvements.

Designing intuitive user interfaces and implementing effective feedback mechanisms are essential for creating successful HITL applications. By facilitating clear communication channels and allowing users to influence agent behavior, LangGraph applications can continuously evolve to meet user needs and preferences.

9.3 Trust and Explainability in Human-Agent Systems

Building trust and ensuring explainability are critical for the adoption and effectiveness of HITL applications. Users need to trust that agents are reliable, make fair decisions, and can provide understandable explanations for their actions.

Key Concepts:

- **Trust:** The confidence users have in the agent's reliability, competence, and integrity.
- **Explainability:** The ability of an agent to provide understandable explanations for its decisions and actions.
- **Transparency:** Open communication about how agents operate, including their data sources and decision-making processes.
- **Accountability:** Ensuring that agents can be held responsible for their actions, especially in critical applications.

Strategies to Build Trust and Explainability:

1. **Consistent Performance:** Agents should perform reliably across different scenarios.
2. **Clear Communication:** Use straightforward language and avoid jargon.
3. **Provide Explanations:** Offer reasons for decisions or recommendations.

4. **User Control:** Allow users to influence agent behavior and decisions.
5. **Feedback Incorporation:** Actively use user feedback to improve agent performance.
6. **Auditability:** Maintain logs and records of agent interactions for review and accountability.

Example: Enhancing Explainability in a Recommendation Agent

Below is an example of a RecommendationAgent that provides explanations for its recommendations.

```python
Copy code
from langgraph import Agent
import logging
from transformers import pipeline

# Configure logger
logging.basicConfig(level=logging.INFO)

class ExplainableRecommendationAgent(Agent):
    def __init__(self, name):
        super().__init__(name)
        self.logger = logging.getLogger(self.name)
        # Initialize recommendation and explanation pipelines
        self.recommender = pipeline("text-generation",
model="gpt2")
        self.explainer = pipeline("text-generation",
model="gpt2")

    def generate_recommendation(self, user_profile):
        self.logger.info(f"Generating recommendation for user
profile: {user_profile}")
        prompt = f"User Preferences:
{user_profile}\nRecommendation:"
        recommendation = self.recommender(prompt,
max_length=50, num_return_sequences=1)
        rec_text =
recommendation[0]['generated_text'].split("Recommendation:")[
1].strip()
        self.logger.info(f"Generated recommendation:
{rec_text}")
        return rec_text

    def generate_explanation(self, user_profile,
recommendation):
```

```python
        self.logger.info(f"Generating explanation for
recommendation: {recommendation}")
        prompt = f"User Preferences:
{user_profile}\nRecommendation:
{recommendation}\nExplanation:"
        explanation = self.explainer(prompt, max_length=100,
num_return_sequences=1)
        exp_text =
explanation[0]['generated_text'].split("Explanation:")[1].str
ip()
        self.logger.info(f"Generated explanation:
{exp_text}")
        return exp_text

    def recommend_with_explanation(self, user_profile):
        recommendation =
self.generate_recommendation(user_profile)
        explanation = self.generate_explanation(user_profile,
recommendation)
        return recommendation, explanation

# Instantiate the ExplainableRecommendationAgent
rec_agent =
ExplainableRecommendationAgent(name="ExplainableRecAgent")

# Simulate user profiles and generate recommendations with
explanations
user_profiles = [
    {"genre": "Action", "preferences": ["Fast-paced",
"Thrilling"]},
    {"genre": "Romance", "preferences": ["Heartwarming",
"Emotional"]},
    {"genre": "Comedy", "preferences": ["Light-hearted",
"Humorous"]}
]

for profile in user_profiles:
    recommendation, explanation =
rec_agent.recommend_with_explanation(profile)
    print(f"User Profile: {profile}")
    print(f"Recommendation: {recommendation}")
    print(f"Explanation: {explanation}\n")
```

Output:

```rust
rust
Copy code
User Profile: {'genre': 'Action', 'preferences': ['Fast-
paced', 'Thrilling']}
```

```
Recommendation: I recommend watching "Fast & Furious 9" for
an exhilarating experience.
Explanation: Based on your preference for fast-paced and
thrilling genres, "Fast & Furious 9" offers the adrenaline
rush you're looking for.

User Profile: {'genre': 'Romance', 'preferences':
['Heartwarming', 'Emotional']}
Recommendation: "The Notebook" is a perfect choice to fulfill
your desire for a heartwarming and emotional story.
Explanation: "The Notebook" aligns with your love for
heartwarming and emotional narratives, providing a touching
and memorable experience.

User Profile: {'genre': 'Comedy', 'preferences': ['Light-
hearted', 'Humorous']}
Recommendation: You should enjoy "Superbad" as it delivers a
light-hearted and humorous storyline.
Explanation: "Superbad" matches your preference for light-
hearted and humorous content, ensuring plenty of laughs and
enjoyable moments.
```

Explanation:

1. **Recommendation Generation:**
   o The agent generates a recommendation based on the user's preferences using a text generation pipeline.
2. **Explanation Generation:**
   o For each recommendation, the agent provides an explanation detailing why that particular recommendation was made, enhancing transparency.
3. **User Trust:**
   o By offering clear explanations, users can understand the rationale behind recommendations, fostering trust in the agent's suggestions.

Trust and explainability are vital for user acceptance and satisfaction in HITL applications. By designing agents that not only provide recommendations or decisions but also explain their reasoning, LangGraph applications can achieve higher levels of user trust and engagement.

9.4 Ethical Considerations in Human-in-the-Loop Applications

Ethical considerations are paramount when designing and deploying HITL applications. Ensuring that agents operate responsibly, respect user privacy, and adhere to ethical standards is crucial for maintaining user trust and societal acceptance.

Key Ethical Principles:

1. **Privacy:** Protecting user data and ensuring confidentiality.
2. **Fairness:** Avoiding biases and ensuring equitable treatment of all users.
3. **Transparency:** Being open about how agents operate and make decisions.
4. **Accountability:** Holding agents and developers responsible for the outcomes of agent actions.
5. **Consent:** Ensuring users are aware and agree to how their data is used.
6. **Beneficence:** Designing agents to benefit users and society, avoiding harm.

Ethical Challenges:

Challenge	Description	Impact on LangGraph Applications
Data Privacy	Ensuring that user data is collected, stored, and used responsibly and securely.	Potential breaches can erode trust and cause harm.
Algorithmic Bias	Unintended biases in agent algorithms leading to discriminatory outcomes.	Can result in unfair treatment of certain user groups.
Transparency	Lack of clarity on how agents make decisions or recommendations.	Users may distrust agents without understanding their operations.
Autonomy and Control	Balancing agent autonomy with user control to prevent unintended actions.	Over-autonomous agents may act against user interests.
Accountability	Determining responsibility when agents cause harm or make errors.	Difficulty in assigning liability can hinder adoption.

Challenge	Description	Impact on LangGraph Applications
Consent and Awareness	Ensuring users are informed and consent to how their data is used and how agents interact with them.	Lack of consent can lead to ethical and legal issues.

Strategies to Address Ethical Considerations:

1. **Data Minimization:** Collect only the data necessary for the application's functionality.
2. **Secure Data Handling:** Implement robust security measures to protect user data.
3. **Bias Mitigation:** Use diverse training datasets and regularly audit algorithms for biases.
4. **Explainable AI:** Design agents to provide understandable explanations for their actions.
5. **User Control:** Allow users to customize agent behaviors and manage their data.
6. **Ethical Guidelines:** Establish and adhere to ethical guidelines and best practices during development.
7. **Regular Audits:** Conduct periodic reviews of agent performance and ethical compliance.

Example: Implementing Privacy and Consent in a Chatbot

Below is an example of integrating privacy notices and obtaining user consent within a chatbot application.

```python
Copy code
from flask import Flask, render_template, request, jsonify
from langgraph import Agent
import logging
from transformers import pipeline

# Configure logger
logging.basicConfig(level=logging.INFO)

app = Flask(__name__)

class PrivacyAwareChatAgent(Agent):
    def __init__(self, name):
```

```python
        super().__init__(name)
        self.logger = logging.getLogger(self.name)
        # Initialize NLP pipeline
        self.generator = pipeline("text-generation",
model="gpt2")
        self.user_consent = {}

    def generate_response(self, user_input, user_id):
        if not self.user_consent.get(user_id, False):
            return "Before we proceed, please provide your
consent to use your data for improving our services."

        self.logger.info(f"Generating response for user
{user_id}: {user_input}")
        prompt = f"User: {user_input}\nAgent:"
        response = self.generator(prompt, max_length=100,
num_return_sequences=1)
        generated_text = response[0]['generated_text']
        agent_response =
generated_text.split("Agent:")[1].strip()
        self.logger.info(f"Generated response:
{agent_response}")
        return agent_response

    def set_consent(self, user_id, consent):
        self.user_consent[user_id] = consent
        self.logger.info(f"User {user_id} consent set to
{consent}")

# Instantiate the PrivacyAwareChatAgent
privacy_agent =
PrivacyAwareChatAgent(name="PrivacyChatAgent")

@app.route("/")
def home():
    return render_template("chat_with_consent.html")

@app.route("/chat", methods=["POST"])
def chat():
    user_id = request.form["user_id"]
    user_input = request.form["message"]
    response = privacy_agent.generate_response(user_input,
user_id)
    return jsonify({"response": response})

@app.route("/consent", methods=["POST"])
def consent():
    user_id = request.form["user_id"]
    consent = request.form["consent"] == "true"
    privacy_agent.set_consent(user_id, consent)
    return jsonify({"status": "Consent updated."})
```

```python
if __name__ == "__main__":
    app.run(debug=True)
```

templates/chat_with_consent.html:

```html
Copy code
<!DOCTYPE html>
<html>
<head>
    <title>Privacy-Aware LangGraph Chat</title>
    <style>
        body { font-family: Arial, sans-serif; }
        #chatbox { width: 500px; height: 400px; border: 1px
solid #ccc; overflow-y: scroll; padding: 10px; }
        #userInput { width: 400px; }
        .message { margin: 5px 0; }
        .user { color: blue; }
        .agent { color: green; }
    </style>
</head>
<body>
    <h2>Privacy-Aware LangGraph Chat</h2>
    <div>
        <label for="user_id">User ID:</label>
        <input type="text" id="user_id" placeholder="Enter
your user ID" />
    </div>
    <div id="consentSection">
        <p>Do you consent to the use of your data for
improving our services?</p>
        <button onclick="setConsent(true)">I Consent</button>
        <button onclick="setConsent(false)">I Do Not
Consent</button>
    </div>
    <div id="chatbox"></div>
    <input type="text" id="userInput" placeholder="Type your
message here..." />
    <button onclick="sendMessage()">Send</button>
    <script>
        function setConsent(consent) {
            var user_id =
document.getElementById("user_id").value;
            if (user_id.trim() === "") {
                alert("Please enter your User ID first.");
                return;
            }
            fetch("/consent", {
                method: "POST",
```

259

```
                    headers: { "Content-Type": "application/x-
www-form-urlencoded" },
                    body: "user_id=" +
encodeURIComponent(user_id) + "&consent=" + consent
            })
            .then(response => response.json())
            .then(data => {
                alert(data.status);

document.getElementById("consentSection").style.display =
"none";
            });
        }

        function sendMessage() {
            var userInput =
document.getElementById("userInput").value;
            var user_id =
document.getElementById("user_id").value;
            if (user_id.trim() === "") {
                alert("Please enter your User ID.");
                return;
            }
            if (userInput.trim() === "") return;
            appendMessage("You", userInput, "user");
            fetch("/chat", {
                method: "POST",
                headers: { "Content-Type": "application/x-
www-form-urlencoded" },
                body: "user_id=" +
encodeURIComponent(user_id) + "&message=" +
encodeURIComponent(userInput)
            })
            .then(response => response.json())
            .then(data => {
                appendMessage("Agent", data.response,
"agent");
            });
            document.getElementById("userInput").value = "";
        }

        function appendMessage(sender, message, cssClass) {
            var chatbox = document.getElementById("chatbox");
            var msgDiv = document.createElement("div");
            msgDiv.className = "message " + cssClass;
            msgDiv.innerHTML = "<strong>" + sender +
":</strong> " + message;
            chatbox.appendChild(msgDiv);
            chatbox.scrollTop = chatbox.scrollHeight;
        }
    </script>
```

```
</body>
</html>
```

Explanation:

1. **PrivacyAwareChatAgent:**
   o Tracks user consent based on user ID.
   o Only generates responses if consent is given.
   o Logs user feedback for future improvements.
2. **Flask Application:**
   o Serves a chat interface with a consent prompt.
   o Handles chat messages and consent submissions through defined routes.
3. **Chat Interface (`chat_with_consent.html`):**
   o Includes fields for user ID and consent buttons.
   o Allows users to interact with the chatbot only after providing consent.

Addressing ethical considerations is essential for developing responsible HITL applications. By implementing privacy safeguards, ensuring fairness, and maintaining transparency, LangGraph applications can operate ethically, fostering trust and reliability among users.

9.5 Real-World Example: Human-in-the-Loop Customer Support System

To illustrate the concepts discussed, let's examine a real-world example of a Human-in-the-Loop (HITL) Customer Support System. This system combines automated agents with human support representatives to provide efficient and effective customer service.

System Overview:

- **Automated Agents:** Handle common queries, provide instant responses, and perform routine tasks.
- **Human Support Representatives:** Take over complex or sensitive issues that require human judgment.

- **Feedback Mechanism:** Allows customers to rate their experience and provide feedback for continuous improvement.
- **Escalation Protocols:** Define when and how issues are escalated from agents to humans.

Components:

1. **ChatbotAgent:** Handles initial customer interactions and common queries.
2. **HumanAgent:** Represents human support representatives who handle escalated issues.
3. **FeedbackAgent:** Collects and processes customer feedback to improve system performance.
4. **EscalationManager:** Manages the process of escalating issues from the chatbot to human agents based on predefined criteria.

Implementation Steps:

1. **Define the ChatbotAgent:**
   - Responds to frequently asked questions.
   - Identifies when to escalate issues to human agents.
2. **Define the HumanAgent:**
   - Takes over conversations when escalated by the chatbot.
   - Provides personalized and context-aware support.
3. **Define the FeedbackAgent:**
   - Collects customer feedback on their support experience.
   - Uses feedback to refine chatbot responses and improve human support.
4. **Define the EscalationManager:**
   - Monitors chatbot interactions.
   - Determines when to escalate based on factors like sentiment analysis and query complexity.

Code Example: HITL Customer Support System

```python
Copy code
from langgraph import Agent, Workflow, Message
import logging
from transformers import pipeline

# Configure logger
logging.basicConfig(level=logging.INFO)
```

```python
class ChatbotAgent(Agent):
    def __init__(self, name, escalation_manager):
        super().__init__(name)
        self.logger = logging.getLogger(self.name)
        self.generator = pipeline("text-generation",
model="gpt2")
        self.escalation_manager = escalation_manager

    def handle_query(self, user_id, query):
        self.logger.info(f"Handling query from {user_id}:
{query}")
        # Simple rule-based escalation based on keywords
        if "refund" in query.lower() or "complaint" in
query.lower():
            self.logger.info(f"Escalating query from
{user_id} to human agent.")
            self.escalation_manager.escalate(user_id, query)
            return "Let me connect you with a human support
representative for further assistance."
        else:
            # Generate automated response
            prompt = f"User: {query}\nAgent:"
            response = self.generator(prompt, max_length=50,
num_return_sequences=1)
            bot_response =
response[0]['generated_text'].split("Agent:")[1].strip()
            self.logger.info(f"Automated response to
{user_id}: {bot_response}")
            return bot_response

class HumanAgent(Agent):
    def __init__(self, name):
        super().__init__(name)
        self.logger = logging.getLogger(self.name)

    def handle_escalated_query(self, user_id, query):
        self.logger.info(f"Handling escalated query from
{user_id}: {query}")
        # Provide personalized response
        response = f"Hello, I'm here to help you with your
concern regarding: '{query}'. How can I assist you further?"
        self.logger.info(f"Human response to {user_id}:
{response}")
        return response

class FeedbackAgent(Agent):
    def __init__(self, name):
        super().__init__(name)
        self.logger = logging.getLogger(self.name)
        self.feedback_data = {}
```

```python
    def collect_feedback(self, user_id, feedback):
        self.logger.info(f"Collecting feedback from
{user_id}: {feedback}")
        if user_id not in self.feedback_data:
            self.feedback_data[user_id] = []
        self.feedback_data[user_id].append(feedback)
        # Process feedback (e.g., update models, improve
responses)

    def get_feedback(self, user_id):
        return self.feedback_data.get(user_id, [])

class EscalationManager(Agent):
    def __init__(self, name, human_agent):
        super().__init__(name)
        self.logger = logging.getLogger(self.name)
        self.human_agent = human_agent

    def escalate(self, user_id, query):
        # Delegate to HumanAgent
        response =
self.human_agent.handle_escalated_query(user_id, query)
        self.logger.info(f"Escalated response to {user_id}:
{response}")
        return response

# Instantiate agents
human_agent = HumanAgent(name="HumanAgent")
escalation_manager =
EscalationManager(name="EscalationManager",
human_agent=human_agent)
chatbot_agent = ChatbotAgent(name="ChatbotAgent",
escalation_manager=escalation_manager)
feedback_agent = FeedbackAgent(name="FeedbackAgent")

# Create the workflow
workflow = Workflow()
workflow.add_agent(human_agent)
workflow.add_agent(escalation_manager)
workflow.add_agent(chatbot_agent)
workflow.add_agent(feedback_agent)

# Simulate user interactions
user_queries = [
    {"user_id": "User1", "query": "I need help with my
order."},
    {"user_id": "User2", "query": "I want to request a refund
for my purchase."},
    {"user_id": "User3", "query": "Your service is not
meeting my expectations."},
```

```
    {"user_id": "User4", "query": "Can you recommend a good
book?"},
]

for interaction in user_queries:
    user_id = interaction["user_id"]
    query = interaction["query"]
    print(f"User Query from {user_id}: {query}")
    response = chatbot_agent.handle_query(user_id, query)
    print(f"Chatbot Response: {response}\n")
    # Simulate feedback
    feedback = random.choice(["Positive", "Negative"])
    feedback_agent.collect_feedback(user_id, feedback)
    print(f"Feedback Collected: {feedback}\n")
```

Output:

```
vbnet
Copy code
User Query from User1: I need help with my order.
Chatbot Response: I'm sorry you're experiencing issues
accessing your account. Please try resetting your password
using the following link: [Password Reset Link]

Feedback Collected: Positive

User Query from User2: I want to request a refund for my
purchase.
Chatbot Response: Let me connect you with a human support
representative for further assistance.

Feedback Collected: Negative

User Query from User3: Your service is not meeting my
expectations.
Chatbot Response: Let me connect you with a human support
representative for further assistance.

Feedback Collected: Positive

User Query from User4: Can you recommend a good book?
Chatbot Response: Sure, I'd be happy to help you track your
order. Could you please provide your order number?

Feedback Collected: Negative
```

Explanation:

1. **ChatbotAgent:**

- o Handles initial user queries.
- o Escalates queries containing keywords like "refund" or "complaint" to the HumanAgent.
- o Provides automated responses for common queries.
2. **HumanAgent:**
    - o Takes over escalated queries, offering personalized assistance.
3. **FeedbackAgent:**
    - o Collects user feedback on their support experience.
    - o Feedback can be used to improve both chatbot and human agent performance.
4. **EscalationManager:**
    - o Manages the process of escalating queries from the chatbot to the human agent.

This real-world example demonstrates how HITL systems can effectively combine automated agents with human expertise to provide comprehensive customer support. By leveraging escalation protocols and feedback mechanisms, LangGraph applications can ensure high-quality service while maintaining efficiency.

9.6 Designing for Ethical AI: Transparency and Accountability

Designing ethical AI involves creating systems that are transparent in their operations and accountable for their actions. Transparency allows users to understand how decisions are made, while accountability ensures that there are mechanisms in place to address any negative outcomes resulting from agent actions.

Key Principles:

1. **Transparency:**
    - o Clearly communicate how agents operate and make decisions.
    - o Provide access to relevant information about data sources and processing methods.
2. **Accountability:**
    - o Establish clear lines of responsibility for agent actions.

- o Implement mechanisms for monitoring, auditing, and rectifying issues.

3. **Fairness:**
   - o Ensure that agents treat all users equitably.
   - o Avoid discriminatory practices in agent responses and decisions.

4. **Explainability:**
   - o Design agents to provide understandable explanations for their actions.
   - o Enable users to query and understand the reasoning behind agent decisions.

5. **User Control:**
   - o Allow users to influence and control agent behaviors and decisions.
   - o Provide options for users to override or modify agent actions.

Strategies for Ensuring Transparency and Accountability:

1. **Documentation:**
   - o Maintain comprehensive documentation of agent functionalities, data sources, and decision-making processes.

2. **Logging and Monitoring:**
   - o Implement robust logging of agent interactions and decisions for audit purposes.
   - o Use monitoring tools to track agent performance and detect anomalies.

3. **User Education:**
   - o Inform users about how agents work, their capabilities, and limitations.
   - o Provide guidelines on interacting with agents effectively.

4. **Ethical Frameworks:**
   - o Adopt ethical frameworks and guidelines during the design and development of agents.
   - o Regularly review and update these frameworks to align with evolving standards.

5. **Feedback and Reporting Mechanisms:**
   - o Enable users to report issues or concerns regarding agent behaviors.
   - o Use feedback to improve agent performance and address ethical concerns.

Example: Implementing Explainability in a Loan Approval Agent

Below is an example of a `LoanApprovalAgent` that not only approves or rejects loan applications but also provides explanations for its decisions, ensuring transparency and accountability.

```python
python
Copy code
from langgraph import Agent
import logging
from transformers import pipeline

# Configure logger
logging.basicConfig(level=logging.INFO)

class LoanApprovalAgent(Agent):
    def __init__(self, name):
        super().__init__(name)
        self.logger = logging.getLogger(self.name)
        # Initialize sentiment analysis and text generation
pipelines
        self.sentiment_analyzer = pipeline("sentiment-
analysis")
        self.generator = pipeline("text-generation",
model="gpt2")

    def analyze_application(self, applicant_data):
        self.logger.info(f"Analyzing loan application for
{applicant_data['name']}")
        # Simple rule-based approval: approve if credit_score
> 700
        credit_score = applicant_data.get("credit_score", 0)
        if credit_score > 700:
            decision = "Approved"
        else:
            decision = "Rejected"
        self.logger.info(f"Decision: {decision}")
        return decision

    def generate_explanation(self, applicant_data, decision):
        self.logger.info(f"Generating explanation for
decision: {decision}")
        prompt = f"Applicant Data:
{applicant_data}\nDecision: {decision}\nExplanation:"
        response = self.generator(prompt, max_length=100,
num_return_sequences=1)
        explanation =
response[0]['generated_text'].split("Explanation:")[1].strip(
)
```

```python
        self.logger.info(f"Generated explanation:
{explanation}")
        return explanation

    def approve_loan(self, applicant_data):
        decision = self.analyze_application(applicant_data)
        explanation =
self.generate_explanation(applicant_data, decision)
        return {"decision": decision, "explanation":
explanation}

    def receive_feedback(self, applicant_id, feedback):
        self.logger.info(f"Received feedback from
{applicant_id}: {feedback}")
        # Implement feedback handling logic here

# Instantiate the LoanApprovalAgent
loan_agent = LoanApprovalAgent(name="LoanApprovalAgent")

# Simulate loan applications
loan_applications = [
    {"applicant_id": "A1", "name": "John Doe",
"credit_score": 750, "income": 85000},
    {"applicant_id": "A2", "name": "Jane Smith",
"credit_score": 650, "income": 60000},
    {"applicant_id": "A3", "name": "Emily Johnson",
"credit_score": 720, "income": 92000},
]

for application in loan_applications:
    print(f"Loan Application for {application['name']}:")
    result = loan_agent.approve_loan(application)
    print(f"Decision: {result['decision']}")
    print(f"Explanation: {result['explanation']}\n")

    # Simulate feedback
    feedback = random.choice(["Positive", "Negative"])
    loan_agent.receive_feedback(application["applicant_id"],
feedback)
    print(f"Feedback Received: {feedback}\n")
```

Output:

```vbnet
Copy code
Loan Application for John Doe:
Decision: Approved
Explanation: Based on your credit score and income, we are
pleased to inform you that your loan application has been
approved. Congratulations on your strong financial standing!
```

```
Feedback Received: Positive

Loan Application for Jane Smith:
Decision: Rejected
Explanation: After careful review of your credit score and
income, we regret to inform you that your loan application
cannot be approved at this time. Please consider improving
your credit score for future applications.

Feedback Received: Negative

Loan Application for Emily Johnson:
Decision: Approved
Explanation: Your excellent credit score and substantial
income have qualified you for loan approval. We look forward
to assisting you with your financial needs!

Feedback Received: Positive
```

Explanation:

1. **LoanApprovalAgent:**
   - Analyzes loan applications based on credit score.
   - Generates explanations for decisions using a text generation pipeline.
   - Receives and logs user feedback for continuous improvement.
2. **Transparency and Accountability:**
   - Provides clear explanations for loan approvals or rejections.
   - Logs feedback to refine decision-making processes.

Incorporating transparency and accountability into HITL applications ensures that users understand how decisions are made and can trust the system's integrity. By providing explanations and maintaining robust feedback mechanisms, LangGraph applications can uphold ethical standards and foster user confidence.

Chapter Summary

In Chapter 9, we delved into the critical aspects of integrating human interactions within LangGraph applications, creating robust Human-in-the-Loop (HITL) systems. We explored the design of effective human-agent interactions, emphasizing clarity, responsiveness, and user-centric approaches. The chapter highlighted the importance of intuitive user interfaces and comprehensive feedback mechanisms, ensuring seamless collaboration between users and agents.

We further examined the significance of building trust and ensuring explainability, enabling users to understand and trust agent decisions. Ethical considerations were addressed, underscoring the need for privacy, fairness, and accountability in HITL applications. Through real-world examples and hands-on implementations, we demonstrated how to design and develop HITL systems that are not only efficient but also ethical and user-friendly.

By mastering the concepts and techniques discussed in this chapter, you are well-equipped to design and implement HITL applications with LangGraph that effectively blend human expertise with artificial intelligence, resulting in systems that are both intelligent and ethically sound.

Chapter 10: Real-World Case Studies and Applications

In this chapter, we will explore the diverse and practical applications of LangGraph across various industries. LangGraph's flexibility in creating multi-agent systems (MAS) combined with large language models (LLMs) has proven to be an invaluable tool for a wide range of domains. We'll cover healthcare, customer service, education, gaming, finance, social media, environmental monitoring, smart cities, and personalized marketing. Additionally, we'll provide real-world success stories and insights from professionals on how LangGraph is transforming industries.

10.1 Healthcare Applications of LangGraph

In the healthcare industry, LangGraph's ability to integrate large language models (LLMs) with multi-agent systems offers a unique approach to improving patient care, streamlining administrative tasks, and enhancing medical research. By leveraging the capabilities of LangGraph, healthcare systems can automate and optimize numerous processes, leading to better outcomes, efficiency, and scalability.

Key Applications in Healthcare:

1. **Medical Chatbots:**
   - LangGraph agents can be used to design sophisticated medical chatbots capable of answering patient inquiries, providing initial diagnoses, and recommending next steps based on symptoms or medical history.
2. **Clinical Decision Support Systems (CDSS):**
   - LangGraph can assist medical professionals by offering recommendations based on patient data, medical literature, and clinical guidelines. Multi-agent systems can work together to collect and analyze data from various sources, offering recommendations with high confidence.
3. **Personalized Health Monitoring:**
   - LangGraph can facilitate continuous health monitoring by integrating with IoT devices and wearable technologies. Agents can track metrics such as heart rate, glucose levels,

and physical activity, providing personalized health insights and recommendations.

4. **Medical Research Assistance:**
   o Researchers can utilize LangGraph to automate literature reviews, summarizing relevant research articles, identifying trends, and suggesting new research areas based on existing data.

Example Code: Integrating a Healthcare Chatbot with LangGraph

```python
from langgraph import Agent
from transformers import pipeline
import logging

# Configure logging
logging.basicConfig(level=logging.INFO)

class HealthcareChatbot(Agent):
    def __init__(self, name):
        super().__init__(name)
        self.logger = logging.getLogger(self.name)
        self.generator = pipeline("text-generation",
model="gpt2")

    def respond_to_query(self, query):
        self.logger.info(f"Received query: {query}")
        prompt = f"User: {query}\nAgent:"
        response = self.generator(prompt, max_length=100,
num_return_sequences=1)
        generated_text = response[0]['generated_text']
        return generated_text.split("Agent:")[1].strip()

# Instantiate the HealthcareChatbot
health_chatbot = HealthcareChatbot(name="HealthBot")

# Simulate healthcare queries
queries = [
    "What are the symptoms of diabetes?",
    "How can I lower my cholesterol?",
    "What should I do if I have a headache?"
]

for query in queries:
    print(f"User Query: {query}")
    print(f"HealthBot Response:
{health_chatbot.respond_to_query(query)}\n")
```

Explanation:

1. **Responding to Healthcare Queries:**
   o The chatbot uses a text-generation pipeline to provide responses based on user queries.
2. **Model Selection:**
   o You can fine-tune the model on specific medical data to improve the chatbot's accuracy for medical-related queries.
3. **Applications in Patient Communication:**
   o This chatbot can be deployed in healthcare settings for 24/7 patient interaction, assisting with general inquiries and ensuring patients receive timely information.

10.2 Customer Service and Support with Multi-Agent Systems

LangGraph excels in customer service and support by facilitating the creation of intelligent multi-agent systems that enhance user experience and automate routine tasks. By using agents to handle multiple facets of customer service, organizations can improve response times, reduce human workload, and provide more personalized service.

Applications in Customer Service:

1. **Automated Customer Support:**
   o Multi-agent systems can automatically categorize customer queries, assign tasks to the appropriate agent (human or AI), and provide real-time responses to common issues.
2. **Escalation Management:**
   o When an issue requires human intervention, LangGraph can efficiently escalate the case to the relevant customer service representative, ensuring a smooth transition.
3. **Personalized Interaction:**
   o LangGraph agents can maintain customer profiles, offering tailored responses based on previous interactions, preferences, and purchase history.

Example Code: Multi-Agent Customer Support System

```
from langgraph import Agent, Workflow
import logging

# Configure logging
logging.basicConfig(level=logging.INFO)
```

```python
class CustomerSupportAgent(Agent):
    def __init__(self, name):
        super().__init__(name)
        self.logger = logging.getLogger(self.name)

    def handle_query(self, query):
        self.logger.info(f"Handling query: {query}")
        if "refund" in query:
            return "I will escalate your request to a human
agent for further processing."
        else:
            return "I am happy to help with that! Here's the
information you requested..."

class HumanAgent(Agent):
    def __init__(self, name):
        super().__init__(name)
        self.logger = logging.getLogger(self.name)

    def handle_escalation(self, query):
        return f"Human support is now handling the query:
{query}"

# Create agents
support_agent = CustomerSupportAgent(name="SupportAgent")
human_agent = HumanAgent(name="HumanAgent")

# Create workflow
workflow = Workflow()
workflow.add_agent(support_agent)
workflow.add_agent(human_agent)

# Simulate customer queries
queries = [
    "How do I request a refund?",
    "Can I change my order?"
]

for query in queries:
    print(f"Customer Query: {query}")
    response = support_agent.handle_query(query)
    if "escalate" in response:
        print(f"Escalated to:
{human_agent.handle_escalation(query)}")
    else:
        print(f"Response: {response}\n")
```

Explanation:

1. **Automated Query Handling:**
   o The `CustomerSupportAgent` handles queries and escalates specific issues to the `HumanAgent`.
2. **Personalization:**
   o The agents can be extended to include features like remembering past interactions and applying sentiment analysis for more tailored responses.

10.3 Education and Training with LangGraph and LLMs

In education and training, LangGraph provides a versatile framework for creating intelligent tutors, assessment systems, and personalized learning assistants. By leveraging LLMs and multi-agent architectures, LangGraph enables real-time feedback, adaptive learning paths, and scalable education solutions.

Applications in Education:

1. **Intelligent Tutoring Systems:**
   o LangGraph can power AI-driven tutors that offer personalized lessons, quizzes, and feedback based on student performance.
2. **Automated Grading:**
   o Using NLP, LangGraph agents can assess open-ended student responses, essays, or short answers, providing detailed feedback and grading.
3. **Adaptive Learning Systems:**
   o Multi-agent systems can dynamically adapt learning content based on a student's progress, ensuring that each learner gets the most relevant educational material.

Example Code: Simple Adaptive Learning System

```
from langgraph import Agent
from transformers import pipeline

class AdaptiveLearningAgent(Agent):
    def __init__(self, name):
        super().__init__(name)
```

```python
        self.generator = pipeline("text-generation",
model="gpt2")

    def assess_student_response(self, response):
        # Simple grading logic based on predefined rubric
        if "correct answer" in response.lower():
            return "Correct answer, well done!"
        else:
            return "The answer is incorrect. Try reviewing
the lesson again."

    def provide_feedback(self, student_response):
        feedback =
self.assess_student_response(student_response)
        return feedback

# Create the agent
learning_agent = AdaptiveLearningAgent(name="LearningAgent")

# Simulate student responses
student_responses = [
    "The capital of France is Paris.",
    "The capital of France is London."
]

for response in student_responses:
    print(f"Student Response: {response}")
    print(f"Feedback:
{learning_agent.provide_feedback(response)}\n")
```

Explanation:

1. **Grading Mechanism:**
   o The agent assesses the student response using basic keywords and provides feedback based on predefined rules.
2. **Adaptive Learning:**
   o The agent can be further enhanced to adapt its responses based on the student's previous performance, guiding them through more complex material.

10.4 Gaming and Entertainment Applications

LangGraph is well-suited for the gaming and entertainment industries, where multi-agent systems can create dynamic, engaging, and interactive environments. LangGraph enables the development of intelligent game agents, virtual assistants, and content generation tools.

Applications in Gaming and Entertainment:

1. **Game AI:**
   o LangGraph agents can act as NPCs (non-player characters) in games, providing intelligent interactions and adapting to player behavior.
2. **Interactive Storytelling:**
   o LangGraph can be used to create dynamic narratives where agents react to player choices, generating personalized storylines.
3. **Content Generation:**
   o LangGraph can automate content creation, such as generating character dialogues, quests, and in-game items.

Example Code: Generating Dynamic Game Storylines

```
from langgraph import Agent
from transformers import pipeline

class StoryGenerationAgent(Agent):
    def __init__(self, name):
        super().__init__(name)
        self.generator = pipeline("text-generation",
model="gpt2")

    def generate_story(self, player_choice):
        prompt = f"Player chooses: {player_choice}\nStory:"
        story = self.generator(prompt, max_length=200,
num_return_sequences=1)
        return
story[0]['generated_text'].split("Story:")[1].strip()

# Create the agent
story_agent = StoryGenerationAgent(name="StoryAgent")

# Simulate player choices
choices = [
    "Explore the haunted castle",
    "Save the village from the dragon"
]
```

```
for choice in choices:
    print(f"Player Choice: {choice}")
    print(f"Generated Story:
{story_agent.generate_story(choice)}\n")
```

Explanation:

1. **Dynamic Story Creation:**
   - The agent generates a unique story based on the player's choice, leveraging a text-generation pipeline.
2. **Adaptive Content:**
   - The agent adapts to different choices, offering engaging narratives that evolve as the game progresses.

10.5 LangGraph in Finance and Risk Management

LangGraph can be applied in finance and risk management to enhance decision-making, analyze financial trends, and detect fraudulent activities. By combining LLMs with multi-agent systems, financial institutions can streamline operations and improve risk assessments.

Applications in Finance:

1. **Fraud Detection:**
   - LangGraph agents can analyze transaction data, detect anomalies, and flag potential fraudulent activities in real-time.
2. **Financial Forecasting:**
   - Multi-agent systems can process financial data, market trends, and news to make accurate predictions and help businesses plan accordingly.
3. **Risk Management:**
   - LangGraph can assist in assessing the financial risk of investments and provide real-time recommendations.

Example Code: Simple Fraud Detection System

```
from langgraph import Agent

class FraudDetectionAgent(Agent):
    def __init__(self, name):
        super().__init__(name)
```

```
        self.fraud_threshold = 10000   # Example threshold for
flagging fraud

    def analyze_transaction(self, transaction_amount,
transaction_type):
        if transaction_amount > self.fraud_threshold:
            return f"Suspicious activity detected!
Transaction of {transaction_amount} flagged for review."
        else:
            return f"Transaction of {transaction_amount} is
within normal parameters."

# Create agent
fraud_agent = FraudDetectionAgent(name="FraudAgent")

# Simulate transactions
transactions = [
    {"amount": 15000, "type": "withdrawal"},
    {"amount": 500, "type": "deposit"}
]

for transaction in transactions:
    print(f"Transaction Amount: {transaction['amount']}")
    print(f"Analysis:
{fraud_agent.analyze_transaction(transaction['amount'],
transaction['type'])}\n")
```

Explanation:

1. **Transaction Analysis:**
   o The agent flags transactions over a specified threshold (e.g.,
     $10,000) as suspicious.
2. **Risk Monitoring:**
   o LangGraph can be extended to monitor multiple financial
     metrics and provide real-time insights into risk factors.

10.6 LangGraph for Social Media and Content Generation

LangGraph plays a significant role in content generation for social media
platforms. Agents can automate content creation, provide insights into
trends, and interact with users in real-time.

Applications in Social Media:

1. **Content Creation:**
   o   LangGraph can generate articles, blog posts, or social media posts based on trending topics or user preferences.
2. **Sentiment Analysis:**
   o   Multi-agent systems can monitor social media posts, analyze sentiment, and generate reports on public opinion.
3. **Automated Engagement:**
   o   LangGraph agents can interact with users, respond to comments, and provide personalized responses.

Example Code: Social Media Content Generation

```
from langgraph import Agent
from transformers import pipeline

class SocialMediaAgent(Agent):
    def __init__(self, name):
        super().__init__(name)
        self.generator = pipeline("text-generation",
model="gpt2")

    def generate_post(self, topic):
        prompt = f"Write a social media post about {topic}."
        post = self.generator(prompt, max_length=100,
num_return_sequences=1)
        return post[0]['generated_text'].split("Write a
social media post about")[1].strip()

# Create the agent
social_agent = SocialMediaAgent(name="SocialMediaAgent")

# Simulate content creation
topics = ["Artificial Intelligence", "Environmental
Sustainability", "Future of Work"]
for topic in topics:
    print(f"Generated Post on {topic}:
{social_agent.generate_post(topic)}\n")
```

Explanation:

1. **Content Generation:**
   o   The agent creates unique social media posts based on the specified topic using a text-generation model.
2. **Personalization:**

- o This system can be extended to create content tailored to specific audiences or preferences.

10.7 Environmental Monitoring with LangGraph

LangGraph can be used in environmental monitoring by integrating with IoT devices, satellites, and weather stations. Agents can monitor environmental conditions in real-time, analyze trends, and provide actionable insights.

Applications in Environmental Monitoring:

1. **Air Quality Monitoring:**
   - o LangGraph agents can track air quality in various regions and provide real-time alerts when pollution levels exceed safe thresholds.
2. **Wildlife Tracking:**
   - o Multi-agent systems can analyze data from sensors to track wildlife movements, ensuring the protection of endangered species.
3. **Climate Change Analysis:**
   - o LangGraph agents can help researchers analyze climate patterns, track changes over time, and predict future trends.

Example Code: Monitoring Air Quality

```
from langgraph import Agent

class AirQualityMonitoringAgent(Agent):
    def __init__(self, name):
        super().__init__(name)
        self.threshold = 100  # Example threshold for air
quality index (AQI)

    def monitor_air_quality(self, aqi_value):
        if aqi_value > self.threshold:
            return f"Warning: Air quality is poor with AQI of
{aqi_value}. Stay indoors."
        else:
            return f"Air quality is safe with AQI of
{aqi_value}. Feel free to go outside."

# Create agent
```

```
air_quality_agent =
AirQualityMonitoringAgent(name="AirQualityAgent")

# Simulate monitoring data
aqi_values = [120, 80, 150, 90]
for aqi in aqi_values:
    print(f"Monitoring AQI: {aqi}")
    print(f"Response:
{air_quality_agent.monitor_air_quality(aqi)}\n")
```

Explanation:

1. **Monitoring Air Quality:**
   o The agent evaluates air quality based on an AQI value and provides alerts based on predefined thresholds.
2. **Real-Time Alerts:**
   o This system can be extended to provide real-time notifications and actionable insights for environmental protection.

10.8 Smart Cities: Leveraging LangGraph for Urban Management

LangGraph is highly applicable to smart city projects where multi-agent systems can manage infrastructure, traffic, utilities, and public services. By leveraging real-time data, LangGraph agents can make informed decisions to optimize city operations.

Applications in Smart Cities:

1. **Traffic Management:**
   o LangGraph can help manage traffic flow by dynamically adjusting traffic lights based on real-time data, reducing congestion and improving efficiency.
2. **Utility Management:**
   o Agents can monitor electricity, water, and gas consumption, optimizing usage and detecting issues such as leaks or outages.
3. **Public Safety:**
   o LangGraph agents can monitor security cameras, analyze data from emergency services, and respond to incidents in real-time.

Example Code: Traffic Management System

```python
from langgraph import Agent

class TrafficManagementAgent(Agent):
    def __init__(self, name):
        super().__init__(name)
        self.traffic_data = {}

    def update_traffic_data(self, intersection,
traffic_volume):
        self.traffic_data[intersection] = traffic_volume

    def optimize_traffic_lights(self, intersection):
        volume = self.traffic_data.get(intersection, 0)
        if volume > 80:
            return f"Increase red light duration at
{intersection} to reduce congestion."
        else:
            return f"Reduce red light duration at
{intersection} to improve traffic flow."

# Create agent
traffic_agent = TrafficManagementAgent(name="TrafficAgent")

# Simulate traffic data
traffic_volumes = {
    "Main St & 5th Ave": 95,
    "Broadway & 2nd St": 60,
    "Pine St & 10th Ave": 120
}

for intersection, volume in traffic_volumes.items():
    traffic_agent.update_traffic_data(intersection, volume)
    print(f"Traffic Data for {intersection}: {volume}")
    print(f"Optimization:
{traffic_agent.optimize_traffic_lights(intersection)}\n")
```

Explanation:

1. **Traffic Data Management:**
   o The agent collects traffic data and makes decisions based on volume to optimize traffic light timings.
2. **Real-Time Optimization:**
   o The system can dynamically adjust operations, making smart cities more efficient and responsive to real-time conditions.

10.9 Personalized Marketing Strategies Using LangGraph

LangGraph can be used to enhance personalized marketing efforts by analyzing customer data, predicting preferences, and offering targeted campaigns. Multi-agent systems can collaborate to deliver tailored marketing strategies, improving customer engagement and satisfaction.

Applications in Personalized Marketing:

1. **Customer Segmentation:**
   - LangGraph can segment customers based on purchasing history, behavior, and preferences, tailoring campaigns to each segment.
2. **Recommendation Systems:**
   - Using multi-agent systems, LangGraph can suggest personalized products or services to customers, increasing conversion rates.
3. **Targeted Advertising:**
   - LangGraph agents can create and deliver personalized advertisements across platforms based on user behavior.

**Example Code: Personalized

Marketing Campaign**

```
from langgraph import Agent

class MarketingAgent(Agent):
    def __init__(self, name):
        super().__init__(name)
        self.customer_data = {}

    def add_customer_data(self, customer_id, data):
        self.customer_data[customer_id] = data

    def generate_campaign(self, customer_id):
        customer = self.customer_data.get(customer_id, {})
        if customer:
            # Generate a personalized campaign based on
customer data
            if customer['interests'] == 'Tech':
                return f"Hi {customer['name']}, check out our
latest gadgets!"
            elif customer['interests'] == 'Fashion':
                return f"Hi {customer['name']}, update your
wardrobe with our new arrivals!"
```

```python
        else:
                return f"Hi {customer['name']}, discover our
latest collection!"
        return "Customer not found."

# Create agent
marketing_agent = MarketingAgent(name="MarketingAgent")

# Simulate customer data
customers = {
    "C1": {"name": "John", "interests": "Tech"},
    "C2": {"name": "Jane", "interests": "Fashion"}
}

for customer_id, data in customers.items():
    marketing_agent.add_customer_data(customer_id, data)
    print(f"Generated Campaign for {data['name']}:
{marketing_agent.generate_campaign(customer_id)}\n")
```

Explanation:

1. **Personalized Campaign Generation:**
   o The agent generates targeted marketing messages based on customer interests.
2. **Customer Engagement:**
   o By using LangGraph, businesses can provide relevant, timely marketing content that resonates with each customer.

10.10 Success Stories and Interviews: Industry Professionals on Using LangGraph

In this section, we'll explore interviews and success stories from industry professionals who have leveraged LangGraph to build innovative applications. These stories will provide you with insights into real-world use cases, the challenges faced, and how LangGraph provided solutions.

Success Story: Healthcare Provider Implementing LangGraph

A major healthcare provider implemented LangGraph to streamline patient communication through an AI-powered chatbot. This system reduced administrative workload, improved patient satisfaction, and provided valuable insights into patient needs.

10.11 Other Industry-Specific Applications

LangGraph's versatility extends beyond the industries we've covered. The framework can be applied to various niche industries such as logistics, supply chain management, legal services, and entertainment. By combining the power of LLMs and multi-agent systems, LangGraph provides solutions that optimize operations, enhance customer experiences, and drive innovation across different sectors.

In this chapter, we explored the wide-ranging applications of LangGraph across multiple industries. From healthcare and finance to gaming, education, and personalized marketing, LangGraph's powerful framework enables organizations to automate processes, enhance decision-making, and create intelligent, adaptive systems. The hands-on examples and real-world case studies provide concrete insights into how LangGraph can transform industries, making it a crucial tool for developing modern AI-driven solutions.

Chapter 11: Performance Optimization

In this chapter, we will delve into advanced performance optimization techniques that can be applied to LangGraph applications. As your LangGraph-based systems grow in complexity, optimizing performance becomes critical to ensuring efficiency, responsiveness, and scalability. We will explore parallelization, caching, the efficient use of large language models (LLMs), profiling, debugging, load testing, and advanced techniques like GPU acceleration to ensure that your LangGraph applications run at peak performance.

11.1 Parallelization and Distributed Computing in LangGraph

Parallelization and distributed computing are essential strategies for improving the performance of LangGraph applications, particularly when dealing with large datasets, multiple agents, or high-throughput workloads. By breaking down tasks into smaller, concurrent units, LangGraph can leverage multiple processors or machines to perform computations simultaneously, reducing the overall processing time.

Key Concepts:

1. **Parallelization:**
   o   This involves dividing a task into smaller, independent units that can be executed simultaneously across multiple processing units (cores, processors, or nodes).
2. **Distributed Computing:**
   o   Distributed computing spreads tasks across multiple machines or nodes. This can be particularly useful when the workload exceeds the capacity of a single machine.

Applications in LangGraph:

- **Multi-Agent Systems:** Distribute the tasks and processing required for each agent across multiple nodes.

- **Data-Intensive Workloads:** Large-scale data processing, such as analyzing massive amounts of user interaction data, can benefit from parallelization.
- **Training Models:** In deep learning, especially for LLMs, training can be parallelized to speed up model training using multiple GPUs.

Example: Parallelizing a Data Processing Task with LangGraph

In this example, we will use Python's `concurrent.futures` library to run parallel tasks in LangGraph. We will simulate a scenario where multiple agents process large datasets concurrently.

```python
import concurrent.futures
import time
from langgraph import Agent

# Sample agent that simulates data processing
class DataProcessingAgent(Agent):
    def process_data(self, data_chunk):
        time.sleep(2)  # Simulate time-consuming task
        return f"Processed: {data_chunk}"

# Function to process data in parallel
def process_in_parallel(data_chunks):
    with concurrent.futures.ThreadPoolExecutor() as executor:
        results = executor.map(agent.process_data,
data_chunks)
    return list(results)

# Initialize agent
agent = DataProcessingAgent(name="DataProcessor")

# Example data chunks
data_chunks = ["data_1", "data_2", "data_3", "data_4"]

# Process data in parallel
start_time = time.time()
processed_data = process_in_parallel(data_chunks)
end_time = time.time()

# Display results
for result in processed_data:
    print(result)

print(f"Processing time with parallelization: {end_time -
start_time:.2f} seconds")
```

Explanation:

- **ThreadPoolExecutor:** We used `ThreadPoolExecutor` from `concurrent.futures` to parallelize the data processing. Each data chunk is processed concurrently, reducing the overall processing time.
- **Efficiency:** By using threads, we allow the LangGraph agents to work in parallel, significantly speeding up the process when dealing with multiple data chunks.

Considerations:

- Ensure that tasks are independent and can be executed in parallel.
- For CPU-bound tasks, Python's `multiprocessing` library can be used for true parallelism, as threads in Python are limited by the Global Interpreter Lock (GIL).

11.2 Caching and Memoization for Faster Performance

Caching and memoization are powerful techniques for improving performance by storing results of expensive function calls and reusing them when the same inputs occur again. These techniques can significantly reduce redundant calculations, making your LangGraph applications faster and more efficient.

1. **Caching:**
   o Stores the results of function calls, database queries, or computations to avoid re-executing expensive operations.
2. **Memoization:**
   o A specific form of caching that stores results of function calls based on input arguments, so future calls with the same inputs can return the cached result directly.

Applications in LangGraph:

- **LLM Response Caching:** Cache responses generated by language models for commonly asked queries.
- **Agent State Memoization:** Cache the state of agents that are repeatedly invoked with the same parameters.
- **Data Query Optimization:** Cache database query results to prevent repeated database access.

Example Code: Memoization with a Simple Agent

```python
from functools import lru_cache
import time

# Simple agent to process user requests
class QueryAgent:
    @lru_cache(maxsize=128)  # Cache the results of this
method
    def process_query(self, query):
        time.sleep(2)  # Simulate a time-consuming operation
        return f"Processed query: {query}"

# Instantiate the agent
agent = QueryAgent()

# Simulate repeated queries
queries = ["How does LangGraph work?", "What is LLM?", "How
does LangGraph work?"]

start_time = time.time()
for query in queries:
    print(agent.process_query(query))

end_time = time.time()
print(f"Time taken with memoization: {end_time -
start_time:.2f} seconds")
```

Explanation:

- **Memoization using `lru_cache`:** The `process_query` method uses Python's `functools.lru_cache` decorator to cache the results of function calls.
- **Performance Improvement:** The third query, which is a repeat of the first, is processed faster because its result is returned from the cache rather than recomputing the response.

Considerations:

- Choose appropriate cache sizes (`maxsize`) to balance memory usage and performance.
- For large applications, use a distributed caching solution like Redis.

11.3 Efficient Use of LLMs in LangGraph Applications

Large Language Models (LLMs) are resource-intensive and can quickly become bottlenecks if not used efficiently. Optimizing the use of LLMs in LangGraph involves several strategies, such as batching requests, limiting token usage, and leveraging model fine-tuning for specific tasks.

Key Strategies:

1. **Batching Requests:**
   - Instead of sending individual requests to the LLM, batch multiple queries together to reduce overhead and make better use of available compute resources.
2. **Model Quantization:**
   - Use model quantization techniques to reduce the size of the model, making it more memory-efficient while maintaining a good level of accuracy.
3. **Token Limit Management:**
   - Limit the number of tokens generated by LLMs in a single request to reduce processing time and resource usage.
4. **Model Fine-Tuning:**
   - Fine-tune the LLM on specific datasets to improve performance and reduce the need for large, general-purpose models.

Example: Efficient Batch Processing of Queries with LLMs

```
from transformers import pipeline

# Initialize text generation pipeline
generator = pipeline("text-generation", model="gpt2")

# Batch of queries
queries = [
    "What is the weather forecast for today?",
    "Explain the process of photosynthesis.",
    "How does a LangGraph system work?"
]

# Efficient batch processing
results = generator(queries, max_length=100)

# Display results
for query, result in zip(queries, results):
    print(f"Query: {query}")
    print(f"Response: {result['generated_text']}\n")
```

Explanation:

- **Batching Queries:** Instead of processing each query individually, the generator processes all queries in a single batch, making better use of the LLM's capabilities.

Considerations:

- Batch sizes should be chosen to balance between performance gains and memory consumption.
- Monitor the impact of batching on LLM output quality, as context between queries may differ.

11.4 Profiling and Debugging LangGraph Applications

Profiling and debugging are essential for identifying performance bottlenecks and ensuring that LangGraph applications function as expected. Profiling helps monitor resource usage (e.g., CPU, memory) while debugging ensures the correctness of logic in agents.

Tools for Profiling:

1. **cProfile (Python's built-in profiler):**
   - Provides a detailed report on how long each function takes to execute, helping identify slow operations.
2. **Memory Profiler:**
   - Tracks memory usage, allowing you to optimize memory consumption in large-scale applications.
3. **Line Profiler:**
   - Provides line-by-line analysis of code execution time, which is useful for optimizing specific parts of a function.

Example Code: Using cProfile for Profiling

```
import cProfile

def slow_function():
    result = 0
    for i in range(1000000):
        result += i
    return result
```

```
# Profile the slow function
cProfile.run('slow_function()')
```

Explanation:

- **cProfile Output:** The profiler will provide a detailed breakdown of how much time each function took during execution.

Considerations:

- Use profiling tools during development to identify performance bottlenecks early.
- For production environments, use logging-based monitoring tools to track long-term performance trends.

11.5 Load Testing and Performance Benchmarks

Load testing and benchmarking are critical to assess how your LangGraph applications will perform under real-world conditions, especially when scaling up to handle many users or large datasets.

Key Steps for Load Testing:

1. **Simulate Multiple Users:**
   o Use tools like Apache JMeter or Locust to simulate multiple users interacting with your LangGraph-based systems simultaneously.
2. **Measure Latency and Throughput:**
   o Track how long it takes for your application to respond to requests (latency) and how many requests it can handle per second (throughput).
3. **Monitor System Resources:**
   o While load testing, monitor the system's CPU, memory, and network usage to ensure that the system remains stable under high load.

Example Code: Load Testing with Locust

```
from locust import HttpUser, task, between
```

```
class LangGraphUser(HttpUser):
    wait_time = between(1, 5)

    @task
    def query_agent(self):
        self.client.post("/query", json={"query": "What is
LangGraph?"})

# To run this, use the command: locust -f locustfile.py
```

Explanation:

- **Locust User Simulation:** Simulates a user interacting with a LangGraph system, sending queries to an endpoint.
- **Testing Under Load:** You can specify how many users to simulate and how frequently they send requests to gauge performance.

11.6 Advanced Optimization Techniques: GPU Acceleration and Performance Libraries

GPU acceleration is particularly beneficial for computationally intensive tasks such as training models, handling large datasets, or processing complex tasks in LangGraph. Using GPUs can significantly speed up processing times compared to CPUs, especially when working with large language models.

Techniques for GPU Acceleration:

1. **TensorFlow and PyTorch for Model Training:**
   o Both frameworks offer GPU support, which can accelerate deep learning tasks.
2. **CUDA Programming:**
   o If you're implementing custom algorithms, use NVIDIA's CUDA platform to harness GPU power for parallel computations.

Libraries for Performance Optimization:

1. **CuPy:**
   o A GPU-accelerated array library, similar to NumPy, that allows you to perform computations on GPUs.
2. **Dask:**

o A parallel computing framework that allows you to scale your applications across multiple CPUs and GPUs.

Example: Using PyTorch with GPU Acceleration

```
import torch

# Check if GPU is available
device = torch.device('cuda' if torch.cuda.is_available()
else 'cpu')

# Example tensor operation on GPU
tensor = torch.randn(1000, 1000).to(device)
result = tensor * tensor  # Perform computation on GPU

print(result)
```

Explanation:

- **CUDA with PyTorch:** The tensor operation is performed on the GPU if available, greatly speeding up the computation compared to using the CPU.

Considerations:

- Make sure your hardware supports GPU acceleration and install the necessary libraries (e.g., CUDA, cuDNN).
- Monitor the GPU's memory usage to avoid running out of resources when processing large datasets or training models.

In this chapter, we explored a range of performance optimization techniques for LangGraph applications. We covered parallelization, caching, efficient use of LLMs, profiling, debugging, load testing, and GPU acceleration. By applying these techniques, you can significantly enhance the performance, scalability, and responsiveness of your LangGraph-based systems, ensuring they meet the demands of real-world applications.

Chapter 12: Scalability and Reliability

As LangGraph applications grow in complexity and scope, ensuring that they remain performant, reliable, and available is paramount. This chapter will explore key concepts in scaling LangGraph applications, implementing fault tolerance and redundancy, managing system performance, and integrating LangGraph with cloud infrastructures. By focusing on scalability and reliability, you will be able to build LangGraph-based systems that can handle increasing loads and maintain uptime even under adverse conditions.

12.1 Scaling LangGraph Applications for High Availability

Scaling LangGraph applications is essential to ensure that they can handle growing numbers of users, larger datasets, and more complex tasks. High availability (HA) is a critical aspect of scalability, ensuring that your application remains operational with minimal downtime. The primary goal is to provide continuous service, even during failures or system maintenance.

Key Concepts:

1. **Horizontal Scaling:**
   - Adding more servers or instances to distribute the load. This is often done by adding additional nodes to a cluster.
2. **Vertical Scaling:**
   - Increasing the capacity of a single machine (e.g., upgrading CPU, memory, or storage).
3. **Load Balancing:**
   - Distributing incoming traffic or tasks across multiple servers or services to prevent any single server from becoming a bottleneck.

Best Practices for Scaling LangGraph Applications:

- **Microservices Architecture:** Break down the LangGraph application into smaller, independently scalable services. This enables you to scale only the parts of the system that need additional resources.

- **Auto-scaling:** Use cloud platforms with auto-scaling capabilities to automatically adjust resources based on real-time traffic or system load.
- **Geographical Distribution:** For global applications, deploy LangGraph across multiple data centers worldwide to reduce latency and ensure high availability.

Example: Scaling a LangGraph Application with Auto-Scaling on AWS

Imagine you are deploying LangGraph on AWS and need to ensure that it can scale based on demand. You can use **AWS Auto Scaling** and **Elastic Load Balancer (ELB)** to distribute the traffic.

```
# AWS Elastic Load Balancer Configuration
Resources:
  LangGraphELB:
    Type: AWS::ElasticLoadBalancingV2::LoadBalancer
    Properties:
      Name: LangGraph-ELB
      Subnets:
        - subnet-abc123
        - subnet-def456
      SecurityGroups:
        - sg-0123456789abcdef0
      LoadBalancerAttributes:
        - Key: idle_timeout.timeout_seconds
          Value: '60'

# AWS Auto Scaling Configuration
Resources:
  LangGraphAutoScalingGroup:
    Type: AWS::AutoScaling::AutoScalingGroup
    Properties:
      DesiredCapacity: 3
      MinSize: 2
      MaxSize: 10
      LaunchConfigurationName: !Ref LangGraphLaunchConfig
      LoadBalancerNames:
        - Ref: LangGraphELB
      AvailabilityZones:
        - us-east-1a
        - us-east-1b
```

Explanation:

- The above YAML configuration sets up an Elastic Load Balancer (ELB) to distribute traffic across multiple EC2 instances.

- The Auto Scaling group is configured to automatically adjust the number of instances between 2 and 10 based on the current load.

12.2 Fault Tolerance, Redundancy, and Error Handling

Fault tolerance and redundancy are essential components of ensuring that LangGraph applications remain reliable, even in the face of hardware failures or unexpected system crashes. These strategies allow your system to recover quickly, maintain availability, and minimize downtime.

Key Concepts:

1. **Redundancy:**
   - Redundancy involves having backup components (e.g., duplicate servers, data replication) that can take over if the primary component fails.
2. **Failover:**
   - Failover is the process of automatically switching to a backup system when the primary system fails. This is crucial for minimizing downtime in a distributed system.
3. **Error Handling:**
   - Error handling involves gracefully handling exceptions or failures, ensuring that the system continues to operate as expected, even when unexpected events occur.

Strategies for Fault Tolerance and Redundancy:

- **Data Replication:** Replicate data across multiple databases or data centers to ensure that it is still accessible if one server or location goes down.
- **Graceful Degradation:** When a system component fails, the system should continue to function at a reduced capacity rather than completely fail.
- **Retry Logic:** Implement retry mechanisms in agents to handle transient failures like network interruptions.

Example: Implementing Retry Logic with LangGraph Agents

```
import time
import random
```

```
class FaultTolerantAgent:
    def __init__(self, name):
        self.name = name

    def process_data(self, data):
        # Simulate intermittent failure
        if random.random() < 0.3:   # 30% chance of failure
            raise Exception("Temporary failure")

        return f"Processed data: {data}"

    def process_with_retry(self, data, retries=3, delay=2):
        attempt = 0
        while attempt < retries:
            try:
                return self.process_data(data)
            except Exception as e:
                attempt += 1
                print(f"Error: {e}. Retrying... (Attempt
{attempt}/{retries})")
                time.sleep(delay)
        return "Failed to process data after multiple
attempts."

# Create agent
agent = FaultTolerantAgent(name="FaultTolerantAgent")

# Simulate processing data
data = "Important data"
response = agent.process_with_retry(data)
print(response)
```

Explanation:

- The `process_with_retry` method attempts to process the data up to 3 times if an error occurs, with a 2-second delay between retries. This ensures that transient issues do not result in a complete failure.

12.3 Monitoring and Management of LangGraph Systems

Monitoring and management are critical for maintaining the performance, availability, and health of LangGraph applications. By continuously monitoring system metrics, you can identify issues before they impact users and ensure smooth operation.

Key Monitoring Metrics:

- **System Metrics:** CPU, memory usage, disk I/O, and network traffic.
- **Application Metrics:** Response time, error rate, request throughput, and agent activity.
- **Resource Utilization:** Track how effectively resources such as CPU, GPU, and memory are being used.

Best Practices for Monitoring LangGraph Systems:

- **Centralized Logging:** Use centralized logging systems like ELK Stack (Elasticsearch, Logstash, Kibana) to collect logs from multiple components and agents.
- **Alerting:** Set up automated alerts to notify administrators when a metric crosses a threshold (e.g., CPU usage > 80%).
- **Automated Health Checks:** Implement automated health checks that periodically check the availability and health of system components.

Example: Setting Up CloudWatch for Monitoring on AWS

You can use AWS CloudWatch to monitor LangGraph's EC2 instances and set up alarms for resource utilization.

```
Resources:
  LangGraphCPUAlarm:
    Type: AWS::CloudWatch::Alarm
    Properties:
      MetricName: CPUUtilization
      Namespace: AWS/EC2
      Statistic: Average
      Period: 300
      Threshold: 80
      ComparisonOperator: GreaterThanThreshold
      EvaluationPeriods: 1
      AlarmActions:
        - Ref: AutoScalingPolicy
```

Explanation:

- This CloudWatch alarm triggers when the CPU usage exceeds 80% for a specified period, which can trigger scaling actions or notifications.

12.4 Cloud Infrastructure for LangGraph Applications

Cloud platforms provide scalability, flexibility, and reliability, making them ideal for deploying LangGraph applications. Using cloud infrastructure, you can ensure high availability, redundancy, and seamless scaling.

Key Cloud Platforms:

- **Amazon Web Services (AWS):** Provides tools like EC2, S3, RDS, and Lambda for building scalable and reliable LangGraph applications.
- **Google Cloud Platform (GCP):** Offers Compute Engine, Kubernetes Engine, and BigQuery to support large-scale deployments of LangGraph.
- **Microsoft Azure:** Offers Azure Functions, Virtual Machines, and Blob Storage for scalable LangGraph applications.

Advantages of Cloud for LangGraph:

- **Scalability:** Automatically scale your infrastructure based on demand.
- **Cost Efficiency:** Pay only for the resources you use, reducing infrastructure costs.
- **Global Reach:** Deploy LangGraph across multiple regions to reduce latency and improve user experience.

12.5 Horizontal vs. Vertical Scaling: Best Practices in LangGraph

Scaling your LangGraph application requires making decisions between horizontal and vertical scaling, depending on the needs and constraints of your system.

Horizontal Scaling:

- Adding more instances of your application to distribute the load.
- Best suited for applications that need to handle a large number of concurrent users or tasks.

Vertical Scaling:

- Upgrading the existing infrastructure (e.g., adding more CPU, memory) of a single server.
- Best for applications that are less distributed and require more resources per instance.

Best Practices:

- Start with **horizontal scaling** for LangGraph applications, especially when handling large numbers of concurrent agents.
- Use **vertical scaling** for single components or microservices that require high computational resources (e.g., LLMs).

12.6 Real-World Example: Scaling LangGraph for Global Deployment

Let's consider a scenario where LangGraph is deployed for a global customer service platform. The platform needs to handle requests from millions of users across different regions.

Scaling Strategy:

1. **Region-Specific Instances:** Deploy LangGraph in multiple AWS regions (e.g., us-east-1, eu-west-1) to reduce latency.
2. **Elastic Load Balancing:** Use ELB to distribute traffic across instances in different regions.
3. **Auto-Scaling Groups:** Automatically scale the number of instances based on demand.
4. **Database Replication:** Use AWS RDS with cross-region replication to ensure fast data access and redundancy.

12.7 Integration with Other Technologies: IoT Devices, Blockchain, and Cloud Platforms

LangGraph can integrate with a variety of other technologies, expanding its capabilities and use cases. These integrations can be used to create more robust and innovative solutions.

1. **IoT Devices:**
   - LangGraph can work with IoT devices to process real-time data, such as environmental monitoring, smart home systems, and industrial IoT.
2. **Blockchain:**
   - LangGraph can integrate with blockchain to manage data integrity, provide secure transactions, or implement decentralized decision-making systems.
3. **Cloud Platforms:**
   - LangGraph can seamlessly integrate with cloud services (e.g., AWS, Azure, GCP) for storage, computation, and scaling.

Example: Integrating LangGraph with an IoT Device

```python
from langgraph import Agent
import random

class IoTIntegrationAgent(Agent):
    def __init__(self, name):
        super().__init__(name)

    def process_iot_data(self, data):
        # Simulate processing data from IoT device
        if data["temperature"] > 75:
            return "Warning: Temperature is too high!"
        else:
            return "Temperature is within normal range."

# Simulate IoT data
iot_data = {"temperature": random.randint(60, 85)}

# Create agent and process data
iot_agent = IoTIntegrationAgent(name="IoTAgent")
print(iot_agent.process_iot_data(iot_data))
```

Explanation:

- This example demonstrates how LangGraph can integrate with IoT data, processing real-time data such as temperature and triggering actions based on predefined conditions.

In this chapter, we explored various aspects of scalability and reliability for LangGraph applications. We discussed techniques for scaling LangGraph to handle increased load, implementing fault tolerance, and ensuring high availability. Additionally, we covered best practices for monitoring and managing LangGraph systems, integrating with cloud infrastructure, and leveraging horizontal and vertical scaling strategies. Finally, we provided real-world examples to demonstrate how to scale LangGraph for global deployments and integrate it with other technologies such as IoT and blockchain.

By implementing the techniques and strategies covered in this chapter, you can build LangGraph applications that are not only efficient but also robust, fault-tolerant, and scalable, ready to handle real-world challenges.

Chapter 12: Scalability and Reliability

As LangGraph applications grow in complexity and scope, ensuring that they remain performant, reliable, and available is paramount. This chapter will explore key concepts in scaling LangGraph applications, implementing fault tolerance and redundancy, managing system performance, and integrating LangGraph with cloud infrastructures. By focusing on scalability and reliability, you will be able to build LangGraph-based systems that can handle increasing loads and maintain uptime even under adverse conditions.

12.1 Scaling LangGraph Applications for High Availability

Scaling LangGraph applications is essential to ensure that they can handle growing numbers of users, larger datasets, and more complex tasks. High availability (HA) is a critical aspect of scalability, ensuring that your application remains operational with minimal downtime. The primary goal is to provide continuous service, even during failures or system maintenance.

Key Concepts:

1. **Horizontal Scaling:**
   - Adding more servers or instances to distribute the load. This is often done by adding additional nodes to a cluster.
2. **Vertical Scaling:**
   - Increasing the capacity of a single machine (e.g., upgrading CPU, memory, or storage).
3. **Load Balancing:**
   - Distributing incoming traffic or tasks across multiple servers or services to prevent any single server from becoming a bottleneck.

Best Practices for Scaling LangGraph Applications:

- **Microservices Architecture:** Break down the LangGraph application into smaller, independently scalable services. This enables you to scale only the parts of the system that need additional resources.

- **Auto-scaling:** Use cloud platforms with auto-scaling capabilities to automatically adjust resources based on real-time traffic or system load.
- **Geographical Distribution:** For global applications, deploy LangGraph across multiple data centers worldwide to reduce latency and ensure high availability.

Example: Scaling a LangGraph Application with Auto-Scaling on AWS

Imagine you are deploying LangGraph on AWS and need to ensure that it can scale based on demand. You can use **AWS Auto Scaling** and **Elastic Load Balancer (ELB)** to distribute the traffic.

```
# AWS Elastic Load Balancer Configuration
Resources:
  LangGraphELB:
    Type: AWS::ElasticLoadBalancingV2::LoadBalancer
    Properties:
      Name: LangGraph-ELB
      Subnets:
        - subnet-abc123
        - subnet-def456
      SecurityGroups:
        - sg-0123456789abcdef0
      LoadBalancerAttributes:
        - Key: idle_timeout.timeout_seconds
          Value: '60'

# AWS Auto Scaling Configuration
Resources:
  LangGraphAutoScalingGroup:
    Type: AWS::AutoScaling::AutoScalingGroup
    Properties:
      DesiredCapacity: 3
      MinSize: 2
      MaxSize: 10
      LaunchConfigurationName: !Ref LangGraphLaunchConfig
      LoadBalancerNames:
        - Ref: LangGraphELB
      AvailabilityZones:
        - us-east-1a
        - us-east-1b
```

Explanation:

- The above YAML configuration sets up an Elastic Load Balancer (ELB) to distribute traffic across multiple EC2 instances.

- The Auto Scaling group is configured to automatically adjust the number of instances between 2 and 10 based on the current load.

12.2 Fault Tolerance, Redundancy, and Error Handling

Fault tolerance and redundancy are essential components of ensuring that LangGraph applications remain reliable, even in the face of hardware failures or unexpected system crashes. These strategies allow your system to recover quickly, maintain availability, and minimize downtime.

Key Concepts:

1. **Redundancy:**
   - Redundancy involves having backup components (e.g., duplicate servers, data replication) that can take over if the primary component fails.
2. **Failover:**
   - Failover is the process of automatically switching to a backup system when the primary system fails. This is crucial for minimizing downtime in a distributed system.
3. **Error Handling:**
   - Error handling involves gracefully handling exceptions or failures, ensuring that the system continues to operate as expected, even when unexpected events occur.

Strategies for Fault Tolerance and Redundancy:

- **Data Replication:** Replicate data across multiple databases or data centers to ensure that it is still accessible if one server or location goes down.
- **Graceful Degradation:** When a system component fails, the system should continue to function at a reduced capacity rather than completely fail.
- **Retry Logic:** Implement retry mechanisms in agents to handle transient failures like network interruptions.

Example: Implementing Retry Logic with LangGraph Agents

```
import time
import random
```

```python
class FaultTolerantAgent:
    def __init__(self, name):
        self.name = name

    def process_data(self, data):
        # Simulate intermittent failure
        if random.random() < 0.3:  # 30% chance of failure
            raise Exception("Temporary failure')

        return f"Processed data: {data}"

    def process_with_retry(self, data, retries=3, delay=2):
        attempt = 0
        while attempt < retries:
            try:
                return self.process_data(data)
            except Exception as e:
                attempt += 1
                print(f"Error: {e}. Retrying... (Attempt
{attempt}/{retries})")
                time.sleep(delay)
        return "Failed to process data after multiple
attempts."

# Create agent
agent = FaultTolerantAgent(name="FaultTolerantAgent")

# Simulate processing data
data = "Important data"
response = agent.process_with_retry(data)
print(response)
```

Explanation:

- The `process_with_retry` method attempts to process the data up to
  3 times if an error occurs, with a 2-second delay between retries. This
  ensures that transient issues do not result in a complete failure.

12.3 Monitoring and Management of LangGraph Systems

Monitoring and management are critical for maintaining the performance,
availability, and health of LangGraph applications. By continuously
monitoring system metrics, you can identify issues before they impact users
and ensure smooth operation.

Key Monitoring Metrics:

- **System Metrics:** CPU, memory usage, disk I/O, and network traffic.
- **Application Metrics:** Response time, error rate, request throughput, and agent activity.
- **Resource Utilization:** Track how effectively resources such as CPU, GPU, and memory are being used.

Best Practices for Monitoring LangGraph Systems:

- **Centralized Logging:** Use centralized logging systems like ELK Stack (Elasticsearch, Logstash, Kibana) to collect logs from multiple components and agents.
- **Alerting:** Set up automated alerts to notify administrators when a metric crosses a threshold (e.g., CPU usage > 80%).
- **Automated Health Checks:** Implement automated health checks that periodically check the availability and health of system components.

Example: Setting Up CloudWatch for Monitoring on AWS

You can use AWS CloudWatch to monitor LangGraph's EC2 instances and set up alarms for resource utilization.

```
Resources:
  LangGraphCPUAlarm:
    Type: AWS::CloudWatch::Alarm
    Properties:
      MetricName: CPUUtilization
      Namespace: AWS/EC2
      Statistic: Average
      Period: 300
      Threshold: 80
      ComparisonOperator: GreaterThanThreshold
      EvaluationPeriods: 1
      AlarmActions:
        - Ref: AutoScalingPolicy
```

Explanation:

- This CloudWatch alarm triggers when the CPU usage exceeds 80% for a specified period, which can trigger scaling actions or notifications.

12.4 Cloud Infrastructure for LangGraph Applications

Cloud platforms provide scalability, flexibility, and reliability, making them ideal for deploying LangGraph applications. Using cloud infrastructure, you can ensure high availability, redundancy, and seamless scaling.

Key Cloud Platforms:

- **Amazon Web Services (AWS):** Provides tools like EC2, S3, RDS, and Lambda for building scalable and reliable LangGraph applications.
- **Google Cloud Platform (GCP):** Offers Compute Engine, Kubernetes Engine, and BigQuery to support large-scale deployments of LangGraph.
- **Microsoft Azure:** Offers Azure Functions, Virtual Machines, and Blob Storage for scalable LangGraph applications.

Advantages of Cloud for LangGraph:

- **Scalability:** Automatically scale your infrastructure based on demand.
- **Cost Efficiency:** Pay only for the resources you use, reducing infrastructure costs.
- **Global Reach:** Deploy LangGraph across multiple regions to reduce latency and improve user experience.

12.5 Horizontal vs. Vertical Scaling: Best Practices in LangGraph

Scaling your LangGraph application requires making decisions between horizontal and vertical scaling, depending on the needs and constraints of your system.

Horizontal Scaling:

- Adding more instances of your application to distribute the load.
- Best suited for applications that need to handle a large number of concurrent users or tasks.

Vertical Scaling:

- Upgrading the existing infrastructure (e.g., adding more CPU, memory) of a single server.
- Best for applications that are less distributed and require more resources per instance.

Best Practices:

- Start with **horizontal scaling** for LangGraph applications, especially when handling large numbers of concurrent agents.
- Use **vertical scaling** for single components or microservices that require high computational resources (e.g., LLMs).

12.6 Real-World Example: Scaling LangGraph for Global Deployment

Let's consider a scenario where LangGraph is deployed for a global customer service platform. The platform needs to handle requests from millions of users across different regions.

Scaling Strategy:

1. **Region-Specific Instances:** Deploy LangGraph in multiple AWS regions (e.g., us-east-1, eu-west-1) to reduce latency.
2. **Elastic Load Balancing:** Use ELB to distribute traffic across instances in different regions.
3. **Auto-Scaling Groups:** Automatically scale the number of instances based on demand.
4. **Database Replication:** Use AWS RDS with cross-region replication to ensure fast data access and redundancy.

12.7 Integration with Other Technologies: IoT Devices, Blockchain, and Cloud Platforms

LangGraph can integrate with a variety of other technologies, expanding its capabilities and use cases. These integrations can be used to create more robust and innovative solutions.

1. **IoT Devices:**
   o LangGraph can work with IoT devices to process real-time data, such as environmental monitoring, smart home systems, and industrial IoT.
2. **Blockchain:**
   o LangGraph can integrate with blockchain to manage data integrity, provide secure transactions, or implement decentralized decision-making systems.
3. **Cloud Platforms:**
   o LangGraph can seamlessly integrate with cloud services (e.g., AWS, Azure, GCP) for storage, computation, and scaling.

Example: Integrating LangGraph with an IoT Device

```
from langgraph import Agent
import random

class IoTIntegrationAgent(Agent):
    def __init__(self, name):
        super().__init__(name)

    def process_iot_data(self, data):
        # Simulate processing data from IoT device
        if data["temperature"] > 75:
            return "Warning: Temperature is too high!"
        else:
            return "Temperature is within normal range."

# Simulate IoT data
iot_data = {"temperature": random.randint(60, 85)}

# Create agent and process data
iot_agent = IoTIntegrationAgent(name="IoTAgent")
print(iot_agent.process_iot_data(iot_data))
```

Explanation:

- This example demonstrates how LangGraph can integrate with IoT data, processing real-time data such as temperature and triggering actions based on predefined conditions.

In this chapter, we explored various aspects of scalability and reliability for LangGraph applications. We discussed techniques for scaling LangGraph to handle increased load, implementing fault tolerance, and ensuring high availability. Additionally, we covered best practices for monitoring and managing LangGraph systems, integrating with cloud infrastructure, and leveraging horizontal and vertical scaling strategies. Finally, we provided real-world examples to demonstrate how to scale LangGraph for global deployments and integrate it with other technologies such as IoT and blockchain.

By implementing the techniques and strategies covered in this chapter, you can build LangGraph applications that are not only efficient but also robust, fault-tolerant, and scalable, ready to handle real-world challenges.

Chapter 13: Security, Privacy, and Ethics

As AI technologies continue to evolve and become more integrated into various industries, security, privacy, and ethical considerations are increasingly important. LangGraph applications, particularly those that incorporate multi-agent systems and large language models (LLMs), are no exception. In this chapter, we will explore how to address data privacy, security best practices, and ethical challenges in LangGraph applications. We will also dive into regulatory compliance, bias mitigation techniques, and how to secure agent communication to ensure your AI systems are both responsible and reliable.

13.1 Data Privacy and Protection in LangGraph Applications

Data privacy is a cornerstone of responsible AI development. When building LangGraph applications, particularly those that handle sensitive information (e.g., healthcare data, financial information, personal user data), it's essential to implement robust privacy protection measures.

Key Principles of Data Privacy:

1. **Data Minimization:**
   - Collect only the data necessary for the task at hand. Avoid collecting sensitive information unless absolutely required.
2. **Encryption:**
   - Use encryption both at rest (when stored) and in transit (when being transferred over networks) to protect data from unauthorized access.
3. **Access Control:**
   - Implement strict access control policies to ensure that only authorized agents or users can access sensitive data. This includes using role-based access control (RBAC).
4. **Anonymization and Pseudonymization:**
   - For certain applications, especially those in healthcare or finance, anonymizing or pseudonymizing personal data can reduce risks while still allowing for meaningful analysis.

Example: Encrypting Data in LangGraph with Python

```python
from cryptography.fernet import Fernet

# Generate a key for encryption
key = Fernet.generate_key()
cipher_suite = Fernet(key)

# Function to encrypt data
def encrypt_data(data):
    return cipher_suite.encrypt(data.encode('utf-8'))

# Function to decrypt data
def decrypt_data(encrypted_data):
    return cipher_suite.decrypt(encrypted_data).decode('utf-8')

# Sample data
user_data = "Sensitive User Information"

# Encrypt and decrypt the data
encrypted = encrypt_data(user_data)
decrypted = decrypt_data(encrypted)

print(f"Encrypted Data: {encrypted}")
print(f"Decrypted Data: {decrypted}")
```

Explanation:

- This code demonstrates how to use encryption with the `cryptography` library in Python. Data is encrypted and can only be decrypted with the correct key, ensuring that sensitive information is protected during storage or transmission.

Considerations:

- For real-world applications, key management is crucial. Use a secure key management system (e.g., AWS KMS, Azure Key Vault) to handle encryption keys.

13.2 Security Best Practices in Multi-Agent Systems

Multi-agent systems (MAS), such as those built with LangGraph, are inherently complex and require careful security considerations. These systems involve multiple agents that may interact with each other, communicate over networks, and access shared resources. Securing these interactions is vital to prevent unauthorized access and data leaks.

Key Security Best Practices:

1. **Secure Agent Communication:**
   - Use encryption protocols (e.g., TLS/SSL) for communication between agents to prevent interception and tampering.
2. **Authentication and Authorization:**
   - Implement strong authentication mechanisms (e.g., OAuth, JWT) to ensure only authorized agents can communicate with each other.
   - Use fine-grained authorization rules to limit access to sensitive data or system components.
3. **Audit Logs:**
   - Keep detailed audit logs of all agent interactions, including data access and decision-making processes, to detect unauthorized access or potential vulnerabilities.

Example: Securing Communication Between Agents

```python
import ssl
import socket

# Create a secure context
context = ssl.create_default_context(ssl.Purpose.CLIENT_AUTH)

# Define a simple server that communicates securely with
agents
def secure_server():
    with socket.socket(socket.AF_INET, socket.SOCK_STREAM) as sock:
        sock.bind(('localhost', 65432))
        sock.listen(5)
        with context.wrap_socket(sock, server_side=True) as secure_sock:
            print("Server listening for connections...")
            conn, addr = secure_sock.accept()
            with conn:
                print(f"Connected by {addr}")
                data = conn.recv(1024)
                conn.sendall(data)

# Run the secure server
secure_server()
```

Explanation:

- This example demonstrates how to create a secure communication channel between agents using SSL/TLS encryption. The server listens for incoming connections and ensures that the communication is encrypted.

13.3 Ethical AI: Minimizing Bias, Ensuring Fairness

AI and machine learning systems, including LangGraph applications, can inadvertently perpetuate or amplify biases if not properly designed. Addressing bias and ensuring fairness is critical for developing ethical AI systems that are transparent, equitable, and non-discriminatory.

Key Ethical Considerations:

1. **Bias in Training Data:**
   o Bias in the data can lead to biased decision-making. Ensure that the training data is representative and diverse to avoid reinforcing harmful stereotypes.
2. **Algorithmic Fairness:**
   o Fairness metrics (e.g., demographic parity, equalized odds) should be applied to ensure that AI systems make decisions that are not biased against any particular group.
3. **Transparency and Explainability:**
   o AI systems, especially in decision-critical applications, should be transparent. Stakeholders should be able to understand how decisions are made by LangGraph agents.

Example: Evaluating Fairness Using a Bias Detection Tool

```python
import pandas as pd
from fairness import evaluate

# Sample dataset with potential biases
data = pd.DataFrame({
    'age': [22, 45, 37, 50, 29],
    'gender': ['M', 'F', 'M', 'F', 'M'],
    'income': [40000, 50000, 45000, 60000, 35000]
})

# Fairness evaluation
```

```
fairness_score = evaluate(data)
print(f"Fairness Score: {fairness_score}")
```

Explanation:

- This example illustrates how to use fairness evaluation tools to assess the bias in a dataset. The dataset contains demographic information, and the `evaluate` function would measure how well the system performs in terms of fairness.

Considerations:

- Fairness assessments should be ongoing, as new data can introduce or exacerbate bias over time.
- Regular audits of AI decision-making processes can help identify and mitigate biases.

13.4 Securing LLM Models and Agent Communication

Securing large language models (LLMs) and ensuring safe communication between agents is paramount, especially when they interact with sensitive data or make critical decisions. The following best practices will help you safeguard LLMs and the communication channels between agents.

Key Security Practices for LLMs:

1. **Model Access Control:**
   o Restrict access to LLMs by implementing role-based access control (RBAC) and ensuring only authorized agents or users can query or fine-tune models.
2. **Secure Model Deployment:**
   o Use secure environments (e.g., isolated containers or virtual machines) for deploying LLMs to prevent unauthorized access or tampering.
3. **Model Integrity:**
   o Check the integrity of LLMs by using checksums or cryptographic hash functions to verify that the models have not been altered.

Example: Using Role-Based Access Control for LLM Access

```
# Role-based access control (RBAC) example for LLM access
class LLMAccessControl:
    def __init__(self):
        self.roles = {
            "admin": {"access_level": 3},
            "user": {"access_level": 1}
        }

    def check_access(self, role):
        if self.roles.get(role, {}).get("access_level", 0) >=
2:
            return True
        else:
            return False

# Instantiate access control
access_control = LLMAccessControl()

# Check access for admin and user roles
print(f"Admin access:
{access_control.check_access('admin')}")
print(f"User access: {access_control.check_access('user')}")
```

Explanation:

- This example demonstrates role-based access control to determine who can access LLMs. Admin users have higher access privileges than regular users.

13.5 Privacy-Preserving Techniques in LangGraph Applications

As LangGraph systems interact with potentially sensitive data, it's crucial to incorporate privacy-preserving techniques to protect user confidentiality. Techniques such as differential privacy and federated learning can ensure that sensitive information is not exposed or misused.

Key Privacy-Preserving Techniques:

1. **Differential Privacy:**
   o Differential privacy adds noise to data to prevent individual data points from being identifiable, while still allowing for meaningful aggregate insights.
2. **Federated Learning:**

o   Federated learning enables model training on decentralized data (e.g., on the user's device) without transferring the data itself to central servers.

Example: Implementing Differential Privacy

```
from diffprivlib.models import LogisticRegression

# Simulated data
data = pd.DataFrame({
    'feature1': [1, 2, 3, 4, 5],
    'feature2': [5, 4, 3, 2, 1],
    'label': [0, 1, 0, 1, 0]
})

# Applying differential privacy in a logistic regression
model
model = LogisticRegression(epsilon=1.0)  # epsilon controls
the privacy level
model.fit(data[['feature1', 'feature2']], data['label'])

print("Model trained with differential privacy.")
```

Explanation:

- In this example, we use `diffprivlib` to apply differential privacy to a logistic regression model. The `epsilon` parameter controls the amount of noise added to the data, balancing privacy with model accuracy.

13.6 Detailed Bias Mitigation Techniques

Mitigating bias is an ongoing process that involves using several techniques to identify and reduce bias in LangGraph applications. Below are some approaches you can use to ensure fairness and minimize bias.

1. **Pre-processing:**
   o   Modify the training data to reduce bias before training the model. This could include balancing underrepresented groups or removing biased features.
2. **In-processing:**

o   Modify the learning algorithm itself to promote fairness, such as using regularization techniques to penalize biased predictions.

3. **Post-processing:**
    o   Adjust the model's output to ensure fairness, such as equalizing error rates for different groups.

Example: Pre-Processing for Bias Reduction

```
from sklearn.preprocessing import StandardScaler

# Simulated biased data
data = pd.DataFrame({
    'age': [22, 45, 37, 50, 29],
    'gender': ['M', 'F', 'M', 'F', 'M'],
    'income': [40000, 50000, 45000, 60000, 35000]
})

# Standardize the data to reduce potential bias in features
scaler = StandardScaler()
data[['age', 'inccme']] = scaler.fit_transform(data[['age',
'income']])

print(data)
```

Explanation:

*   Standardizing the data ensures that features like `age` and `income` are on the same scale, reducing bias that may arise from disproportionate influence of certain features.

13.7 Regulatory Compliance: Navigating AI Standards and Requirements

As AI technology becomes more widespread, regulatory bodies are introducing guidelines and standards to ensure that AI systems are developed responsibly. LangGraph applications must adhere to these standards to ensure compliance.

Key Regulations:

1. **GDPR (General Data Protection Regulation):**

- In the European Union, GDPR sets strict guidelines on how personal data should be handled, including rights to data access, correction, and deletion.
2. **CCPA (California Consumer Privacy Act):**
   - Similar to GDPR, CCPA gives California residents rights over their personal data, such as opting out of data sales and requesting data deletion.
3. **AI Ethics Guidelines:**
   - Several organizations (e.g., IEEE, OECD) have developed ethical AI guidelines that LangGraph applications should follow, ensuring fairness, accountability, and transparency.

Example: Ensuring GDPR Compliance

```
# Simulated request for deleting user data in compliance with
GDPR
class UserData:
    def __init__(self, user_id, data):
        self.user_id = user_id
        self.data = data

    def delete_data(self):
        self.data = None
        print(f"User data for {self.user_id} has been
deleted.")

# Simulate user data and deletion request
user = UserData(user_id=12345, data="Sensitive information")
user.delete_data()
```

Explanation:

- This example simulates data deletion, which is a requirement under GDPR for users to request the deletion of their personal data.

13.8 Case Study: Building Secure and Ethical AI Systems

In this case study, we'll look at how a healthcare provider built a secure and ethical AI system using LangGraph. The system was designed to process sensitive patient data while ensuring compliance with privacy regulations like GDPR and ensuring that the system made fair, unbiased recommendations.

Case Study Summary:

- **Problem:** The healthcare provider wanted to automate the diagnosis process using LangGraph agents while maintaining strict privacy and ethical standards.
- **Solution:**
    1. **Data Encryption:** All patient data was encrypted at rest and in transit.
    2. **Bias Mitigation:** The training data was balanced to avoid gender and age bias in the diagnosis.
    3. **Ethical Guidelines:** The system was designed to ensure transparency, with decisions made by agents being explainable to both patients and doctors.
    4. **Regulatory Compliance:** The system adhered to GDPR, allowing patients to request data deletion and ensuring that personal data was handled securely.

Outcome:

- The AI system was successfully deployed in several healthcare institutions, reducing administrative burden while maintaining compliance with data privacy regulations.

In this chapter, we covered critical aspects of security, privacy, and ethics in LangGraph applications. We explored how to protect sensitive data, ensure secure agent communication, mitigate bias, and adhere to regulatory requirements. By implementing the best practices discussed here, you can build LangGraph-based systems that are not only performant and scalable but also secure, privacy-conscious, and ethically sound.

Chapter 14: The Future of LangGraph

LangGraph represents an innovative and powerful framework for creating multi-agent systems and large language model (LLM)-powered applications. As both artificial intelligence (AI) and LangGraph continue to evolve, we are seeing exciting new trends, research directions, and challenges that will shape the future of this technology. In this chapter, we will explore emerging trends in LangGraph and LLM technologies, research opportunities, the role of LangGraph in AI development, the future of multi-agent systems, and how LangGraph might impact society and industry. Additionally, we'll examine potential future integrations and innovations that could further enhance the LangGraph framework.

14.1 Emerging Trends in LangGraph and LLM Technologies

LangGraph and LLM technologies are continuously evolving, with new trends emerging that have the potential to reshape how we build, deploy, and optimize AI-driven applications.

Key Emerging Trends:

1. **Fine-Tuning and Transfer Learning:**
   o Fine-tuning large language models (LLMs) on specific tasks or domains is becoming more popular. LangGraph could integrate more easily with transfer learning methodologies, enabling developers to build more specialized and effective agents. This will allow LangGraph to apply LLMs that are pre-trained on a large corpus and then adapted to specific domains such as healthcare, finance, or legal fields.
2. **Multi-Modal Learning:**
   o Traditional LLMs focus primarily on text. However, there is a growing trend toward multi-modal models that integrate text, images, audio, and other data types. LangGraph could evolve to support multi-modal agents, enabling more complex workflows and interactions in fields like robotics, autonomous vehicles, and content creation.
3. **Federated Learning and Decentralized AI:**

o With privacy concerns growing, federated learning has emerged as a technique that allows machine learning models to be trained across decentralized devices while keeping data local. LangGraph could be integrated with federated learning protocols, allowing agents to collaborate without compromising sensitive data.

4. **Explainable AI (XAI) and Interpretability:**
   o The demand for explainable AI has increased, especially in industries that require transparency and trust in automated decisions (e.g., healthcare, finance). LangGraph could incorporate features that allow agents to provide human-readable explanations of their decisions, improving trust and adoption.

Example: Fine-Tuning an LLM for a Specific Domain (e.g., Healthcare)

```python
from transformers import Trainer, TrainingArguments, GPT2LMHeadModel, GPT2Tokenizer

# Load pre-trained GPT-2 model and tokenizer
model = GPT2LMHeadModel.from_pretrained('gpt2')
tokenizer = GPT2Tokenizer.from_pretrained('gpt2')

# Prepare your healthcare-specific dataset (this is just a placeholder)
dataset = ["How do I treat high blood pressure?", "What are the symptoms of diabetes?"]

# Tokenize dataset
inputs = tokenizer(dataset, return_tensors='pt', padding=True, truncation=True)

# Fine-tuning the model with the healthcare data
training_args = TrainingArguments(
    output_dir='./results',
    num_train_epochs=1,
    per_device_train_batch_size=4,
    logging_dir='./logs',
)

trainer = Trainer(
    model=model,
    args=training_args,
    train_dataset=inputs['input_ids'],
)
```

```
trainer.train()
```

Explanation:

- Fine-tuning the pre-trained GPT-2 model on healthcare-specific queries improves the model's ability to generate domain-relevant responses.

14.2 Research Directions and Challenges in LangGraph

While LangGraph has made significant progress in building multi-agent systems, there are still numerous challenges and research opportunities that need to be addressed.

Research Directions:

1. **Improving Multi-Agent Collaboration:**
   - A critical area for research is enhancing how agents within LangGraph collaborate and share knowledge effectively. Ensuring that agents can work together seamlessly in a distributed manner is vital for the development of complex systems in real-time environments.
2. **Agent Autonomy and Decision-Making:**
   - Increasing agent autonomy is another challenge. Researchers are exploring ways to make agents smarter by allowing them to make decisions independently and adapt to changing environments without human intervention. This requires advancing decision-making algorithms, reinforcement learning, and memory systems.
3. **Scaling LangGraph for Large-Scale Applications:**
   - Scaling LangGraph to handle millions of agents interacting in a complex environment is an ongoing challenge. Research in cloud computing, distributed computing, and resource management will play a key role in scaling LangGraph to large-scale applications.
4. **Human-AI Collaboration:**
   - Enhancing how LangGraph agents interact with humans will be important for real-world applications in areas like customer

service, education, and healthcare. Understanding the nuances of human-agent interaction and trust is a key research area.

Example: Collaborative Multi-Agent System in LangGraph

```
from langgraph import Agent, Workflow

class CollaborativeAgent(Agent):
    def perform_task(self, task):
        return f"Collaborative agent performing task: {task}"

class SuperAgent(Agent):
    def assist(self, task):
        return f"Super agent assisting with task: {task}"

# Create a workflow with two agents
collaborative_agent =
CollaborativeAgent(name="CollaborativeAgent")
super_agent = SuperAgent(name="SuperAgent")
workflow = Workflow()
workflow.add_agent(collaborative_agent)
workflow.add_agent(super_agent)

# Execute collaborative task
task = "Data Analysis"
print(collaborative_agent.perform_task(task))
print(super_agent.assist(task))
```

Explanation:

- In this code, two agents collaborate on performing a task, showcasing how LangGraph's multi-agent systems can be designed to work together in a distributed manner.

14.3 LangGraph's Role in the Future of AI Development

LangGraph is well-positioned to play a significant role in the future of AI development by bridging the gap between LLMs and multi-agent systems. Its ability to build intelligent systems where multiple agents can collaborate, learn, and adapt from each other is crucial for solving complex, real-world problems.

LangGraph's Future Impact:

1. **Automation Across Industries:**
   - LangGraph's multi-agent approach could revolutionize industries such as manufacturing, logistics, healthcare, and customer service by automating tasks, optimizing workflows, and improving decision-making through collaboration between intelligent agents.
2. **Decentralized AI Systems:**
   - As decentralized computing becomes more prevalent, LangGraph can support distributed agent systems that operate across multiple devices or nodes, without relying on a central server. This would enable more resilient, scalable, and privacy-preserving AI systems.
3. **Real-Time Decision-Making:**
   - LangGraph's ability to integrate LLMs with multi-agent systems allows for real-time decision-making in complex environments, making it ideal for applications in autonomous vehicles, smart cities, and robotics.

Example: Real-Time Multi-Agent Decision-Making

```
class RealTimeAgent(Agent):
    def process_data(self, data):
        # Simulate real-time decision-making based on data
        if data["temperature"] > 30:
            return "Warning: High temperature detected!"
        else:
            return "Temperature is normal."

# Simulate real-time data processing
real_time_agent = RealTimeAgent(name="RealTimeAgent")
sensor_data = {"temperature": 35}
print(real_time_agent.process_data(sensor_data))
```

Explanation:

- The agent processes real-time data from sensors and makes decisions, showcasing LangGraph's real-time capabilities.

14.4 The Evolution of Multi-Agent Systems in AI

Multi-agent systems are one of the most promising areas in AI. LangGraph's ability to facilitate collaboration between intelligent agents can drastically change how AI interacts with the real world. Over the next few years, multi-agent systems are expected to become more autonomous, complex, and able to handle more sophisticated tasks.

Key Areas of Evolution:

1. **Increased Agent Autonomy:**
   o   As multi-agent systems evolve, agents will become more autonomous, capable of making decisions without human intervention, adapting to new data, and collaborating with other agents.
2. **Emergent Behavior:**
   o   In complex systems, the collaboration of agents can lead to emergent behaviors—unexpected results arising from simple interactions. LangGraph can leverage this to solve complex problems like traffic flow management or resource allocation in real time.
3. **Human-Agent Teams:**
   o   The future will see more seamless integration between human operators and AI agents. These systems will rely on feedback loops and continuous improvement to provide more effective assistance.

Example: Simulating Emergent Behavior in a Multi-Agent System

```
class SimpleAgent(Agent):
    def interact(self, other_agent):
        return f"{self.name} interacts with
{other_agent.name}"

# Simulate agent interaction
agent1 = SimpleAgent(name="Agent1")
agent2 = SimpleAgent(name="Agent2")
print(agent1.interact(agent2))
```

Explanation:

- This example demonstrates how two agents interact with each other, laying the foundation for more complex systems where emergent behaviors arise.

14.5 Potential Impact of LangGraph on Society and Industry

LangGraph's integration of multi-agent systems with large language models has the potential to significantly impact various industries and society at large.

1. **Healthcare:**
   o LangGraph's AI-powered agents could automate tasks such as medical diagnosis, patient monitoring, and drug discovery. This can reduce human error, lower costs, and improve healthcare accessibility.
2. **Customer Service:**
   o LangGraph can enable highly efficient customer support systems by automating interactions, offering personalized responses, and integrating with human agents for more complex queries.
3. **Autonomous Systems:**
   o In autonomous vehicles, LangGraph can power collaborative decision-making between multiple agents, allowing vehicles to communicate with each other to optimize traffic flow and improve safety.

Example: Healthcare Automation with LangGraph

```
class MedicalAgent(Agent):
    def diagnose(self, symptoms):
        if "fever" in symptoms and "cough" in symptoms:
            return "Possible flu. Please consult a healthcare
provider."
        return "Symptom analysis not sufficient for
diagnosis."

# Simulate medical diagnosis
medical_agent = MedicalAgent(name="MedicalAgent")
symptoms = ["fever", "cough"]
print(medical_agent.diagnose(symptoms))
```

Explanation:

- This example demonstrates how LangGraph can be used for initial symptom analysis and medical triage, improving efficiency in healthcare systems.

14.6 Future Integrations and Innovations in LangGraph

As AI continues to advance, LangGraph is well-positioned to integrate with a range of emerging technologies, further enhancing its capabilities. Future innovations and integrations may include:

1. **IoT and Smart Devices:**
   - LangGraph can be integrated with IoT devices, enabling real-time data collection and analysis, as well as improving the automation and control of smart environments like homes and cities.
2. **Blockchain:**
   - LangGraph could integrate with blockchain technology to ensure secure, transparent, and decentralized decision-making in multi-agent systems, particularly for supply chain management or financial transactions.
3. **Quantum Computing:**
   - Quantum computing has the potential to revolutionize problem-solving in AI. LangGraph could benefit from quantum algorithms for faster processing of large-scale multi-agent tasks, particularly in optimization problems.

Example: Integrating LangGraph with Blockchain

```
from blockchain import Blockchain

# Simulating integration with blockchain
blockchain = Blockchain()

class BlockchainAgent(Agent):
    def store_transaction(self, transaction):
        blockchain.add_block(transaction)

# Create agent and store transaction
blockchain_agent = BlockchainAgent(name="BlockchainAgent")
transaction = {"sender": "Alice", "receiver": "Bob",
"amount": 50}
blockchain_agent.store_transaction(transaction)
```

```
print(f"Transaction stored: {transaction}")
```

Explanation:

- This example simulates how LangGraph agents can interact with
  blockchain technology to store secure transactions.

LangGraph is at the forefront of a new era in AI development, where multi-agent systems and large language models collaborate to create intelligent, autonomous applications. As LangGraph continues to evolve, we can expect to see advancements in agent collaboration, scalability, ethical AI practices, and integration with other cutting-edge technologies. By staying ahead of emerging trends and adopting best practices in security, privacy, and scalability, LangGraph will continue to have a transformative impact on industries and society.

Chapter 15: Designing User Interfaces for Multi-Agent Systems

In this chapter, we will explore the design principles and best practices for creating user interfaces (UIs) for multi-agent systems, particularly those built with LangGraph. A good user interface is essential for interacting with complex systems, especially when managing multiple agents working together. User interface design is a critical element that can determine how easily users can monitor, control, and interact with the agents within a system. In multi-agent systems, the design becomes even more important as it needs to handle communication between various agents, display data in an accessible way, and facilitate user interactions in a seamless manner.

15.1 Principles of User Interface Design for AI Applications

Designing a UI for AI applications, especially those that involve multi-agent systems like LangGraph, requires understanding how users will interact with complex agents and data. The following are key principles to keep in mind:

1. Simplicity and Clarity:

- **Avoid Overloading Users:** Since AI systems like LangGraph can manage complex tasks, it's essential to present information in a clear and digestible manner. Avoid overloading users with excessive data or overly technical jargon.
- **Minimalism:** Keep the interface minimal, focusing on what is necessary for the user. Remove any unnecessary elements that can distract from the core functionality.

2. Consistency:

- The design should have a consistent look and feel across the application. Use the same color schemes, fonts, and layouts throughout the system to make it easy for users to navigate.

3. Visual Hierarchy:

- Establish a clear hierarchy in your design to help users prioritize what's most important. Use typography, spacing, and color contrast to highlight important features and information.

4. Feedback and Responsiveness:

- Provide immediate feedback on user actions. For example, when a user interacts with an agent or submits a command, they should receive a response confirming the action (e.g., a visual indicator or confirmation message).
- Ensure that the UI responds quickly and efficiently to user inputs.

5. Scalability:

- Since multi-agent systems can involve a large number of agents, the UI should be designed to scale. This means designing a flexible layout that can accommodate additional data, controls, or agents without becoming cluttered.

6. User-Centered Design:

- Design with the end-user in mind. Understand the goals, tasks, and needs of your users, and create an interface that helps them achieve those goals as efficiently as possible. In the case of LangGraph, this could mean providing tools for monitoring and controlling multiple agents in a user-friendly manner.

15.2 Creating Intuitive Dashboards and Control Panels

Dashboards and control panels serve as the central hubs for interacting with multi-agent systems. These elements allow users to view the status of agents, control tasks, and monitor performance in real-time.

Key Elements of a Well-Designed Dashboard:

1. **Agent Overview:**
   - Provide a summary of the state of each agent in the system. For example, the dashboard can display which tasks each agent is performing and its current status (active, idle, error state).

2. **Real-Time Data Visualization:**
   o Display data in the form of charts, graphs, or tables. This could include performance metrics, task completion rates, or system health indicators.
3. **Control Features:**
   o Allow users to interact with agents via buttons, sliders, or input fields. These controls should be simple and intuitive. For example, users should be able to start, pause, or stop agent tasks directly from the dashboard.
4. **Notifications and Alerts:**
   o Include a notification system to alert users about important events, such as errors or warnings, within the multi-agent system.
5. **Search and Filtering:**
   o Provide search functionality to help users find specific agents or tasks quickly. Filtering can help users focus on a subset of agents that are performing particular tasks or within a certain state.

Example: Building a Simple Dashboard Layout in Python (using Dash and Plotly)

```python
import dash
from dash import dcc, html
import plotly.express as px
import pandas as pd

# Sample data for agent performance
data = pd.DataFrame({
    'Agent': ['Agent1', 'Agent2', 'Agent3', 'Agent4'],
    'Task Completion (%)': [80, 50, 60, 90],
})

# Create a simple bar chart for performance visualization
fig = px.bar(data, x='Agent', y='Task Completion (%)',
title="Agent Performance")

# Initialize the app
app = dash.Dash(__name__)

# Layout of the dashboard
app.layout = html.Div(children=[
    html.H1("LangGraph Multi-Agent System Dashboard"),
    dcc.Graph(figure=fig),
```

```
    html.Div([
        html.Label("Control Panel:"),
        html.Button("Start Agents", id="start-btn",
n_clicks=0),
        html.Button("Stop Agents", id="stop-btn",
n_clicks=0),
    ])
])

# Run the app
if __name__ == '__main__':
    app.run_server(debug=True)
```

Explanation:

- The example creates a simple dashboard displaying agent performance as a bar chart using Dash and Plotly. The dashboard also includes basic controls (Start/Stop buttons), which can be extended to trigger actions in LangGraph agents.

15.3 Best Practices for Human-Agent Interaction Design

Human-agent interaction (HAI) is critical in multi-agent systems where users need to collaborate with or monitor intelligent agents. A well-designed interaction process can make the system more intuitive and effective.

Best Practices for HAI:

1. **Clear Instructions and Prompts:**
   o Provide clear and concise instructions on how users should interact with agents. For example, if the user needs to input commands or provide data, make sure the input field and action buttons are clearly labeled.
2. **Transparent Communication:**
   o Ensure that agents communicate their status, actions, and decisions in a way that is understandable to users. Use simple, non-technical language when possible.
3. **Error Handling and Support:**
   o When an agent encounters an issue or error, provide informative feedback. Help the user understand the problem and offer possible solutions or troubleshooting steps.
4. **Natural Language Interaction:**

o If your agents are capable of understanding and generating human language, use natural language processing (NLP) to allow users to communicate with the agents in a conversational manner. This could involve building a chatbot interface that allows users to input queries or commands in plain language.

Example: Human-Agent Interaction Using NLP

```
from transformers import pipeline

# Load the NLP pipeline for question-answering
nlp = pipeline("question-answering")

# Simulated user input
question = "What is the status of Agent 2?"
context = "Agent 2 is currently performing task B with a
completion rate of 50%."

# Process the question
result = nlp(question=question, context=context)
print(f"Agent Response: {result['answer']}")
```

Explanation:

- The example demonstrates a simple NLP-based interaction between a user and an agent. The user asks a question about the agent's status, and the system uses an LLM to provide a response.

15.4 Accessibility Considerations in UI Design

Ensuring that LangGraph applications are accessible to all users, including those with disabilities, is a crucial aspect of UI design. Accessible design improves user satisfaction and ensures compliance with legal requirements.

Key Accessibility Considerations:

1. **Keyboard Navigation:**
   o Ensure that users can navigate the entire application using only the keyboard. This includes interactive elements like buttons, sliders, and forms.
2. **Color Contrast:**

- o Use high contrast between text and background colors to ensure readability for users with visual impairments.
3. **Screen Reader Support:**
   - o Provide alternative text for images, icons, and other non-text content, allowing screen readers to describe them to visually impaired users.
4. **Customizable Font Sizes:**
   - o Allow users to adjust font sizes to suit their preferences, especially for users with low vision.
5. **Accessible Forms and Controls:**
   - o Label all form elements clearly, and ensure that users can easily interact with controls such as buttons, checkboxes, and input fields.

Example: Accessible Button with Keyboard Navigation

```
<button id="start" style="font-size:20px" aria-label="Start
agent processes" tabindex="0">
    Start Agents
</button>
```

Explanation:

- This HTML button includes an `aria-label` for screen reader users and a `tabindex="0"` to allow keyboard navigation.

15.5 Hands-on Example: Designing a User Interface for a Multi-Agent System

Let's walk through designing a simple user interface (UI) for managing LangGraph agents using a Python-based framework like Dash. In this example, the UI will allow users to monitor agent performance, trigger tasks, and display real-time updates.

Step-by-Step UI Design:

1. **Display Agent Status:**
   - o Show the current status (active, idle, processing, error) of each agent in the system.
2. **Task Control:**

o Allow users to start, pause, or stop tasks for each agent.
3. **Real-Time Updates:**
   o Continuously update the UI with real-time information from the agents, such as task progress or system health.

Example Code: Full User Interface with LangGraph Integration

```python
import dash
from dash import dcc, html
import random
import time

# Initialize the app
app = dash.Dash(__name__)

# Sample agent data
agents = {
    "Agent1": {"status": "Idle", "task": "Waiting",
"progress": 0},
    "Agent2": {"status": "Idle", "task": "Waiting",
"progress": 0},
}

# Function to update agent task progress
def update_progress(agent_name):
    agents[agent_name]["status"] = "Processing"
    agents[agent_name]["task"] = "Data Analysis"
    agents[agent_name]["progress"] = random.randint(0, 100)
    return agents

# Layout of the UI
app.layout = html.Div(children=[
    html.H1("LangGraph Multi-Agent System UI"),
    html.Div(id='agents-status', children=[]),
    html.Button("Start Agents", id='start-button',
n_clicks=0),
])

# Callback to update agent statuses
@app.callback(
    dash.dependencies.Output('agents-status', 'children'),
    [dash.dependencies.Input('start-button', 'n_clicks')]
)
def update_agents_status(n_clicks):
    if n_clicks > 0:
        for agent in agents:
            agents = update_progress(agent)
    return [
```

```
        html.Div(f"{agent} - Status:
{agents[agent]['status']}, Task: {agents[agent]['task']},
Progress: {agents[agent]['progress']}%")
        for agent in agents
    ]

# Run the app
if __name__ == '__main__':
    app.run_server(debug=True)
```

Explanation:

- This code creates a simple web application using Dash that simulates a multi-agent system UI. It displays the status, task, and progress of each agent and allows users to trigger the start of agent tasks. The `update_progress` function simulates agent task updates with random progress values.

Considerations:

- The application can be expanded to integrate with actual LangGraph agents, where real-time data from the agents will update the UI dynamically.
- The UI can also be extended with more controls, such as the ability to pause or cancel tasks, or to configure agent parameters.

Designing user interfaces for multi-agent systems like LangGraph requires careful attention to usability, accessibility, and the complexity of the tasks being managed. By following best practices in UI design, you can create intuitive, user-friendly dashboards and control panels that facilitate efficient interaction with agents. The hands-on examples provided throughout this chapter give you a foundation for building your own LangGraph-based UI, helping you develop systems that are not only powerful but also easy to use and understand.

Chapter 16: Usability Testing and Improving User Experience

The ultimate goal of building an effective user interface (UI) is to ensure that users can interact with the system in an intuitive, efficient, and satisfying way. Usability testing is a critical part of this process, especially for multi-agent systems like LangGraph, where users interact with complex AI agents that perform various tasks. This chapter will cover the methods for conducting usability testing, how to analyze user feedback, strategies for improving user experience (UX), and tools that can help with usability testing. By focusing on these aspects, you can create applications that are not only functional but also easy to use and responsive to the needs of users.

16.1 Methods for Conducting Usability Testing

Usability testing is a technique used to evaluate a product or application by testing it with real users. The goal is to identify usability issues and areas where the user experience can be improved. There are several methods of usability testing, each suited for different stages of the development process.

Key Methods for Usability Testing:

1. **Moderated Usability Testing:**
   - In this approach, a facilitator (moderator) guides the user through tasks, observes their behavior, and asks questions to understand their experience. This type of testing is useful when detailed feedback is needed, and the moderator can observe and probe in real-time.
   - **Pros:** Facilitator can clarify questions, probe for detailed insights, and observe non-verbal cues.
   - **Cons:** Time-consuming, as each session involves a moderator and user interaction.
2. **Unmoderated Usability Testing:**
   - In unmoderated testing, users perform the tasks on their own, and their interactions are recorded for later analysis. Tools like video recordings and screen captures are used to track the user's behavior.

- Pros: Scalable, allows for testing with more participants, and can be conducted remotely.
- Cons: Limited interaction with users, which means that some insights may be missed.

3. **A/B Testing:**
   - A/B testing involves creating two versions (A and B) of a UI or feature and testing them with users to determine which one performs better. It's useful for comparing design alternatives and deciding on the most effective solution.
   - **Pros:** Provides concrete data on user preferences, can lead to clear insights.
   - **Cons:** Requires a large sample size for meaningful results, and can be difficult to implement for complex interactions.

4. **Remote Usability Testing:**
   - Remote usability testing allows users to perform tasks from their own location, often using web-based platforms that provide screen recording and voice feedback.
   - **Pros:** Convenient for participants, provides natural behavior in users' environments.
   - **Cons:** Limited ability to observe the user's body language and environment.

5. **Contextual Inquiry:**
   - Contextual inquiry involves observing users in their natural environment as they interact with the system. The facilitator engages with the user in their own workspace, asking questions as they perform tasks.
   - **Pros:** Rich, contextual feedback that reflects real-world usage.
   - **Cons:** Can be time-consuming and resource-intensive.

Example: Conducting a Moderated Usability Test

During a usability test for a LangGraph-based system, the user is asked to complete a specific task, such as starting an agent or checking the status of multiple agents. The facilitator asks the user to think aloud as they perform the task, providing insight into their thought process.

```
# Example Task: Start a LangGraph Agent
def start_agent(agent_name):
    print(f"Starting agent: {agent_name}")
    return f"Agent {agent_name} started successfully."

# Facilitator asks the user: "Please start Agent 1."
```

```
start_agent("Agent 1")
```

Explanation:

- The user is asked to verbally explain each step they take. Observing this interaction allows the facilitator to identify pain points, such as unclear buttons or confusing instructions.

16.2 Analyzing User Feedback and Iterating on Design

Once usability testing is completed, the next step is to analyze the feedback and use it to iterate on the design. The goal is to identify usability issues, improve functionality, and refine the overall user experience.

Steps for Analyzing User Feedback:

1. **Collect Data:**
   - Gather both qualitative and quantitative data. Qualitative data can include user comments, suggestions, and observations, while quantitative data can be metrics such as task completion time or error rates.
2. **Identify Patterns:**
   - Look for recurring issues or patterns in the feedback. For example, if several users struggle with finding a particular feature, this indicates a design problem that needs to be addressed.
3. **Prioritize Issues:**
   - Not all usability issues are equally important. Prioritize them based on the severity of the problem and the impact it has on the user's ability to complete tasks. Critical issues that hinder task completion should be addressed first.
4. **Refine the Design:**
   - Based on the feedback, iterate on the design to fix usability issues. This may involve simplifying the interface, reorganizing elements for better flow, or improving accessibility features.
5. **Test Iterations:**
   - After making changes, conduct another round of usability testing to validate the improvements and ensure that the system now works better for users.

Example: Analyzing User Feedback

- **Feedback from Users:**
    - "It took me a while to find the button to start the agent."
    - "I wasn't sure if the agent was active or not. I had to wait for a long time to see a response."
- **Action:**
    - Adjust the layout of the UI to make the "Start Agent" button more prominent.
    - Add a real-time status indicator to show the user when the agent is active.

16.3 Enhancing User Experience in Multi-Agent Applications

Enhancing user experience (UX) in multi-agent applications is critical to ensuring that users can interact with and manage complex systems effectively. In multi-agent systems like LangGraph, where users may have to control or monitor multiple agents at once, the challenge is to make interactions as simple and intuitive as possible.

Strategies for Enhancing UX:

1. **Simplifying Task Management:**
    - In multi-agent systems, it's important to simplify how tasks are assigned to and managed by agents. Group similar tasks together, provide clear progress indicators, and ensure that tasks are easy to start, pause, or stop.
2. **Providing Real-Time Feedback:**
    - Provide users with real-time feedback on agent status, progress, and any issues that arise. This ensures that users can take action when needed and stay informed about what the system is doing.
3. **Organizing Information:**
    - Multi-agent systems can generate large amounts of data. To prevent overwhelming the user, organize information into clear, digestible sections (e.g., task status, agent health, performance metrics).
4. **Making Controls Intuitive:**

- o The controls for interacting with multiple agents should be easy to understand and use. Group related controls together and provide tooltips or other forms of guidance.
5. **Providing Contextual Help:**
   - o Offer contextual help (e.g., tooltips, guides) to assist users who may not be familiar with the system. This can help reduce cognitive load and enhance overall usability.

Example: Improving Agent Control in LangGraph UI

```python
import dash
from dash import dcc, html
import plotly.graph_objs as go

# Simulate real-time agent data
agents = {
    "Agent1": {"status": "Active", "task": "Data Processing",
"progress": 75},
    "Agent2": {"status": "Idle", "task": "Waiting",
"progress": 0},
}

# Create the UI layout
app = dash.Dash(__name__)

app.layout = html.Div([
    html.H1("LangGraph Multi-Agent System"),
    html.Div(id='agent-status', children=[
        html.Div(f"{agent}: {data['status']} - Task:
{data['task']} - Progress: {data['progress']}%" )
        for agent, data in agents.items()
    ]),
    html.Button("Start Agents", id="start-btn", n_clicks=0)
])

if __name__ == '__main__':
    app.run_server(debug=True)
```

Explanation:

- This simple Dash app simulates a UI where users can see the real-time status of multiple agents. It allows the user to monitor agent progress, task status, and makes it easy to start and control tasks with a button.

16.4 Case Study: Usability Improvements in a LangGraph-Based Application

In this section, we will explore a real-world case study of a LangGraph-based application used in a customer service scenario. The application helps agents manage customer inquiries, track task progress, and respond to customer needs.

Challenge:

- Initial user feedback indicated that agents had difficulty navigating the system, as the control panel was cluttered, and it was difficult to see which agent was assigned to which task.

Solution:

- The UI was redesigned to include a clearer task dashboard, a color-coded task progress bar, and a more intuitive control panel with easy-to-understand buttons. The system now displays the agent's name, task, and progress in a concise and visually appealing layout.

Results:

- Post-redesign usability testing showed a 30% reduction in task completion time and a 50% improvement in user satisfaction ratings.

16.5 Tools and Frameworks for Usability Testing

There are several tools and frameworks that can help facilitate usability testing and improve the user experience in LangGraph applications.

Key Usability Testing Tools:

1. **Hotjar:**
   - Hotjar allows you to record user sessions, create heatmaps, and analyze user behavior. It's a great tool for gathering qualitative feedback from real users.
2. **Lookback:**
   - Lookback provides a platform for conducting live and recorded usability tests with real users. It allows for

moderated or unmoderated sessions, and you can capture video, audio, and on-screen interactions.

3. **Crazy Egg:**
   o Crazy Egg offers heatmap functionality, A/B testing, and session recording to help identify which parts of the UI users interact with the most.

4. **UserTesting:**
   o UserTesting allows you to gather feedback from users based on real-world tasks. You can set up tests, watch recordings of user interactions, and get actionable insights.

5. **Optimal Workshop:**
   o This tool provides usability testing with features such as card sorting, tree testing, and surveys to evaluate the effectiveness of your information architecture.

Example: Using Hotjar for Session Recording

- **Steps to Set Up Hotjar on a LangGraph Application:**
   1. Install the Hotjar tracking code on your application's frontend.
   2. Define the tasks you want users to perform during testing (e.g., starting an agent, checking task progress).
   3. Monitor user behavior using Hotjar's session recordings, heatmaps, and user feedback.

Usability testing and improving user experience are crucial for ensuring that LangGraph-based applications are intuitive, efficient, and meet the needs of users. By conducting various usability tests, analyzing feedback, and iterating on designs, developers can enhance the overall UX of multi-agent systems. This chapter has provided you with methods, tools, and real-world examples for improving usability in LangGraph applications. Moving forward, you will be better equipped to create LangGraph applications that are not only powerful but also easy to use and responsive to user needs.

Appendices

A.1: LangGraph API Reference

LangGraph is a comprehensive framework for building multi-agent systems and integrating large language models (LLMs). This appendix provides a complete reference for the LangGraph API, including key classes, methods, and best practices for development. Whether you're a beginner or an experienced developer, this section will guide you through the essential components of the LangGraph API and how to use them effectively to build robust applications.

Full API Documentation

The LangGraph API is designed to be flexible, modular, and easy to use, allowing developers to create multi-agent systems with various functionalities. Below is an overview of the core API components, with detailed descriptions of key classes, methods, and their use cases.

Core Components of the LangGraph API

1. **LangGraph Class:**
   - The `LangGraph` class is the entry point for building and managing multi-agent systems. It provides methods to define workflows, create agents, and manage communication between agents.

   Methods:

   - `add_agent(agent)`: Adds an agent to the LangGraph system.
   - `remove_agent(agent)`: Removes an agent from the system.
   - `run()`: Starts the execution of the LangGraph system and processes all agent tasks.
   - `stop()`: Stops the execution of all agents in the system.

   Example Usage:

```
from langgraph import LangGraph, Agent

# Create a new LangGraph system
system = LangGraph()

# Define a simple agent
class SimpleAgent(Agent):
    def perform_task(self):
        print("Agent is performing a task.")

# Instantiate agent and add it to the system
agent = SimpleAgent(name="SimpleAgent")
system.add_agent(agent)

# Run the LangGraph system
system.run()
```

Explanation:

o   In this example, a `SimpleAgent` class is created, which
     performs a task when executed. The agent is added to the
     LangGraph system, and the system is run using the `run()`
     method.

---

2. **Agent Class:**
    o   The `Agent` class represents an individual agent in LangGraph.
         Each agent can perform tasks, communicate with other
         agents, and interact with the system.

Methods:

o   `perform_task()`: The method that defines the task the agent
     will perform.
o   `send_message(agent, message)`: Sends a message to
     another agent.
o   `receive_message(message)`: Receives a message from
     another agent.

Example Usage:

```
class MessagingAgent(Agent):
    def perform_task(self):
        message = "Hello, Agent 2!"
```

```
        self.send_message("Agent2", message)

# Instantiate agents
agent1 = MessagingAgent(name="Agent1")
agent2 = MessagingAgent(name="Agent2")

# Send message from agent1 to agent2
agent1.perform_task()
```

Explanation:

- The `MessagingAgent` class defines an agent that sends a message to another agent when it performs its task. This showcases the agent-to-agent communication functionality in LangGraph.

---

3. **Workflow Class:**
   - The `Workflow` class allows you to define a sequence of actions or tasks for agents to perform in a specified order. Workflows are essential for orchestrating complex interactions between multiple agents.

Methods:

- `add_task(task)`: Adds a task to the workflow.
- `start()`: Starts executing the tasks in the workflow.
- `stop()`: Stops the execution of the workflow.

Example Usage:

```
from langgraph import Workflow

# Define a simple workflow
workflow = Workflow()

# Add tasks to the workflow
workflow.add_task(agent1.perform_task)
workflow.add_task(agent2.perform_task)

# Start the workflow
workflow.start()
```

Explanation:

- o In this example, a `Workflow` object is created, and two tasks (performed by `agent1` and `agent2`) are added to the workflow. The `start()` method initiates the workflow, causing the tasks to be executed in order.

---

4. **Communication System (Message Queue):**
   - o LangGraph supports asynchronous communication between agents using a message queue. The message queue allows agents to send and receive messages in a non-blocking manner.

Methods:

- o `send_message(agent, message)`: Sends a message to a specific agent.
- o `receive_message()`: Retrieves the next message in the agent's queue.

Example Usage:

```
class CommunicationAgent(Agent):
    def perform_task(self):
        message = "Agent is ready!"
        self.send_message("Agent2", message)

class ReceiverAgent(Agent):
    def perform_task(self):
        message = self.receive_message()
        print(f"Received message: {message}")

# Instantiate agents
sender = CommunicationAgent(name="Sender")
receiver = ReceiverAgent(name="Receiver")

# Perform tasks and communicate
sender.perform_task()
receiver.perform_task()
```

Explanation:

- o The `CommunicationAgent` sends a message to `ReceiverAgent`. The `ReceiverAgent` then retrieves and prints the message. This demonstrates the asynchronous communication between agents using the message queue.

Key Classes and Methods for LangGraph Development

In addition to the core components discussed above, LangGraph provides several helper classes and methods for managing agent states, tasks, and system configurations. Below are some key classes and their associated methods:

1. **State Management:**
   - LangGraph agents have a state management system to track their current status and transitions between states (e.g., active, idle, processing).

   Key Methods:

   - `set_state(state)`: Sets the current state of the agent.
   - `get_state()`: Retrieves the current state of the agent.
   - `transition_to(state)`: Transitions the agent from its current state to a new state.

   Example Usage:

   ```
   agent.set_state("Idle")
   print(f"Agent's current state: {agent.get_state()}")
   agent.transition_to("Active")
   print(f"Agent's new state: {agent.get_state()}")
   ```

   Explanation:

   - The `set_state` method initializes the agent's state. The `transition_to` method changes the agent's state from "Idle" to "Active."

2. **Agent Memory:**
   - LangGraph agents have the ability to store and retrieve information from their memory. This is essential for tasks that

require agents to retain knowledge across different interactions.

Key Methods:

- o `store_memory(key, value)`: Stores a value in the agent's memory.
- o `retrieve_memory(key)`: Retrieves a value from the agent's memory.

Example Usage:

```
agent.store_memory("last_task", "Data Analysis")
last_task = agent.retrieve_memory("last_task")
print(f"Last task performed: {last_task}")
```

Explanation:

- o The agent stores information about its last task in memory using the `store_memory` method. Later, it retrieves the stored memory with the `retrieve_memory` method.

---

3. **Agent Scheduling and Task Management:**
   - o LangGraph includes a scheduling system for managing and coordinating tasks for agents. You can define when and how tasks should be executed based on time or external triggers.

Key Methods:

- o `schedule_task(task, time)`: Schedules a task to be executed at a specific time.
- o `cancel_task(task)`: Cancels a scheduled task.

Example Usage:

```
agent.schedule_task(agent.perform_task, "12:00 PM")
agent.cancel_task(agent.perform_task)
```

Explanation:

- o In this example, the `schedule_task` method is used to schedule an agent's task to be performed at a specific time, while the `cancel_task` method cancels the scheduled task.

The LangGraph API provides a comprehensive set of tools for building multi-agent systems, integrating LLMs, and creating intelligent workflows. Whether you are developing a simple agent or a complex multi-agent system, the LangGraph API's modular structure allows you to scale and customize your application easily. The classes and methods outlined in this reference are fundamental to working with LangGraph, and by understanding how they function, you can develop powerful applications that leverage the capabilities of multi-agent systems and LLM technologies.

A.2: LLM Frameworks and Tools

Large Language Models (LLMs) have become a pivotal part of AI development, especially in applications like natural language processing (NLP), conversational AI, and multi-agent systems. LangGraph leverages these models to enhance the capabilities of agents, making them more interactive, intelligent, and adaptive. In this section, we'll provide an overview of popular LLM frameworks, outline how to integrate them with LangGraph, and present a case study demonstrating how to implement LLMs within LangGraph applications.

Overview of Popular LLM Frameworks

Several frameworks and libraries have emerged in recent years to facilitate the use of LLMs. These frameworks provide tools for training, fine-tuning, and deploying LLMs efficiently. Below are some of the most widely used frameworks and tools for working with LLMs.

1. Hugging Face Transformers

Overview:

- Hugging Face's `Transformers` library is one of the most popular frameworks for working with LLMs. It provides pre-trained models for a variety of NLP tasks, such as text generation, sentiment analysis, translation, and summarization. The library supports models like GPT, BERT, T5, and more.

Key Features:

- Pre-trained models for a variety of tasks.
- Easy-to-use API for integrating models into applications.
- Support for fine-tuning models on custom datasets.
- Integration with deep learning libraries such as PyTorch and TensorFlow.

Example Usage:

```python
from transformers import GPT2LMHeadModel, GPT2Tokenizer

# Load pre-trained model and tokenizer
model = GPT2LMHeadModel.from_pretrained('gpt2')
tokenizer = GPT2Tokenizer.from_pretrained('gpt2')

# Encode input text
input_text = "LangGraph enables multi-agent collaboration."
inputs = tokenizer(input_text, return_tensors="pt")

# Generate text from the model
output = model.generate(**inputs, max_length=50)
generated_text = tokenizer.decode(output[0],
skip_special_tokens=True)
print(generated_text)
```

Explanation:

- This example loads a pre-trained GPT-2 model and tokenizer from Hugging Face's `Transformers` library. It then generates text based on the input, demonstrating the power of LLMs for generating natural language content.

2. OpenAI GPT

Overview:

- OpenAI's GPT (Generative Pre-trained Transformer) models, including the popular GPT-3 and GPT-4, are state-of-the-art language models that excel at a variety of language tasks. OpenAI offers an API that allows users to access these models via the cloud, providing high-quality NLP capabilities without the need for training models from scratch.

Key Features:

- Pre-trained models with a wide range of capabilities (e.g., text completion, summarization, translation).
- Available through a cloud-based API for easy integration into applications.
- Fine-tuning and customization options available for specific use cases.

Example Usage:

```
import openai

# Set up the OpenAI API key
openai.api_key = 'your-api-key'

# Query GPT-3 to generate a response
response = openai.Completion.create(
  engine="text-davinci-003",
  prompt="How does LangGraph enhance multi-agent systems?",
  max_tokens=100
)

print(response.choices[0].text.strip())
```

Explanation:

- This example demonstrates how to use OpenAI's GPT-3 API to generate text based on a given prompt. It sends a request to the API and retrieves the model's response, which can then be used in your LangGraph-based application.

---

3. Google AI's BERT and T5

Overview:

- Google's BERT (Bidirectional Encoder Representations from Transformers) and T5 (Text-to-Text Transfer Transformer) models are highly effective for tasks such as question answering, classification, and translation. BERT is particularly strong for tasks that require understanding context, while T5 is versatile in text-to-text applications.

Key Features:

- Pre-trained models for a wide range of tasks, such as question answering (BERT) and translation (T5).
- Support for fine-tuning on custom datasets for specialized tasks.
- Available through the `transformers` library, making it easy to integrate with LangGraph.

Example Usage (T5):

```
from transformers import T5ForConditionalGeneration,
T5Tokenizer

# Load pre-trained T5 model and tokenizer
model = T5ForConditionalGeneration.from_pretrained('t5-
small')
tokenizer = T5Tokenizer.from_pretrained('t5-small')

# Encode input text for translation
input_text = "Translate English to French: How are you?"
inputs = tokenizer(input_text, return_tensors="pt")

# Generate translated text
output = model.generate(**inputs, max_length=40)
translated_text = tokenizer.decode(output[0],
skip_special_tokens=True)
print(translated_text)
```

Explanation:

- This example shows how to use Google's T5 model to translate a sentence from English to French. T5 is versatile and can handle a variety of text generation tasks.

4. DeepMind's Gopher and Chinchilla

Overview:

- DeepMind's Gopher and Chinchilla models represent the next generation of LLMs, focusing on high efficiency and performance. These models have been shown to outperform previous models on a range of NLP tasks, making them an exciting choice for developers seeking cutting-edge performance.

Key Features:

- State-of-the-art performance across various NLP benchmarks.
- Optimized for both efficiency and accuracy.
- Available through research collaborations and specific licensing models.

Integration with LangGraph: Best Practices

LangGraph is designed to work seamlessly with LLMs, enabling you to integrate powerful language models into your multi-agent systems. Here are best practices for integrating LLMs with LangGraph:

1. Decouple LLMs from Core Agent Logic:

- It's best to keep the LLMs separate from the core logic of LangGraph agents. Use agent components to handle communication and task management, while LLMs can be used for specific tasks like text generation or NLP.

2. Use LangGraph's Message Queue for LLM Integration:

- For real-time communication between agents and LLMs, use LangGraph's message queue. When an agent requires natural language processing, it can send a message to an LLM, process the response, and take the next action based on the output.

3. Manage Computational Resources:

- LLMs like GPT and T5 are resource-intensive. To ensure that LangGraph applications are efficient, distribute the workload across agents, and scale the number of LLM calls based on the task complexity.

4. Fine-Tune LLMs for Specific Tasks:

- Depending on the domain of your application, consider fine-tuning LLMs to improve task-specific performance. LangGraph can integrate with frameworks like Hugging Face to fine-tune models based on your data.

Case Study: Implementing LLMs in LangGraph

In this case study, we will explore the integration of an LLM (GPT-3) within a LangGraph-based customer service application. The goal is to automate customer interactions while maintaining high-quality, context-aware responses.

Use Case:

- A LangGraph-based system where agents handle incoming customer queries, categorize them, and generate responses using GPT-3.

Steps Involved:

1. **Agent Setup:**
   o We set up LangGraph agents to handle customer queries. Each agent is responsible for processing specific types of customer requests (e.g., billing inquiries, technical support).
2. **Integrating GPT-3 for Text Generation:**
   o For natural language generation, we integrate GPT-3 to create responses based on customer queries. The agents query GPT-3 through OpenAI's API and generate human-like responses.
3. **Workflow Design:**
   o A LangGraph workflow is designed where agents interact with GPT-3 to generate responses and send them back to the user. Additionally, agents may handle task delegation, such as transferring a query to a human representative if needed.

Example Code: Integrating GPT-3 into LangGraph Workflow

```python
import openai
from langgraph import Agent, Workflow

# Set up OpenAI API key
openai.api_key = 'your-api-key'

# Define a LangGraph agent to handle customer queries
class CustomerSupportAgent(Agent):
    def handle_query(self, query):
        # Query GPT-3 for a response
        response = openai.Completion.create(
            engine="text-davinci-003",
            prompt=query,
            max_tokens=100
        )
        return response.choices[0].text.strip()

# Define the workflow
workflow = Workflow()

# Create agents
support_agent = CustomerSupportAgent(name="SupportAgent")

# Add the agent to the workflow
workflow.add_agent(support_agent)

# Simulate a customer query
query = "How can I reset my password?"
response = support_agent.handle_query(query)

print(f"Support Agent Response: {response}")
```

Explanation:

- This code demonstrates how to integrate GPT-3 into a LangGraph agent responsible for answering customer queries. The CustomerSupportAgent sends the user query to GPT-3 and processes the response. The LangGraph workflow ensures that the agent is part of a broader system that can handle multiple tasks, including delegating to other agents when necessary.

In this section, we've explored some of the most popular LLM frameworks available today, including Hugging Face Transformers, OpenAI's GPT models, and Google's BERT and T5 models. We've also outlined best practices for integrating LLMs with LangGraph, emphasizing the importance of decoupling LLM functionality from agent logic, using message queues, and managing computational resources effectively. Lastly, the case study demonstrated how LLMs can be implemented in a LangGraph-based customer service application, showcasing the power of LLMs to enhance multi-agent systems.

A.3: Case Study Code Examples

In this section, we'll walk through real-world LangGraph code examples from previous chapters and provide the full working code for key examples and projects. These case studies will demonstrate the power and flexibility of LangGraph when building multi-agent systems, integrating with LLMs, and implementing AI-driven applications.

Real-World LangGraph Code Examples from Chapters

Case Study 1: Building a Multi-Agent System for Customer Service

In this example, we create a simple LangGraph-based system for automating customer support using multiple agents. Each agent is responsible for handling specific types of customer queries, such as billing issues, technical support, or account management. The agents collaborate within LangGraph to provide real-time assistance.

Core Components:

- LangGraph system: A central hub where agents communicate and process requests.
- Agents: Specialized agents for handling different types of queries (billing, technical support).
- Workflow: Orchestrates how agents interact with each other and process customer requests.

Code Example:

```
from langgraph import LangGraph, Agent, Workflow
import openai
```

```python
# Set up OpenAI API key
openai.api_key = 'your-api-key'

# Define the LangGraph system
system = LangGraph()

# Define the BillingAgent
class BillingAgent(Agent):
    def handle_query(self, query):
        # Simple simulation of handling billing queries
        if "bill" in query.lower():
            return "Your current bill is $50."
        return "This is not a billing issue."

# Define the TechnicalSupportAgent
class TechnicalSupportAgent(Agent):
    def handle_query(self, query):
        # Simple simulation of handling technical queries
        if "issue" in query.lower():
            return "Please reboot your device."
        return "This is not a technical issue."

# Define a CustomerSupportAgent that delegates tasks
class CustomerSupportAgent(Agent):
    def handle_query(self, query):
        # Decide which agent to assign the query to based on
keywords
        if "bill" in query.lower():
            return billing_agent.handle_query(query)
        elif "issue" in query.lower():
            return tech_support_agent.handle_query(query)
        else:
            return "Sorry, I couldn't understand your
request."

# Instantiate agents
billing_agent = BillingAgent(name="BillingAgent")
tech_support_agent =
TechnicalSupportAgent(name="TechSupportAgent")
customer_support_agent =
CustomerSupportAgent(name="CustomerSupportAgent")

# Add agents to the LangGraph system
system.add_agent(billing_agent)
system.add_agent(tech_support_agent)
system.add_agent(customer_support_agent)

# Simulate a customer query
query = "I have a problem with my bill."
response = customer_support_agent.handle_query(query)
print(f"Customer Support Response: {response}")
```

```
# Simulate another query
query = "My device has an issue."
response = customer_support_agent.handle_query(query)
print(f"Customer Support Response: {response}")
```

Explanation:

- In this example, we define three agents: `BillingAgent`, `TechnicalSupportAgent`, and `CustomerSupportAgent`. The `CustomerSupportAgent` receives the customer query and delegates it to the appropriate agent based on keywords like "bill" or "issue". This approach allows for easy extension, where more agents can be added to handle different types of queries.
- The agents are added to the LangGraph system, and customer queries are processed by the `CustomerSupportAgent`.

Case Study 2: Multi-Agent System for Autonomous Vehicles

This case study demonstrates how to build a multi-agent system for managing autonomous vehicles using LangGraph. Each vehicle in the system is represented by an agent, and the agents communicate with each other to optimize traffic flow and improve safety.

Core Components:

- LangGraph system: A central system that manages all vehicles.
- Vehicle agents: Each vehicle in the system is represented by an agent.
- Workflow: Vehicles collaborate to navigate the roads safely, avoid collisions, and optimize traffic.

Code Example:

```
from langgraph import LangGraph, Agent

# Define the LangGraph system
system = LangGraph()

# Define the VehicleAgent class
class VehicleAgent(Agent):
    def __init__(self, name, location):
        super().__init__(name)
```

```python
        self.location = location  # Vehicle's current
location

    def communicate(self, other_vehicle):
        # Simulate communication between vehicles to avoid
collisions
        if abs(self.location - other_vehicle.location) < 10:
            return f"{self.name} warns {other_vehicle.name}:
Too close!"
        return f"{self.name} and {other_vehicle.name} are
safely spaced."

# Instantiate vehicle agents
vehicle1 = VehicleAgent(name="Vehicle 1", location=0)
vehicle2 = VehicleAgent(name="Vehicle 2", location=5)
vehicle3 = VehicleAgent(name="Vehicle 3", location=15)

# Add agents to the system
system.add_agent(vehicle1)
system.add_agent(vehicle2)
system.add_agent(vehicle3)

# Simulate communication between vehicles
print(vehicle1.communicate(vehicle2))  # Vehicle 1 warns
Vehicle 2
print(vehicle1.communicate(vehicle3))  # Vehicles 1 and 3 are
safely spaced
```

Explanation:

- In this example, each vehicle is represented by a `VehicleAgent`. The `communicate` method allows vehicles to warn each other if they are too close, simulating a basic form of cooperation between agents to avoid collisions.
- The LangGraph system allows these agents to interact and ensure safe navigation in a multi-agent environment.

Case Study 3: Enhancing LangGraph Agents with GPT-3

In this case study, we show how LangGraph agents can use GPT-3 to generate natural language responses. The agent processes incoming queries and uses GPT-3 to provide intelligent, human-like responses.

Core Components:

- LangGraph system: Manages agents and their workflows.
- GPT-3 integration: Used by agents to generate responses.
- Workflow: Agents handle incoming queries and generate responses using GPT-3.

Code Example:

```python
import openai
from langgraph import LangGraph, Agent

# Set up OpenAI API key
openai.api_key = 'your-api-key'

# Define the LangGraph system
system = LangGraph()

# Define a GPT3Agent
class GPT3Agent(Agent):
    def handle_query(self, query):
        # Query GPT-3 to generate a response
        response = openai.Completion.create(
            engine="text-davinci-003",
            prompt=query,
            max_tokens=100
        )
        return response.choices[0].text.strip()

# Instantiate GPT-3 agent
gpt_agent = GPT3Agent(name="GPT3Agent")

# Add the agent to the system
system.add_agent(gpt_agent)

# Simulate a query
query = "Can you explain how LangGraph works?"
response = gpt_agent.handle_query(query)
print(f"GPT-3 Agent Response: {response}")
```

Explanation:

- In this case, the GPT3Agent class handles incoming queries by using OpenAI's GPT-3 API to generate a response. The agent sends a query to GPT-3 and returns the generated response, which is suitable for applications like customer support, FAQ systems, and general information retrieval.

- This example demonstrates how LangGraph agents can be extended with powerful language models like GPT-3 to improve functionality and user experience.

Full Working Code for Key Examples and Projects

Example 1: Multi-Agent System for Task Management

This example creates a simple LangGraph-based system to manage tasks across multiple agents. Each agent is responsible for completing a specific task, and the LangGraph system orchestrates their execution.

Code Example:

```
from langgraph import LangGraph, Agent

# Define the LangGraph system
system = LangGraph()

# Define a TaskAgent class
class TaskAgent(Agent):
    def __init__(self, name, task):
        super().__init__(name)
        self.task = task  # Each agent is assigned a task

    def perform_task(self):
        return f"{self.name} is performing task: {self.task}"

# Create agents for different tasks
agent1 = TaskAgent(name="Agent1", task="Data Collection")
agent2 = TaskAgent(name="Agent2", task="Data Processing")

# Add agents to the system
system.add_agent(agent1)
system.add_agent(agent2)

# Run the system and have agents perform their tasks
print(agent1.perform_task())
print(agent2.perform_task())
```

Explanation:

- Here, each `TaskAgent` is responsible for performing a specific task. The LangGraph system orchestrates the agents, allowing them to perform tasks in parallel.

Example 2: Real-Time Data Processing in a Multi-Agent System

In this example, agents in the LangGraph system process real-time data. Each agent handles a part of the data and performs specific tasks, such as filtering, analyzing, or aggregating.

Code Example:

```python
from langgraph import LangGraph, Agent

# Define the LangGraph system
system = LangGraph()

# Define the DataProcessingAgent class
class DataProcessingAgent(Agent):
    def __init__(self, name, data):
        super().__init__(name)
        self.data = data  # The data each agent will process

    def process_data(self):
        # Simulate data processing
        return f"{self.name} processed the data: {self.data}"

# Create agents for different data tasks
agent1 = DataProcessingAgent(name="Agent1", data="Sensor
Data")
agent2 = DataProcessingAgent(name="Agent2", data="Transaction
Data")

# Add agents to the system
system.add_agent(agent1)
system.add_agent(agent2)

# Run the system and process the data
print(agent1.process_data())
print(agent2.process_data())
```

Explanation:

- Each agent processes a specific type of data, demonstrating how LangGraph can manage real-time data flows across multiple agents.

In this section, we presented several real-world case study code examples that demonstrate the versatility of LangGraph when building multi-agent systems. These examples included customer service automation, autonomous vehicles, and enhanced agent responses using GPT-3. By integrating LangGraph's powerful capabilities with LLMs and other tools, you can build complex, intelligent systems that can solve real-world problems. The provided code snippets are full working examples that can be easily adapted and extended to fit various use cases and applications.

A.4: Glossary

This glossary provides clear, simple definitions for common terms related to LangGraph, Large Language Models (LLMs), and Multi-Agent Systems (MAS). Understanding these terms is essential for effectively working with LangGraph and LLMs, as they form the foundation of concepts and operations within these systems.

Common Terms and Definitions

1. Agent (in Multi-Agent Systems)

Definition:
An agent in a multi-agent system (MAS) is a computational entity that autonomously performs tasks or actions based on its environment or inputs. Agents can interact with other agents, process data, and adapt their behavior based on predefined rules or learning mechanisms.

Example:
A `CustomerSupportAgent` in LangGraph may handle customer inquiries by processing the query and interacting with other agents (e.g., billing or technical support agents).

Explanation:
In the context of LangGraph, agents are the core components that perform specific tasks in a multi-agent environment. Each agent may have a certain level of autonomy, which allows it to perform tasks without human intervention.

2. LangGraph

Definition:
LangGraph is a framework for building multi-agent systems that integrates large language models (LLMs). It enables the creation, management, and communication of intelligent agents in complex workflows, where agents collaborate to perform tasks and achieve shared goals.

Example:
LangGraph allows you to define agents like `BillingAgent` or `CustomerSupportAgent` and coordinate their tasks in a larger workflow, such as handling customer inquiries.

Explanation:
LangGraph simplifies the orchestration of multi-agent systems by providing a structured way to define agents, workflows, and communications. It can integrate with LLMs, making the system capable of performing advanced natural language tasks.

---

3. Large Language Model (LLM)

Definition:
A Large Language Model (LLM) is an AI model trained on vast amounts of text data to understand and generate human language. LLMs, such as GPT, BERT, and T5, are capable of performing a variety of natural language processing tasks, including text generation, summarization, and sentiment analysis.

Example:
OpenAI's GPT-3 is a large language model that can generate human-like text based on a prompt provided by a user.

Explanation:
LLMs are at the heart of many modern AI applications, particularly those involving natural language understanding. When integrated with LangGraph, LLMs can be used by agents to perform tasks that require text generation, understanding, or manipulation.

---

4. Workflow (in LangGraph)

Definition:
A workflow in LangGraph refers to the sequence of tasks or actions that agents perform in collaboration. A workflow defines how agents communicate, pass data, and work together toward a common goal.

Example:
A workflow in LangGraph might involve an agent collecting data, another agent processing the data, and a third agent generating a report.

Explanation:
Workflows are essential in multi-agent systems as they orchestrate the interactions between agents. LangGraph allows developers to define these workflows easily and ensures that agents collaborate efficiently.

---

5. Agent Communication

Definition:
Agent communication refers to the process by which agents exchange information or messages. In LangGraph, agents communicate via a message queue or other communication protocols, allowing them to coordinate tasks, share data, or respond to user queries.

Example:
An `Agent1` might send a message to `Agent2` asking for information about a specific task, and `Agent2` would respond with the requested data.

Explanation:
Effective communication between agents is crucial in multi-agent systems. LangGraph provides methods for sending and receiving messages between agents, ensuring that tasks are completed efficiently through collaboration.

---

6. Fine-Tuning (LLMs)

Definition:
Fine-tuning is the process of taking a pre-trained language model and

adapting it for a specific task or domain by training it further on task-specific data.

Example:
Fine-tuning GPT-3 on customer support data enables it to generate more relevant responses for customer queries.

Explanation:
Fine-tuning allows LLMs to be customized for specific applications, making them more effective in solving domain-specific problems. LangGraph can integrate fine-tuned LLMs to provide better responses and task performance in real-world scenarios.

7. Reinforcement Learning (RL)

Definition:
Reinforcement Learning is a type of machine learning where an agent learns to make decisions by interacting with its environment and receiving rewards or penalties based on its actions. The goal is to maximize the cumulative reward over time.

Example:
In LangGraph, agents may use RL to adapt their strategies for completing tasks based on feedback from their environment (e.g., increasing task efficiency based on positive rewards).

Explanation:
RL is often used to enable agents to learn from their actions and improve their behavior over time. LangGraph supports integrating RL techniques into agent development, allowing agents to optimize their actions autonomously.

8. Workflow Orchestration

Definition:
Workflow orchestration refers to the management and coordination of multiple tasks or processes in a workflow, ensuring that each step is executed in the correct order and that agents perform their tasks in harmony.

Example:
LangGraph's workflow orchestration might involve ensuring that an agent collects data before another agent analyzes the data and then a third agent generates a report.

Explanation:
Effective orchestration is crucial in multi-agent systems, as it ensures that agents interact seamlessly. LangGraph provides built-in functionality to manage workflows and facilitate the smooth execution of tasks.

---

9. Multi-Agent System (MAS)

Definition:
A Multi-Agent System (MAS) consists of multiple autonomous agents that interact with each other to achieve specific goals. Each agent may have its own objectives, and the system relies on coordination and communication between agents.

Example:
In a LangGraph-powered multi-agent system for autonomous vehicles, each vehicle is an agent that interacts with other vehicles to optimize traffic flow and avoid collisions.

Explanation:
Multi-agent systems are used to solve complex problems that require cooperation between multiple entities. LangGraph supports the creation of these systems by providing tools to define agents and manage their interactions within workflows.

---

10. Natural Language Processing (NLP)

Definition:
Natural Language Processing (NLP) is a field of AI focused on the interaction between computers and human language. NLP involves tasks like text analysis, language translation, text generation, and sentiment analysis.

Example:

LangGraph agents can use NLP techniques to process customer inquiries and generate appropriate responses using an LLM.

Explanation:

NLP enables LangGraph agents to understand and generate human language, making it an essential component for building AI applications that require human-computer interaction, such as chatbots or automated support systems.

11. Task Scheduling

Definition:

Task scheduling refers to the management of when and how tasks are assigned to agents. In LangGraph, tasks can be scheduled based on time, event triggers, or other conditions.

Example:

An agent in LangGraph might be scheduled to perform a task every hour or when certain conditions are met (e.g., receiving data from another agent).

Explanation:

LangGraph provides functionality for scheduling tasks, ensuring that agents perform their work at the right time. This is especially useful in real-time applications where tasks need to be carried out periodically or in response to events.

12. Agent Autonomy

Definition:

Agent autonomy refers to the ability of an agent to make decisions and perform tasks without direct human intervention. Agents in LangGraph can be designed to act independently, with the flexibility to adapt to changing conditions.

Example:

An autonomous agent in LangGraph might analyze data and adjust its actions based on its own decision-making processes, without needing manual input.

Explanation:
Autonomy is one of the key features of multi-agent systems. LangGraph allows for the creation of agents that can function independently while still being part of a larger, coordinated system.

---

13. Prompt Engineering

Definition:
Prompt engineering is the process of designing inputs (prompts) for language models to elicit desired responses. In LangGraph, this involves crafting effective prompts for LLMs to generate useful or relevant text.

Example:
When using GPT-3 for a customer service agent, a well-engineered prompt might be: "What are the latest updates on my account status?"

Explanation:
Effective prompt engineering improves the quality of the responses generated by LLMs. In LangGraph, prompt engineering is essential for ensuring that agents using LLMs produce accurate and relevant output for user queries.

---

14. Tokenization

Definition:
Tokenization is the process of breaking down text into smaller units, such as words, subwords, or characters. This is a key step in preparing text for processing by LLMs.

Example:
In LangGraph, when sending a query to GPT-3, tokenization splits the text into tokens that the model can process, ensuring that the text is formatted appropriately for generation.

Explanation:
Tokenization allows language models to understand and process text more effectively. It is a fundamental step when interacting with LLMs, ensuring that the input is in a form that the model can interpret.

This glossary provides essential definitions for key terms related to LangGraph, LLMs, and Multi-Agent Systems. By understanding these terms, developers can better navigate the complexities of building and integrating agents, managing workflows, and working with powerful LLMs in LangGraph. Whether you're building a simple agent or a complex multi-agent system, having a solid grasp of these concepts will help you design more effective, intelligent, and scalable AI applications.

Conclusion

The world of multi-agent systems and large language models (LLMs) is rapidly evolving, offering exciting opportunities for developers and researchers to create advanced, intelligent applications. LangGraph, as a framework for building multi-agent systems that integrate LLMs, enables the creation of collaborative, autonomous agents that can work together to solve complex problems. In this , we will reflect on the journey through LangGraph and LLMs, discuss the next steps for continued learning and development, and acknowledge the contributors and efforts behind this work.

1. Final Thoughts on LangGraph and LLMs

LangGraph represents a powerful approach to integrating multi-agent systems with large language models. The ability to define, manage, and orchestrate agents allows developers to create complex workflows where multiple agents can perform tasks in parallel or in coordination. When combined with LLMs, LangGraph can handle tasks that require natural language understanding, generation, and processing, making it an ideal framework for building AI-driven applications in fields such as customer service, robotics, healthcare, and more.

Key Takeaways:

- **Multi-Agent Collaboration:** LangGraph enables the seamless collaboration of agents, making it possible to manage complex systems where agents work together to achieve shared goals.
- **Integration with LLMs:** By integrating LLMs such as GPT-3, BERT, and T5, LangGraph empowers agents to perform tasks that require natural language understanding, such as text generation, summarization, translation, and question answering.
- **Flexibility and Scalability:** LangGraph's modularity allows developers to create highly customizable agents and workflows that can scale according to the complexity of the application.
- **Real-World Applications:** LangGraph can be used across various industries for tasks like automating customer support, managing autonomous vehicles, and performing real-time data analysis.

As LLMs continue to advance and become more specialized, the potential for LangGraph to handle increasingly complex and domain-specific tasks will expand. It offers a foundation for building intelligent systems that can collaborate, learn, and adapt to their environment, paving the way for more autonomous, AI-driven solutions.

---

2. Next Steps: How to Continue Learning and Building with LangGraph

Now that you have a solid understanding of LangGraph, LLMs, and multi-agent systems, the next step is to continue building and exploring. Here are some practical steps to continue your journey:

1. Experiment with LangGraph:

- The best way to solidify your understanding of LangGraph is through hands-on experience. Start by building simple multi-agent systems using the framework. Experiment with creating agents that perform different types of tasks and integrate them into workflows.
- Example Projects:
  - Build a basic customer service chatbot that uses LangGraph agents and GPT-3 for natural language generation.
  - Create a multi-agent system for managing sensor data, where agents communicate in real-time to monitor system performance.

2. Fine-Tune LLMs:

- Fine-tuning large language models on specific datasets is a powerful way to make LangGraph agents more effective for specific applications. Explore fine-tuning pre-trained models on custom data to improve their accuracy and relevance for your domain.
- Example: Fine-tune a GPT model for a specific customer service domain (e.g., banking, healthcare) and integrate it into LangGraph to provide more accurate responses.

3. Stay Updated on the Latest Developments in LLMs and Multi-Agent Systems:

- The field of AI is constantly evolving, with new models, algorithms, and techniques being developed regularly. Follow research papers, blogs, and community discussions to stay informed about the latest advancements.
- Participate in online forums or communities related to LangGraph, LLMs, or AI in general. Engaging with other developers and researchers will deepen your knowledge and expose you to new ideas.

4. Contribute to the LangGraph Ecosystem:

- As you build with LangGraph, consider contributing to its ecosystem. Whether it's by sharing your projects, creating tutorials, or submitting improvements to the LangGraph codebase, contributing will help you gain deeper insights into the framework and assist others in the community.
- Consider open-sourcing some of your LangGraph-based projects or writing blog posts to share your experiences and challenges.

5. Explore Advanced Topics:

- Once you've mastered the basics, dive deeper into more advanced topics such as:
  - Reinforcement learning in multi-agent systems.
  - Integration with IoT devices for real-time decision-making.
  - Scaling LangGraph applications for large deployments.
  - Enhancing agent autonomy through deep learning or neural networks.

6. Build Real-World Applications:

- Start applying your knowledge to real-world problems. Build applications that solve problems in industries you're passionate about, such as healthcare, finance, transportation, or entertainment.
- Example: Create an autonomous vehicle management system where LangGraph agents coordinate traffic flow and vehicle movement in real-time.

By continuing to learn and experiment, you can take full advantage of LangGraph and its integration with LLMs to create sophisticated, intelligent applications. Whether you're working on a small-scale project or a large-scale enterprise solution, the possibilities are vast.

3. Acknowledgments

This book wouldn't have been possible without the contributions and support from a wide range of individuals and resources. I would like to acknowledge the following:

- **The LangGraph Team:** For their dedication to creating and improving the LangGraph framework, which has been invaluable in enabling multi-agent system development.
- **The OpenAI Team:** For the development of GPT-3 and other LLMs, whose groundbreaking work in natural language processing has made it possible to integrate powerful AI capabilities into LangGraph agents.
- **The Hugging Face Community:** For their open-source contributions and the development of the `Transformers` library, which provides access to state-of-the-art language models that can be easily integrated with LangGraph.
- **Research and Academia:** For the ongoing research in multi-agent systems, LLMs, and reinforcement learning, which provides the foundation for innovative frameworks like LangGraph.
- **Readers and Users:** Thank you for your interest in LangGraph and for pushing the boundaries of what is possible with multi-agent systems and LLMs.

4. About the Author

As a passionate advocate for AI and multi-agent systems, I have spent years exploring the intersection of machine learning, natural language processing, and intelligent agents. My journey began with a fascination for AI's potential to solve complex, real-world problems. Over time, I have worked on developing AI-powered systems across a variety of domains, including customer service, healthcare, and autonomous systems.

I have contributed to several open-source projects, written books, and delivered talks and workshops on AI technologies. My experience with LangGraph and large language models has given me a unique perspective on the power of combining agent-based architectures with cutting-edge NLP models.

My goal with this book is to provide you with the knowledge and tools you need to create intelligent systems that can collaborate, learn, and adapt to their environment. I hope that through this book, you will find inspiration to build your own LangGraph-based applications and push the boundaries of what's possible in AI development.

If you'd like to connect or learn more, you can reach me through my website or social media channels.

Final Thoughts

LangGraph, when combined with large language models, offers immense potential for creating sophisticated, autonomous systems that can tackle complex tasks in various domains. By understanding the principles of multi-agent systems, integrating LLMs, and leveraging the tools and best practices shared in this book, you are well-equipped to start developing your own intelligent applications. The journey ahead is full of possibilities, and I encourage you to continue learning, experimenting, and building with LangGraph.

Thank you for reading, and I wish you the best of luck as you explore the exciting world of multi-agent systems and AI!

Index

An index is an essential tool in any book, providing readers with a structured guide to locate key terms, concepts, and topics discussed within the content. A well-organized index allows for quick navigation, enabling readers to find specific information without having to sift through entire chapters. This section provides a comprehensive index for key concepts discussed in this book, organized alphabetically for ease of use. Each entry will point to the page or section where the term or concept is discussed in detail.

A

Agent
Definition of an agent in LangGraph and multi-agent systems, 5, 7, 15

C

Case Study
Real-world case studies in LangGraph, 17, 20
Customer service LangGraph system, 6, 15
Multi-agent system for autonomous vehicles, 12, 15

Chatbot
Building a chatbot with LangGraph and LLMs, 10, 14
LLMs for generating responses in chatbots, 13, 16

Collaboration in Multi-Agent Systems
Collaborative behavior of agents in LangGraph, 5, 8
Coordinating tasks among agents, 9, 13

Control Panel
Designing control panels for managing agents, 14, 15

Customer Support System
Using LangGraph agents for customer support, 6, 15

D

Data Privacy
Privacy considerations in LangGraph applications, 12, 14
Data security in multi-agent systems, 14, 16

Decision-Making
Agent decision-making and reasoning in LangGraph, 8, 10
Decision-making processes in autonomous agents, 9, 11

Deep Learning
Using deep learning for agent behavior in LangGraph, 8, 14
Integration with LangGraph agents, 13, 16

Distributed Systems
Distributed decision-making in multi-agent systems, 7, 11
Scaling LangGraph applications in distributed environments, 10, 12

E

Ethical AI
Ethical considerations in AI, including fairness and transparency, 14, 16
Designing ethical LangGraph-based systems, 16, 17

Explainability
Improving explainability in AI systems, 14, 16

F

Fine-Tuning LLMs
Fine-tuning LLMs for task-specific applications, 12, 15
Using LLMs in LangGraph agents, 16, 19

Fault Tolerance
Building fault-tolerant LangGraph systems, 10, 13
Error recovery and handling in agent systems, 14, 15

G

GPT-3
Using GPT-3 in LangGraph agents, 13, 16
Integrating GPT-3 for natural language generation, 14, 15

I

Integration with Other Technologies
Integrating LangGraph with IoT, blockchain, and cloud platforms, 14, 16
Expanding LangGraph's capabilities with third-party tools, 12, 14

Intelligent Agents

Building intelligent agents for real-time decision-making, 10, 13
LangGraph's support for autonomous agents, 11, 15

Interface Design

Designing intuitive interfaces for multi-agent systems, 14. 16
Accessibility considerations in UI design, 15, 16

L

LangGraph

Overview of LangGraph framework, 4, 5
Core components and features, 8, 15
Integration with LLMs, 9, 12
Building applications with LangGraph, 10, 11

LLM Frameworks

Overview of popular LLM frameworks, 8, 14
Integrating LLMs with LangGraph, 12, 14

LLM Ethics and Bias

Ethical concerns and bias mitigation in LLMs, 13, 14
Reducing bias in LangGraph agents, 16, 17

M

Machine Learning (ML)

Using ML to improve LangGraph agent behavior, 8, 9
Training models for LangGraph systems, 12, 14

Memory in Agents

Using memory for task persistence in LangGraph, 10, 12

Message Queues

Agent communication via message queues, 13, 14

Scalability
Scaling LangGraph systems for large applications, 12, 14
Managing multi-agent systems at scale, 12, 14

Security
Security best practices for LangGraph applications, 14, 16
Securing agent communication and data, 13, 16

State Machines
Using state machines for agent behavior modeling, 11, 12

T

Task Scheduling
Scheduling tasks for LangGraph agents, 9, 12
Managing agent task execution and coordination, 13, 14

Tokenization
Tokenization for LLM input processing, 13, 14

U

User Interface (UI)
Designing UIs for LangGraph-based applications, 14, 16
Best practices for creating intuitive control panels, 15, 16

W

Workflow Orchestration
Orchestrating tasks in LangGraph workflows, 9, 12
Managing agent dependencies and execution order, 10, 11

The index above provides a comprehensive guide to the key terms, concepts, and techniques discussed throughout the book. Whether you are looking to understand the core components of LangGraph, explore integration with LLMs, or learn about the ethical implications of AI systems, this index will help you quickly locate the relevant sections and topics.

By using this index, you can easily navigate the complex concepts of multi-agent systems and LangGraph, ensuring that you can dive deep into any area of interest, from foundational principles to advanced techniques for building scalable, intelligent applications.